Hard Passage

A Mennonite Family's Long Journey from Russia to Canada

To Margaret Maes.

Arthur Kroeger

ARTHUR KROEGER

Hard Passage

*A Mennonite Family's Long Journey
from Russia to Canada*

THE UNIVERSITY OF ALBERTA PRESS

Published by

The University of Alberta Press
Ring House 2
Edmonton, Alberta, Canada   T6G 2E1

LIBRARY AND ARCHIVES CANADA CATALOGUING IN PUBLICATION

Kroeger, Arthur
    Hard passage : a Mennonite family's long journey from Russia to Canada / Arthur Kroeger.

Includes bibliographical references and index.
ISBN–13: 978–0–88864–473–2
ISBN–10: 0–88864–473–6

    1. Kroeger family. 2. Mennonites—Canada—Genealogy. 3. Mennonites—Russia—Genealogy.
4. Canada—Genealogy. 5. Russia—Genealogy. I. Title.

CS90.K762 2006   929'.20971   C2006–905163–1

This book was copyedited by Brenda Belokrinicev and the maps were done by Wendy Johnson.

The University of Alberta Press is committed to protecting our natural environment. As part of our efforts, this book is printed on Enviro: it contains 100% post-consumer recycled fibres and is acid- and chlorine-free.

The University of Alberta Press gratefully acknowledges the support received for its publishing program from The Canada Council for the Arts. The University of Alberta Press also gratefully acknowledges the financial support of the Government of Canada through the Book Publishing Industry Development Program (BPIDP) and from the Alberta Foundation for the Arts for our publishing activities.

Canada Council   Conseil des Arts
for the Arts   du Canada

Canadä

In memory of Heinrich and Helena Kroeger

Contents

Preface

THE EVENTS RECOUNTED IN THIS BOOK all happened. The story of Heinrich and Helena Kroeger as I have set it out is the product of extensive examinations of family documents, some of them fragmentary, supplemented by reading, research and many interviews. Only in cases where something in a notebook, a letter or a diary was ambiguous have I provided my own interpretation.

The book is more than the story of one family. The Kroegers' experiences of Russian Mennonite society before 1914, and then of war, civil war, famine, typhus, hyperinflation, and emigration were paralleled by the experiences of literally thousands of Mennonites living in Russia during this period.

In the same vein, our family's life after we had settled in Alberta had a good deal in common with the experiences of many who came to Canada from different parts of the world in the first part of the twentieth century. Such experiences form a part of Canadian history.

A few words of explanation about several subjects may be useful. Throughout the book, I have spoken of the Mennonite colonies in "Russia," even though the principal ones were located in what is now the Ukraine. This usage reflects the way the Mennonites thought of themselves. When they had to deal with a government, it was the czar's officials who were their interlocutors. Those who came to Canada in the 1920s were referred to by their co-religionists as "Russlaender."

In czarist times, it was actually illegal to use the term "Ukraine" in print. In any case, the Mennonites' focus was generally on matters within their self-contained colonies, and they had only limited contact with the Ukrainian population around them.

In Part I, which deals with the family's life in Russia, I have generally expressed distances and quantities in standard metric terms. However, in Part II, which is set in Western Canada, I have reverted to the imperial system. The West was surveyed in miles, ranges, and townships, and agricultural yields are still commonly expressed in bushels per acre and dollars per bushel. To have spoken in terms of kilograms per hectare and the like would have rendered the manuscript largely unintelligible to readers on the prairies.

Finally, insofar as temperatures are concerned, my only observation is that extremes of heat and cold are the norm in that part of Canada, whether expressed in Celsius or Fahrenheit.

Acknowledgements

I OWE A PARTICULAR DEBT OF GRATITUDE to Charlotte Gray, who spent many hours reading my early drafts and telling me what was wrong with them. For a first-time author, such advice from an accomplished writer was invaluable in getting me on the right track.

Patrick Kavanagh demonstrated to me how many good ideas a skilled editor can come up with.

The late Dr. George Harder spent many hours translating my father's documents after they had come into my possession in 1971. In doing so, he enabled me to get insights into my parents' lives in Russia and in Canada, that I had never had before.

Professor Emeritus Ted Regehr in Calgary, author Rudy Wiebe in Edmonton, and Mennonite historian Paul Toews in Fresno, California all provided valuable advice about drafts of my manuscript.

Professor Harvey Dyck at the University of Toronto was instrumental in getting me copies of documents about my family from the archives in Zaporozhe, Ukraine. The archivist, Aleksandr Tedeev, extended his full co-operation to Professor Dyck.

I discovered that archivists really enjoy being helpful. This proved to be true of the staff at the National Archives of Canada, the Mennonite Heritage Centre and the Centre for Mennonite Brethern Studies, both in Winnipeg, the Glenbow Alberta Museum in Calgary, and the Canadian Pacific Archives in Montreal.

Dealing with the University of Alberta Press has been a pleasure. In its website the Press says, "We treat our authors well." I agree.

Arthur Kroeger
Ottawa, September 2006

PROLOGUE   *Mennonite Roots*

Now go, write it before them in a table, and note it in a book,
that it may be for the time to come…

—*ISAIAH 30:8*

WHEN I WAS GROWING UP IN ALBERTA in the 1930s and 1940s, there were some things about my family that puzzled me.

I once asked, "Since we come from Russia, aren't we Russians?" and was firmly told, "No, we're Mennonites."

During World War II, children in Canada who showed a disinterest in the food placed before them were commonly reproached by their mothers to "Think of the starving children in Europe" (or China, or elsewhere). My mother's enjoinder was different: "The time is going to come when you will be glad to find *anything* to eat." What was she talking about?

Like most boys, I liked playing cops and robbers and other games that involved guns. However, when a school friend gave me a wooden toy gun that had been cut out of a board, I knew that I had to keep it hidden because if my father ever saw it he would burn it. I was not quite sure why.

In later years, I sometimes wondered about my mother's sudden death in the winter of 1958, when I was twenty-five and studying at Oxford University. She had died of a stroke, brought on by anxiety about a violent incident. A Polish-Canadian farmer, after a quarrel with his son, had shot and killed the son's wife. These tragic events had taken place some twenty miles from where my parents lived, and involved people with whom they were acquainted but with whom they had no particular relationship. What had caused her to be so frightened?

It would be some years before I was to find the answers to these and many other questions.

In March 1971, while I was serving at the Canadian Embassy in Washington, one of my brothers called from Alberta. Our 87-year-old father, who had been in failing health, had died.

While I was at home for the funeral, I sought and obtained my family's agreement that I could take back with me a wooden box containing papers that he had often revisited over the years. I wanted to know about the contents of the box because of a growing curiosity about my parents' past, concerning which I realized I knew very little.

This subject had been of hardly any interest to me in my earlier years. When I was an adolescent, my goal had been to become as much like my peer group as possible. While I respect the sincerity of those who earnestly explain to all comers that Canada "is not a melting pot like the United States," I have also observed that these people usually bear Anglo-Saxon names. To have been an "ethnic" was to experience the power of conformist pressures, and to grow up on the prairies with a German name during the war was to know the discomforts of being different. The conversations that my parents regularly had with each other about life in Russia, their religion, the Low German language we spoke at home, and many other factors were daily, but not particularly welcome, reminders that my background was different from that of my schoolmates.

The documents in that wooden box were mostly hand-written and in German. There were also a few official documents in Russian, such as the internal passports that residents were required to possess. I could not read most of these documents, but Dr. George Harder, a retired Mennonite who had known our family during the early years in Alberta, generously translated many of them for me. These documents gave me my first real insights into my parents' lives.

One of Heinrich Kroeger's notebooks and the box in which Heinrich Kroeger kept his papers. The box was originally made by his great-grandfather for his maternal grandmother in 1857.

There was a diary from 1911, when my father had been a young man in quest of a wife, and another, from early 1914, that ended in September when he was called up for military service. There were letters, postcards, and photos. With the papers was a white felt patch bearing a red cross and three letters in Cyrillic script, which my father had cut from the sleeve of his uniform jacket when he was demobilized from the Russian army's medical corps.

Several notebooks recording income and expenditures provided, in deceptively laconic terms, pictures of events in wartime Moscow, the Russian civil war, a typhus epidemic, the famine of 1921 to 1922, and then the hyperinflation that had for several years made currency all but worthless. There were the Soviet passports that my parents had been issued for their 1926 emigration, several more notebooks dealing with the hard years of drought and depression that followed their arrival in Canada, and the naturalization certificates issued to them by the Canadian government in 1933.

Because of my work and other activities, it took me a while to get to all of these documents and to comprehend the story that lay within them. Not until 2002 did I begin to make a systematic effort to understand the various documents and their relationships to one another. I read the 1911 diary perhaps twenty times and, with each reading, its flat, factual entries conveyed an increasingly three-dimensional picture of my father's life in his Russian Mennonite community during the comfortable, happy years before the cataclysmic events that began with the outbreak of World War I. From the well-worn notebooks, with their entries of income and expenditure, I found I was able to piece together a picture of life during the post-revolutionary period.

Turning to published Mennonite histories, I found eyewitness accounts of violence and anarchy in my parents' village during the Russian civil war. As my reading progressed, my eyes would widen from time to time, and I would catch myself on the point of saying aloud, "Mother and Dad lived through *that?*"

The years in Canada after my parents' immigration in 1926 were easier to reconstruct. There were the recollections of my older brothers and surviving sister, together with my own personal experiences and the accounts of friends and neighbours. In addition, the archives of the Mennonite Land Settlement Board and the Canadian Pacific Railway brought to light correspondence about our parents' prolonged efforts to find a farm they could live on, while the notebooks conveyed a picture of their struggle to survive in a Canada where there was as yet no social safety net.

Going through the documents was a humbling experience. I came to realize that my brothers and sisters and I had only partly known our parents during their lifetimes. This book is my account of what I learned.

PART I *Russia*

ONE   *Before the Flood*

*For as in the days that were before the flood, they were eating and
drinking, marrying and giving in marriage....
And knew not until the flood came and took them all away.*
— MATTHEW 24:38–39

MY FATHER, Heinrich Kroeger, was born in 1883 in the Mennonite village
of Rosental, across the Dnieper River from the present-day city of
Zaporozhe (formerly Alexandrovsk) in the Ukraine. The period during
which he grew up is today regarded as the golden age of the Mennonite
colonies in czarist Russia. The pattern of his life paralleled that of many
young men in the colonies.

The Mennonites were an offshoot of the Anabaptists, a radical Protestant
group that had emerged in the 1500s, early in the Reformation. They took
their name from Menno Simons, a sixteenth-century Dutch priest who
had converted from Roman Catholicism.

The key tenets of the Anabaptist, and later the Mennonite, religion
were an emphasis on an individual's personal relationship with God,
adult baptism, a rejection of state or official religion, a refusal to swear
oaths, non-resistance in the face of aggression, and a refusal of military service. In some respects, the Mennonites' religion had a good deal

in common with that of groups such as the Quakers and the Amish. Religious leaders were elected by their congregations.

Harsh persecution in the Netherlands during the sixteenth century had led many Mennonites to seek refuge in other countries. Somewhat like the Jews, they moved about Europe and settled in places where they felt they would be free to practice their religion. In the eyes of the authorities, the Mennonites were a stubborn, awkward, idealistic people who refused to conform to local norms. Their resistance to military service was viewed as particularly troublesome.

Beginning in the 1530s, a substantial number of Mennonites migrated from the Netherlands to the relatively tolerant Kingdom of Poland. They brought with them Dutch skills in the use of dykes and dams, which they applied to the water-logged and overgrown lands of the Vistula delta. As a result, the estate owners of the region found them useful and gave them a qualified welcome. Although they were never afforded the full rights of citizens, they were tolerated by the Polish monarchy and left relatively undisturbed for some two hundred and fifty years. In time, they became culturally German and their Dutch language gave way to Low German, the North German language which, mixed with some Dutch words, later became the *lingua franca* of the Mennonites in Russia. By 1777, there were some twelve thousand Mennonites living in the area outside Danzig.[1]

The partition of Poland in the late eighteenth century brought the Mennonites under Prussian rule. With this change came increasing restrictions on their ability to acquire land; more important for some, there was also the prospect that their historic exemption from military service might end.

It was at this juncture that an emissary from Empress Catherine the Great of Russia arrived, offering guarantees of religious freedom and exemption from military service if the Mennonites would colonize some of her largely empty lands. Her missive proved to be very timely. To some, it came as a godsend. Despite obstacles placed by the Prussian authorities, a number of families managed to leave. The first wagon trains moved across the Russian border in 1788 and arrived at their destination in July 1789.

The first colony, as the Mennonite settlements were called, was established in Chortiza, across the Dnieper River from Alexandrovsk (now known as Zaporozhe), a city of modest size. In 1803, in response to a further set of restrictive measures by the Prussian regime, a second and much larger Mennonite exodus got under way.

After the death of Empress Catherine in 1796, the colonists entered into negotiations with representatives of her son and successor, Czar Paul I, to formalize the rights they had been given by his mother. The outcome was a *Privilegium* issued by the czar in 1800. It praised the Mennonites for their "excellent industry and morality," and spoke of them as "a model for the foreigners settled here." Its guarantees included freedom of religion; the allocation of 65 *dessiatines* (roughly 75 hectares) of land to each family; a ten-year exemption from taxes; the right to brew beer, vinegar, and to distill corn brandy; and, of primary importance, that "none…will ever be taken into military service."[2]

Through the nineteenth century and well into the twentieth, the *Privilegium* was the Mennonites' *magna carta*. It governed their dealings with the authorities, and at times was even cited when there were internal disputes in the colonies. Among Heinrich Kroeger's papers was a family account book recording transactions for the years 1878 to 1883, in which the text of the *Privilegium* had been carefully copied.

Most of the settlers who arrived after 1803 migrated to an area that had become available south of Chortiza, where they established a new colony that came to be known as the Molochna. Over time, Molochna became larger and more prosperous than the Old Colony, as Chortiza was called. Although as the Mennonite population grew a number of other colonies would be created in other regions, the Chortiza and Molochna colonies remained the heart of the Mennonite presence in Russia. The Chortiza colony was comprised of eighteen villages, the Molochna fifty-eight.

While poverty and hardship were the hallmarks of the early years in both colonies, the traditional virtues of hard work and thrift eventually produced results. As time went on, crops yielded increased harvests, improved strains of cattle were introduced, and more substantial houses were built. Visitors to the colonies were impressed by the well-tilled fields, abundant orchards, and fine herds of livestock. The colonies' progress attracted favourable notice in St. Petersburg, and in the first part of the nineteenth century they received visits from Czar Alexander I and his successor Nicholas I.

Even though in an era when the Russian Ministry of Education was hostile to the notion of educating the general public, the Mennonites from the outset created schools, albeit ones that were primitive in the early years. An important motivating factor was that they considered an ability to read the Bible to be essential for the practice of their religious beliefs. In 1820, the first secondary school and a teachers' college were established. Other educational institutions followed as the nineteenth century unfolded. In the 1920s, when large numbers of Russian Mennonites emigrated to Canada, they proved to be better educated than those who had been in Canada since the 1870s.[3]

Russia in the nineteenth century was a relatively under-governed country. The reach of the czar's government did not extend beyond the eighty-nine provincial capitals. In this environment, the thousands of rural colonists who had been attracted to Russia from Western Europe over the years were largely left to govern themselves.

Autonomy was especially important to the Mennonites because of their religious beliefs. The czar was 1,500 kilometres away in St. Petersburg. They gave him their loyalty, and in return asked only to be left alone. Their colonies were fully self-sufficient and self-governing. They financed and managed their own schools, colleges, hospitals, courts, credit unions, fire insurance, taxes, orphanages, and systems of poor relief. Only for the rare cases of serious crimes and events such as raids by local nomads, did they have recourse to government law enforcement agencies. General oversight of the colonies was the responsibility of the Office of Guardianship of New Russian Foreign Settlers in Ekaterinaslav.[4]

The late nineteenth and early twentieth centuries are often referred to as the Golden Age of Mennonite society in Russia. There were some four hundred Mennonite villages, with a total population of over a hundred thousand. Education was universal for girls and boys alike, and the literacy rate was over ninety per cent. There were two teacher-training colleges, a special school for the deaf, a business college, two trade schools, and institutions for training nurses. In 1914, the eighteen villages of the Chortiza colony had thirty flour mills and three plants manufacturing farm machinery. The villages were characterized by comfortable homes, well-stocked barns, and up-to-date agricultural machinery.[5]

The Mennonites commonly referred to themselves as *die Stillen im Land* (the quiet ones in the land). They steered clear of political controversies and avoided any actions that could attract unwelcome attention.

It was an approach that would serve them well for many decades. But not forever.

The first serious turbulence for the Mennonite colonies came late in the 1860s, when the government launched a program of Russification, under which Russian was to become the language of instruction in all schools. Most important of all in the eyes of the Mennonites was an 1870 decree making military service universal, which meant that their historic exemption was to come to an end.

The reaction in the colonies was prompt, and whole villages began making preparations to leave. Alarmed at the prospect of losing forty thousand of their most industrious and productive farmers, the czar's government sought a compromise. In the ensuing negotiations, the Mennonites based their position on the provisions of Paul I's *Privilegium*. The outcome in 1874 was an agreement to replace the Mennonites' military exemption with an obligation for non-combatant service, which in peacetime would take the form of forestry work, and in wartime would take the form of service in forestry or in the army medical corps.

This compromise was acceptable to many in the colonies, but by no means to all. Some had been shaken by the government's attempt to end their historic exemption and were determined to leave. In Canada, the new province of Manitoba had come into existence, and the Canadian authorities were eager to attract settlers. Guarantees of religious freedom and exemption from military service were forthcoming, and large tracts of land were set aside in the south of the province. The United States was also prepared to welcome the colonists. By 1880, some ten thousand

Mennonites had left Russia for the United States, mainly Kansas, and eight thousand had left for Canada.

Those who chose this option were spared the much harsher events that were to unfold in Russia in the early twentieth century.

Among the group who migrated to Russia in 1803 was Heinrich's ancestor, Johann Kruger. Johann was a clockmaker from Marienburg (now Marbork, Poland) in the Vistula area of Prussia who settled in the Chortiza colony. He found a need for his skills in the new land, and passed those skills on to his descendants.

Over the next 125 years, Kroeger clocks were a common artifact in Russian Mennonite households (various documents show a casual approach to the spelling of our name, including for example Kruger, Kroger, Koeker, Kroeger) The clocks were manufactured in the village of Rosental by successive generations of Kroegers until the 1920s. The mechanism of the clocks was simple, consisting of a pendulum and a set of weights that drove the inner works and the chimes. The faces were about thirty centimetres square and were usually painted with floral designs. In many Mennonite households, the end of the day was marked by the father winding the Kroeger clock before the family retired for the night.

Heinrich was a member of the extended Kroeger family, but was not from the branch that manufactured the clocks. He was the eldest of four, the others being his brothers Peter and Abram, and his sister Maria, who was the youngest. Heinrich came from an average family: neither rich nor prominent in the community, nor a member of the landless proletariat. His father was a carpenter and, with his sons, also farmed the family landholding of 65 *dessiatines* bestowed by the *Privilegium* in the early years to Mennonite colonists.

The family lived in the village of Rosental, which adjoined the village of Chortiza (somewhat confusingly, Chortiza was both a village and the name of the colony). Heinrich attended the village school, and then the *Zentralschule* (secondary school). The surviving report cards show that he attained average-to-good marks. During Heinrich's time there, the *Zentralschule* had a tall tower surmounted by a large, specially designed clock known as the *Kroegeruhre* (Kroeger clock).

The Kroeger clock brought to Canada by Heinrich and Helena.

Heinrich's mother died at the age of twenty-seven, when he was eight. His father remarried, and the young Heinrich came to dislike his step-mother. Fortunately, there was a strong emotional bond between him and his maternal grandparents. They visited him when he was in the forestry camp, and wrote to him regularly with parental counsel as well as news of current happenings. His grandfather died in 1910, and one of the first entries in the 1911 diary deals with a visit to his grave. His grand-mother came to live with him after that, and late in the year fell ill. Sadly, in January 1912, she also died.

Among her effects that Heinrich inherited was a finely crafted wooden box. An inscription in German is penciled on the bottom of the box:

Heinrich Kroeger gehort die Dose. Diese Dose hat meine Grossmamma zu Weihnachten 1857 bekommen; ihr Vater Jacob FAST hat sie gemacht.

The band at the Azov forestry camp, c.1908. Heinrich Kroeger is seated at the right end of the second row.

(The box belongs to Heinrich Kroeger. This box was given to my grandmother at Christmas, 1857; Jacob Fast, her father, made it.)

It was in this box that Heinrich would keep his notebooks and papers for the rest of his life, including a number of letters he had received from his maternal grandparents.

When in 1905 he reached the age of twenty-one, Heinrich was inducted into the forestry service and was assigned to a camp near the Sea of Azov, which was one of the first established under the Compromise of 1874. The Mennonite colonies operated the camps, bore all of the costs, and assigned Mennonite chaplains to look after the spiritual life of the inductees. The young men lived in barracks and were outfitted with uniforms. Their daily work included management of a nursery, planting saplings, logging, and removal of dead trees.[6]

To relieve the isolation and tedium of life in the camps, the colonies supported the creation of choirs and bands, and engaged conductors locally. They also provided the camps with libraries. Nevertheless, the young men looked forward to periods of leave, when they were allowed to return home.

Heinrich Kroeger's papers included a professionally taken photograph of a brass band in which he played. He formed some lasting friendships in those times, and in later years looked forward to the camp reunions that were held periodically.

After completing his three years of forestry service, Heinrich rejoined his family in Rosental. During the next few years, he led the agreeable life of a young Mennonite man, farming the family's land and, in his leisure time, enjoying the company of his friends, singing in a choir, travelling to visit relatives in nearby villages, attending church, and swimming in the nearby Dnieper River.

The annual farm cycle began in March, when there were still periods of frost. Together with his father, his brothers, and hired Russian workers, Heinrich harrowed the fields, spread manure to fertilize them, and then seeded the crops. The family's holdings were divided into five relatively small fields on which they grew a variety of crops: barley, rye, corn, wheat, oats, melons, cucumbers, pumpkins, and hay.

The period of peak activity began in early July, when harvest got under way. Heinrich's 1911 diary contains a succession of entries about long days of work with his brother Peter (Abram was by then taking his turn in the forestry service):

> We threshed the load that was left over before breakfast. Then we went for the last two loads of wheat, which we did not thresh until after lunch. We also brought in one load of rye and threshed it. We went to the Dnieper for a swim towards evening. The hired man trimmed the straw stacks. I kept the man who was hired by the

Heinrich Kroeger's house in Rosental.

Heinrich Kroeger and hired men at work on the farm.

month until threshing was finished for another three days paying him by the day.

Harvesting the cereal crops took some six weeks; after the cereal harvest, Heinrich and Peter brought in pumpkins, melons, cucumbers, and corn. They sold some of their production, ground some for early consumption, and stored some for the winter. They and the hired man then ploughed the fields to prepare them for spring planting. Sunday was always observed as a day of rest in the colonies, even in periods of high activity such as seeding and harvest.

Under Russian law, title to land in the Mennonite colonies was initially vested in the villages rather than in individuals. While over time some individuals came to hold titles, the lands were managed communally. In July 1911, Heinrich attended a meeting at which it was decided which fields were to be planted in various crops the following year. Crop rotation was managed by the village, with individual fields being planted in cereals for three consecutive years, followed in the fourth year by a planting of vegetables such as melons and pumpkins. Village meetings also decided the number of cattle and other animals an individual was allowed to keep in the common pastures. During the ripening season, guards were posted at night to protect the crops from marauders—animal or human.

From today's perspective, an irony emerges from Heinrich's account of farming in the Chortiza colony. If in the 1920s the Bolsheviks had chosen to examine Mennonite practices—which they decidedly did not—they would likely have found a model of community agricultural management that worked, unlike the collective farms that Stalin imposed on the population in the first five-year plan.

Agricultural management was only one element of village self-government as practiced by the Mennonites. Adult male landowners made up the governing body, and village meetings were held approximately every few weeks, perhaps with more regularity outside of the busy times of planting and harvest. The subjects dealt with over the thirteen months of Heinrich's diary included the establishment of a credit union in the

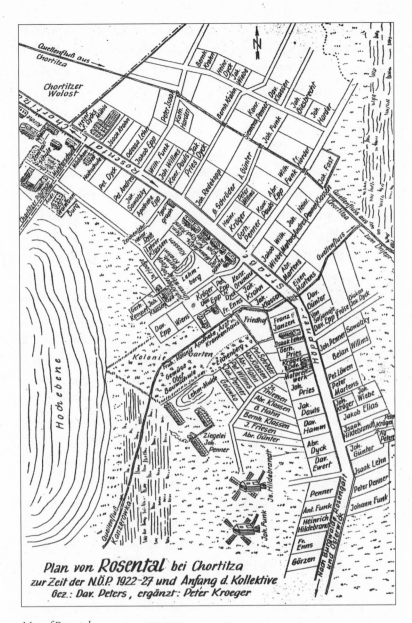

Map of Rosental. (Russian Dance of Death, 8)

colony, living quarters for a teacher, and a loan for construction projects in the schoolyard. Self-government was equally practiced in the field of religion. On April 15th, 1912, Heinrich attended a meeting that chose the preachers for the coming year.

Part of the responsibility of village residents was to engage regularly in communal work. Over the course of a year, Heinrich and his hired man between them contributed some four weeks of communal labour, repairing roads, clearing trees, painting street signs, and hauling bricks to the school. Residents of the colonies were also required to contribute to security arrangements, and Heinrich recorded standing guard duty with the village police.

Although farming involved a good deal of hard work, especially during seeding and harvest seasons, residents of the colony were also able to enjoy leisure time. The recurring pattern in Heinrich's diary entries for Sundays was church in the morning, visiting in the afternoon, and then a film in the early evening at the village "biograph," which showed silent films dealing with subjects such as Biblical events and Napoleon's invasion of Russia in 1812. A place that Heinrich particularly liked to visit with his friends was the *Koloniesgarten*, a park beside a stream in Rosental. The park was described by one resident as having "big oaks and stately poplars, dozens of varieties of flowers and hosts of birds singing overhead."

In 1910, the village of Rosental established a *Naturschutzverein* (Society for the Protection of Nature). The following year, Heinrich recorded attending "a public lecture about nature," and on April 1st, 1912, he paid a visit to an orchard being established by the Society. The functions of the Society would be readily recognizable to environmentalists today: publicizing the impacts of industrial development, opposing heavy deforestation, calling for better regulation of fishing in the Dnieper, protecting animals from cruel treatment, promoting the control of erosion. At the time the Society was established, the village granted it one *dessiatine* (one hectare) of land for twenty-five years to grow an evergreen forest. In December 1911, the Society purchased an additional two *dessiatines*, in the words of one resident, "to supply the population with young fruit trees, shrubs for berries and decorative purposes, selling seedlings at a low price, giving them for free to the poorest people."[7]

At the outbreak of World War I, the czarist government ordered the Society to disband. It was considered a risk because of its German-speaking members.

Music has always played an important part in Mennonite society, and still does. Congregations at church services in Russia sang hymns in four-part harmony, and at some Mennonite churches in Canada today this is still the case. Rosental had several choirs, an orchestra, and a brass band.

Heinrich's 1911 diary contains frequent references to music:

June 12
    In the evening I was in the garden, where an orchestra of
    stringed instruments played.
September 5
    The first choir practice in the evening in the auditorium of the
    Zentralschule.
December 25
    Some songs were practiced for the evening of the last day of
    Christmas [a three-day festival in the Mennonite calendar]
December 27
    We had a choir practice in the forenoon in the depot of Lepp
    and Wallman [farm machinery] factory and decorated the
    Christmas trees. The Christmas program lasted from about
    five thirty to eight oclock. There were three choirs singing.
May 15, the last day of Whitsuntide
    It is a Tuesday. An excursion of the choir to the Porogi [a set of
    cataracts on the Dnieper River]. The excursion lasted all day.

During this period Heinrich, age twenty-seven, was actively looking for a wife. One of the first entries in his 1911 diary reads:

Tuesday, May 10

> I got myself ready and went to A., the daughter of P. Loewen,
> to propose.

The response was evidently disappointing, since there are no further references in the diary to the lady in question. Then, towards the end of the year, Heinrich's younger brother Peter married an attractive young woman from a distant village. When Heinrich met her sister, he developed a strong interest in her. In early 1912, he made several long train trips to visit her and her family, but ultimately without result. However, that summer a friend told him of a young woman, Helena Rempel, who was working in a nearby village. He sought her out, and they were married after a two-week courtship. It was the beginning of forty-five years together.

One of the unusual features of Chortiza/Rosental was that, while the population was predominantly Mennonite, there were also a number of Jewish businesses and residences, and a large synagogue. The Rabbi lived down the street from the Kroegers, where he operated a small store, and his son played in the village orchestra. Heinrich's and Helena's wedding picture was taken by a Jewish photographer, Kogan.

Given the harsh anti-Semitism that characterized czarist Russia and the brutal pogroms that were a regular occurrence in town and country alike, it is not surprising that Jews would have chosen to settle in the more stable and tolerant environment of a Mennonite village. There were some instances of Jews being sheltered by Mennonites during pogroms. They learned to speak Low German, and some of their children attended the Mennonite schools in Chortiza, while others crossed the river each day to Alexandrovsk, neatly dressed in school uniforms.[8]

While the colonies were not completely free of anti-Semitism, relations between Jews and Mennonites were generally good. Heinrich's diary regularly records transactions with Jewish businesses, whether selling them agricultural produce or making purchases in their stores. He enjoyed particularly cordial relations with a local merchant, baker, and bookbinder named Israelski, with whom he recorded making a number of trips to neighbouring villages. On March 1, they went to Alexandrovsk together to get matzo bread from the synagogue there for Israelski's mother. The following month Heinrich rented land to him because Israelski wanted to plant melons. They also shared a hired man for a time.

Another unusual feature of Chortiza/Rosental was that it had some five hundred Russian residents and a Russian Orthodox Church (built by Mennonite industrialists). Most of the Russians would have been workers in the three large farm machinery factories that the Mennonites had established, but a number also worked as farm labourers. Heinrich employed at least one hired man year-round, and engaged a second on a month-by-month basis when required. At the peak of harvest activity, he engaged as many as six additional Russians, sometimes including women.

Employment on Mennonite farms was attractive to the local peasants. First, they were paid relatively well. Secondly, although they were subject to the sometimes harsh disciplinary regimes that were common at the time, they were better housed and fed than if they had worked for Russian landowners. The hired workers, who in their villages typically lived in crude huts, were given accommodation by the Mennonites in what amounted to servants' quarters in people's houses. At harvest time, the man Heinrich hired temporarily brought his wife to stay with him in the two rooms that Heinrich allocated to him. In January 1912, Heinrich recorded the death and funeral of a hired man's child. He also provided a helping hand when needed. On January 18th, 1912, he wrote, "Russians arrived in their broken down sleigh and we repaired it."

There was little difference between the work done by the hired peasants and that done by their Mennonite employers. Making bricks of manure and chopped straw, the standard fuel in the region, was done mainly by hired labourers, but other duties were equally shared. On June 20th, Heinrich recorded weeding a field while his two hired men cut straw, and on September 3rd he wrote, "Peter and the wife of the hired man and K.K. had winnowed enough wheat and had it bagged." The following April 4th he wrote, "We harrowed both small fields and also the wheat and the school hill. Then I and Tina, the wife of my brother, and the hired man went out to plant beans." This kind of interchange-ability between the functions of a hired man and his employer would be normal on a Canadian farm, but was not common on the estates of Russian landowners.

While relationships with Russian workers appear to have been gener-ally civil and constructive, there was a clear gulf between the Mennonites and the local population. There was no social interaction of any kind between the Mennonites and the local Russians, and for a young Mennonite man to marry a local Russian girl was virtually unheard of. The few who did generally left the colonies. For what it may be worth, there is also no reference anywhere in the literature I have seen to sexual exploitation of female Russian employees. One explanation could be the strict religious standards that prevailed in the communities.

There is one reference in the 1911 diary to a royal visit:

Wednesday, September 14th
> In the morning I and Anna [his stepmother] went to Einlage to Unger's place to get two bolts for the plough. I couldn't get them since it was a Russian holiday and furthermore a motorcade was proceeding from Ekaterinoslav-Alexandrovsk via Einlage, and the people had poured out on to the streets to watch the proces-sion since the successor to the throne of our Russian Emperor was supposed to be in it; we too watched the spectacle.

In 1981, a book was published providing a visual retrospective of life during this period. It comprised a set of portraits by Peter Rempel, who had been a professional photographer in Rosental, and provides an idyllic picture of well-dressed people enjoying life and each other's company in a prosperous and stable society. The nostalgia with which Mennonites in Canada looked back on the golden era of their society was captured by the title of the book: *Immer Sommer, Immer Sontag* (Forever Summer, Forever Sunday). One of the photographs is of a spring choir picnic beside the cataracts on the Dnieper; it took place a year after the one recorded in Heinrich's diary.

A group of young Mennonite women photographed by Peter Rempel of Rosenthal.

Henry Regier, Professor Emeritus at the University of Toronto, recounts that one of the photographs in the book includes his mother, Margaretha Kröger, with several close friends. On several occasions, he had urged her to talk about her friends and the photograph in which they appeared, but she always declined. The subject was too painful for her, because she knew from first-hand experience what had happened in the years after the photograph was taken.

Even in the late nineteenth and early twentieth centuries, all was not as idyllic in the Mennonite colonies as a nostalgic retrospective might suggest. The colonies were periodically riven by religious disagreement, and in 1860 a substantial group, reacting against growing secularism, split off to form what became known as the Mennonite Brethren.

With increasing prosperity also came social inequalities. By the beginning of the twentieth century, some estates had grown to comprise
thousands of *dessiatines,* while at the other end of the spectrum about
twenty-five per cent of the population had little or no land, partly because
of a prohibition by the czarist government on the subdivision of Mennonite
holdings. Being landless, members of this group could not participate in
village meetings.[9]

Conformist pressures, social as well as religious, were strong in the
tightly knit colonies. Together, the village assembly and the congregation—both groups were largely made up of the same people—controlled
the life of the community. Some individuals, particularly young people,
found the regime irksome. After the October 1917 revolution there were
cases of young Mennonites allying themselves with the Bolsheviks in
pursuit of—they thought—a freer and less materialistic society.

Ominous for the future of the Mennonite colonies were periodic
tremors in the Russian socio-political landscape. By the early twentieth
century, the country was rife with civil unrest. In 1905, following Russia's
defeat in the war with Japan and the "Bloody Sunday" suppression of a
demonstration in St. Petersburg, disturbances flared across the country.
Between 1907 and 1914 there were some 20,000 peasant attacks on landowners and wealthy individuals.[10] There were manifestations of nationalism
and xenophobia. Military interventions were frequently required to deal
with peasant uprisings and urban disorders until the outbreak of war in
1914. There were also a number of mutinies in the army.

The spreading unrest made itself felt in the Mennonite colonies. Among
Heinrich's papers is a letter of April 1906, sent to him at his forestry camp
by his maternal grandfather, which recounts an attack by ten "bandits"
who killed the village watchman and broke into several houses. Another
letter in September speaks of a village resident being killed and his wife
severely beaten in an attack. Elsewhere, there are contemporary accounts
of mobs gathering at the gates of Mennonite factories, and of rocks being
thrown at Mennonites when they drove through local villages. During
the same period, there were attacks on Jewish residents of Alexandrovsk.

Such attacks reflected the growing contrast between the prosperous living conditions of the Mennonite colonists and those of the peasants in the surrounding countryside, who were 85 per cent illiterate and lived in crude huts. Sensing the significance of the trends around him, a highly respected church elder and community leader in Rosental, Isaac Dyck, in 1909 privately expressed the view to a visiting Mennonite from Canada that the colonists should leave Russia and seek to establish themselves in another country.[11] He did not however feel sufficiently confident of his assessment that he could advocate it publicly. Given the comfortable circumstances prevailing in the colonies at the time, there was in any case little chance that such a suggestion would have elicited a positive response.

Resentment of Mennonite prosperity by the Russian peasantry was inevitable; that this resentment would grow in step with the growing disparity between the peasants' standard of living and that of the colonists was also inevitable. While some peasants benefited from employment and housing in the colonies, this group was a very small fraction of the millions who lived on the margins of survival, for whom the poverty and random violence in their villages were permanent realities, and in whose eyes those who were well off were exploiters and oppressors.

Consequently, when the Revolution came and governmental authority collapsed across the country, the Mennonite colonies were certain to become targets.

Heinrich Kroeger's father was apprenticed to a carpenter when he was young, and in turn passed on the craft to his eldest son.

On the inside back cover of one of Heinrich's notebooks is a sketch with accompanying instructions on how to make a coffin. It was knowledge he would be required to draw upon in the succeeding years.

TWO *War, 1914–1918*

One event happeneth to them all.
　—*ECCLESIASTES 2:14*

HEINRICH KROEGER and Helena Rempel were married on October 20th, 1912. He was twenty-eight, she twenty-six.

Heinrich's work as a carpenter, together with the products of the family farm, had given him a moderately comfortable life as a resident of the village of Rosental.

The young woman he married, Helena Rempel, was one of eight children in a Mennonite family. Some members of her family farmed, some operated flour mills, and in 1913 two of her brothers opened a plant that manufactured wagons. Aside from a school photograph, there are virtually no records of Helena's early life. The only document dealing with her parents is one about her attendance at her father's funeral in February 1915. One family legend has it that she left home at the age of thirteen because of difficult relations with her stepmother—an experience she had in common with her new husband, who disliked his own stepmother. On the other hand, she had a strong attachment to her brothers and sisters, and particularly to her older brother George.

Helena was literate, but had spent only four or five years in school; all the letters sent to members of their family over the years came from

Heinrich and Helena Kroeger's wedding photo, Rosental, October 1912.

Heinrich, never from her. She was a spirited person, warm and affectionate. While Heinrich's religious observances may have been largely *pro forma*, Helena's reflected a strong if simple faith. The fact that she was of very limited means and working for wages in a nearby village when she married Heinrich elicited some disapproving comments from his stepmother, who drew an unfavourable comparison with the marriage his younger brother Peter had made. Heinrich never forgot her comments and still spoke of them disparagingly some fifty years later.

For the first year of their marriage, they lived in Rosental, probably with Heinrich's parents as often happened in Mennonite families. However, in October 1913, Helena's brothers, George and Peter, invited Heinrich to become a partner in a wagon plant they were preparing to open in the district of Voronezh, some six hundred kilometres north of Rosental. He found this offer attractive on its own terms, and perhaps also because it gave him and his new wife an opportunity to strike out on their own.

Heinrich's share in the plant cost him 1,500 rubles—about 750 Canadian dollars, a large sum at the time. On October 31st, 1913, he wrote enthusiastically to his younger brother, Abram, who was still doing his national service at a forestry camp:

> Well, what do you think, we have an offer to become partners in the Olchowatka area. We do not want to sell our share (of the family farm), but we have to use cattle and equipment in order to make a down payment. Write soon what you think of this.

In January 1914, Heinrich and Helena arrived in the village of Olchowatka, where the plant was to be. It was an exciting time for them, and the future seemed full of promise. The diary entries for the late winter deal in rapid succession with the erection of the building, and with the installation of machinery and an engine to drive it. March 21st was a landmark day: work began on the first wagons. As production gathered momentum, there followed regular entries about making spokes, pegs, hubs, and other components. The work force of the plant included four Russian workers, a blacksmith, and an apprentice. Production continued through

Heinrich Kroeger at his wagon plant, Spring 1914.

the spring months, interrupted only in mid-May, when Heinrich and
Helena returned to Rosental for a reunion with Heinrich's contempo-
raries in the forestry service.

Olchowatka was a predominantly Russian village. The number of
Mennonite residents appears to have been fairly small. There was no
church, and on Sundays religious services were held in one or another
of the Mennonites' homes. There is no record of what led the Rempel
brothers to select it as the site of their plant, but potential market opportunities would be a plausible explanation. Russian towns generally had
fewer manufacturing facilities than the Mennonite colonies where the

brothers had grown up. In addition to the wagon plant, George and Peter operated a flour mill and a sunflower press in Olchowatka.

This period may well have been the happiest in Heinrich's and Helena's lives. During their later years in Canada, a photo of Heinrich at the door of the plant with a new wagon wheel always hung in their living room.

Yet there was a shadow on this happiness. By now they had a baby daughter, named Helena after her mother. On April 15th, Heinrich recorded that she had contracted measles. At that time, measles was a much more serious disease than it is today. In early May, the child's parents made a series of visits with her to the local doctor, and purchased the medicine he had prescribed. She apparently improved, and in May her parents took her along to the forestry reunion in Rosental. Reflecting the hope that she would make a complete recovery, Heinrich noted on June 20th that he had completed assembling a baby carriage that he had ordered for her in March.

During the following days, the child became seriously ill, and there were repeated visits to the doctor. Heinrich's diary then contains the following entries:

Tuesday, July 8
> At six o'clock this morning our daughter Helena finally passed away after a long illness. At once we made preparations for burial. Sent out telegrams.

July 9
> Began work on the coffin yesterday and got it finished today. The workmen have dug the grave in the Russian cemetery not far from the plant. The dear wife and others are busy preparing for the funeral.

July 10
> This afternoon our dear child was buried in the presence of the German people of this locality. There was a brief divine service.

July 12

I and Helena have put a fence around the grave of our Helena.

July 13, Sunday

Were at home in the afternoon. After that we went for a little while to the hill to look at the crops. We then stopped at the cemetery on the way home.

July 20, Sunday

Went to the cemetery to Helena's grave. Stayed at home the rest of the day.

After the tragedy of their child's death, Heinrich returned to work at the plant, and his diary again began to record the routine events of daily life. But this return to routine proved to be short-lived.

The chain of events that led to World War I was set in motion on June 28th, when Archduke Franz Ferdinand, heir to the Austro-Hungarian throne, was assassinated in Sarajevo. European governments exchanged communications; the pitch rose; and the military obligations enshrined in existing alliances were invoked. On July 28th, the czar ordered partial mobilization of the Russian army. Full mobilization followed on the 31st, and on August 1st, Germany declared war on Russia.

Under the Mennonites' 1874 agreement with the Russian government, they were exempt from bearing arms in wartime. However, they were required to enter national service either in forestry or the medical corps, known as the *Sanitatsdienst*. Between the summer of 1914 and the end of 1917, when Russia left the war, some twelve thousand to fourteen thousand Mennonite young men were enrolled.

As the trains bearing the first troops moved off to the front, there was a surge of patriotism in the major European countries. Volunteer organizations sprang up, well-born young women undertook training to become nurses, funds were raised for various causes.

Although the Mennonites did not join in the general cheering about the prospect of armed conflict, their reaction in other respects had a good deal in common with that of the general population. Their leaders sent telegrams of loyalty to the czar, and urged the young men to volunteer for medical service without waiting to be called up.[1] An editorial in a Mennonite newspaper stated, "We need to show that we have kept the promise of faithfulness made by our forefathers. Our confession forbids us to spill blood, but binding wounds we hold to be a sacred duty."[2]

Some of the Mennonites' displays of loyalty were likely prompted by worry that they could become the target of hostile actions by the Russian populace against the large German-origin minority in the country, which in 1914 numbered some two million. The risk was real, and the early months of the war saw some anti-German legislative measures. The Mennonites therefore had good reason to make a vigorous display of loyalty to their adopted country. The evidence suggests, however, that their manifestations of support for their Russian homeland were genuine. For well over a century, Russia had largely respected the undertakings it had given them about freedom of religion and exemption from military service. It was also in Russia that their communities had flourished and grown prosperous. For the Mennonites, their German links were cultural and religious rather than political. Russia was their home.[3]

Consequently, when the war broke out, the Mennonites responded promptly. Large donations were made in cash and kind, including funds for distribution to needy Russian families whose men had been called up. There were calls to establish a hospital in the Chortiza colony to care for wounded soldiers. Mennonite leaders and newspapers urged members of the community to assist local Russian families with the harvest.[4]

The first reference to the war in Heinrich's diary came on July 25th. He and Helena had received a telegram reporting the death of a beloved uncle and religious elder who had officiated at their wedding. They set off immediately to attend the funeral in Rosental, but were able to get only part way before they had to turn back because all the trains had been commandeered in anticipation of general mobilization. On July 29th, Heinrich recorded that his two brothers-in-law intended to volunteer as medical orderlies. He for his part focused on the local situation. On August 4th, he wrote, "Used the large grain separator and motor for threshing the crops of soldiers' wives whose husbands had gone to war." Further entries about threshing for Russian families in local villages continued for the next two weeks.

On August 5th, Abram wrote from Alexandrovsk, asking whether he should proceed with shipping various materials Heinrich had ordered for the wagon plant, in view of the likelihood that Heinrich would be called up. On August 20th, Heinrich wrote: "Because it appears that we will have to report for military service as medical orderlies, we are getting ready to leave." The wagon plant was closed and five cartloads of materials were taken to a warehouse. The young couple set off for Rosental. When they arrived on August 22nd, Heinrich reported for duty at the district office.

On the morning of September 1st, a train of horse-drawn wagons bearing Mennonite reservists moved out of the Chortiza colony. They were travelling to Ekaterinoslav (now Dniepropetrovsk), eighty kilometres to the north. When they arrived at the end of the following day, the reservists, including Heinrich and his younger brother Abram, reported to the military commandant. They were given physical examinations, followed by some initial training in their future duties. On September 7th, 1914, Heinrich sent the following postcard to his wife:

> Finally it seems to be definite what I shall be doing. The figures are approximately as follows: 2,000 men to be employed in the forests and 700–800 as orderlies. Abram and I want to serve as orderlies, and today it was decided. But we do not know where we will be sent. We leave here immediately.

In the event, their departure was delayed, which made it possible for Helena to come to Ekaterinoslav and stay for a week. On September 23rd, a group of 283 Mennonite orderlies boarded boxcars adapted for transporting people, known as *teplushki*. They were taken north to Moscow, where they arrived on the 26th. Heinrich and Helena were not to see each other again until the following June. He was thirty, she twenty-eight. She was also pregnant with their first son.

In Russia, much of the support for the war effort was provided by organizations known as *zemstvos*, which served as local assemblies of self-government and were dominated by local nobles. With the outbreak of war in 1914, the individual *zemstvos* were grouped into two national bodies. The largest, known as the All-Russian *Zemstvo Soyuz* (union) was to be Heinrich's employer for the duration of the war.

One of the first tasks undertaken by the *Zemstvo Soyuz* was the organization of medical services for the army in collaboration with the Red Cross. A component of the program was the outfitting of fifty trains to transport the wounded to hospitals in the interior. Mennonites were to staff forty-eight of these trains. The *Soyuz* also established 1,600 hospitals to receive the wounded.[5]

When Heinrich and the other prospective Mennonite orderlies arrived in Moscow, they were issued with uniforms. On the sleeve of each jacket was a white felt patch bearing a red cross and the three initials of the *Zemstvo* in Cyrillic script. The orderlies were then billeted in a former factory and given basic instructions.

Some were assigned to hospitals, others to the ambulance corps. Only a few became stretcher-bearers, because the authorities believed that persons of German origin could not be trusted on the battlefield to pick up the wounded. The great majority were assigned to the trains and were put to work cleaning old freight cars, installing bunk beds, and furnishing the cars with bedding and medical supplies. The trains comprised thirty to forty *teplushki*, with twelve bunks in each. Although the figures varied, the normal complement for a train was two doctors, six nurses, and thirty-four Mennonite orderlies, or approximately one per car. There were also three cars carrying medical supplies.[6]

On October 14th, Heinrich left Moscow for Brest Litovsk, some 150 kilometres east of Warsaw, where he was assigned to Train 195. He then wrote:

Within a few days we left Brest-Litovsk for Rovno. From there we went to Dubno…we were called out in early November…to go to Galicia to get wounded soldiers in Brody…

From Brody we went to Kiev the distance amounts to 450 *versty* [roughly 450 kilometres]. We travelled this route a long time. Made 13 trips. Made four trips in a different direction.

On one occasion, Heinrich's train was shunted on to a siding to let the czar's train go by.

The area served by Heinrich's train was the scene of heavy fighting. The normal practice was for the medical trains to move as close as possible to the front and then to load the wounded into the *teplushki*. Sometimes the trains would come under fire. One assessment found that some 120 Mennonite orderlies serving on the trains lost their lives, either to enemy fire or to disease.[7]

Much has been written about the carnage of World War I, in which the numbers of military casualties far exceeded those of the next world conflict over two decades later. Casualties were especially heavy on the Russian front. The Russian army took little cognizance of the machine-gun, rapid-firing artillery or other new military technologies. Even more than the armies in other countries, it continued to rely on traditional military practices, such as cavalry and bayonet charges. The army was also handicapped by badly organized support. Heinrich witnessed a case in which a shipment to the front of what was to have been rifles turned out to be shovels.

In the first five months of the war, more than one million men in the Russian army were killed, wounded, or taken prisoner.[8] During the winter of 1915, Heinrich saw frozen bodies piled like cordwood in the combat areas. As the casualties mounted, Russian medical support services rapidly became over-taxed. A field hospital built for 200 patients struggled to care for over 3,000 sick and wounded men, with only four doctors to attend to them.[9]

The experiences of the orderlies in the *teplushki* bringing the wounded back from the front could be horrific. Following is an account written by a young Mennonite in the same period that Heinrich's train was making its runs to Galicia:

Heinrich Kroeger as a medical orderly in the Czar's army, March 1915.

Heinrich Kroeger's shoulder badge, which he cut from his uniform when he was demobilized in 1918.

The service is really rather difficult. For two consecutive nights I did not sleep. Some (of the wounded) die in our arms. One hears much moaning and groaning. I had one young fellow in my car who was wounded near the mouth: both lips were shattered, the front teeth and tongue tip were missing. The mouth was badly swollen. He refused to eat and drink. Several times I was close to tears.[10]

On January 15th, Heinrich received a telegram from his wife in Rosental which read, "A son is born." They named the boy Nicholas.

Heinrich's papers include postcard-sized professional photos of himself, his two younger brothers, and his brother-in-law George all wearing the uniform of the *Zemstvo Soyuz*. Heinrich had his photo taken during a layover in Rovno on March 20th, 1915, and sent it home to his wife. His expression in the photo is sombre and his face shows the stresses he had been experiencing.

In early April, Heinrich's service was cut short by health problems. He was hospitalized for three weeks in Moscow and then was on convalescent leave until early June. A probable diagnosis would be rheumatic fever. In his notebook he recorded that his departure from Moscow in October had been delayed by "rheumatism in the legs." "Rheumatism" is also given as the reason he had to leave his train in April. Whatever the explanation, he was never able to return to duty on the hospital trains. He served the balance of the war in Moscow, and his time there was interrupted by recurrent periods of sick leave and convalescence.

Heinrich's ill health caused Helena great concern, and in June 1915 she boarded a wartime train and embarked on a three-day trip to Moscow, accompanied by her five-month-old baby. It was an act of considerable bravery. Moscow was then the scene of attacks on German-owned shops, factories, and houses. When she arrived, it was the first time Heinrich saw his new son, and he recorded his pleasure: "My dear wife with the small son Nicolai came here on June 20th."

After spending three weeks with her husband, Helena made a five-hundred-kilometre trip to Olchowatka to check the effects from the family wagon plant that had been placed in storage in August 1914. It

Helena Kroeger and her infant son Nick, with whom she made a three-day train trip in wartime to visit her ailing husband in Moscow, June 1915.

is probable that her brothers' wives and families were still living in the area, as she stayed for two weeks. She returned to Moscow on July 23rd, and then on August 8th embarked on the thousand-kilometre train trip back to Rosental. A month later, Heinrich took the risk of going absent without leave for two weeks because "I had to look after a great many things" in Rosental. Apparently his absence went unnoticed. On October 24th, Helena rejoined him in Moscow and stayed for a lengthy period.

From the summer of 1915 until he was demobilized in January 1918, Heinrich continued to work for the *Zemstvo Soyuz* in Moscow. At times he worked in the kitchens or made bandages. In November 1915, he acquired a sewing machine and began sewing for the orderlies and others on military service. His notebooks contain references to blouses, trousers, cartridge belts, and shoulder straps for epaulets. It appears that he was paid on a piece-work basis. It was not lucrative: his notebooks record returns of around seven rubles a week, which would not have gone far in the inflationary wartime economy. In February 1916, he was again hospitalized, and there followed a period of convalescence during which he was cared for by Helena.

In May 1916, Heinrich became a night watchman in the clothing department of the *Zemstvo Soyuz*. At the end of June, he was given three months' sick leave, which enabled him to spend the summer in Rosental, where he helped with harvesting and other farm work. During the winter of 1916 and 1917, his wife was again with him in Moscow, and worked for a time in a hospital to supplement their income.

During these years, Heinrich no longer kept a diary. Instead, he made entries from time to time in his notebooks about past events: injuring his hand in the planer at the wagon plant in the spring of 1914, the death of their daughter, his service on the trains, his work in Moscow. His retrospectives indicate periods of reflection about the changes in his life, and perhaps also uncertainty about the future.

In February 1917, bread shortages in Petrograd (the Russified name that had been given to St. Petersburg at the beginning of the war) triggered demonstrations that spread rapidly throughout the city. The old regime tottered towards disaster. Faced with widespread rioting and bloodshed, and with mutinies spreading through the army and the police, Czar Nicholas II was persuaded by his senior military commanders to recognize the inevitable. He abdicated on March 15th. The Provisional Government under Alexandre Kerensky took power.

Thirteen days later, the Kroeger's second son Henry was born in Moscow.

There is no indication of when Helena returned to Rosental, but it may well have been soon after the birth of the baby. Heinrich evidently continued to work for the *Zemstvo Soyuz* in Moscow, although there is virtually no documentation about his activities in 1917, nor about conditions back in Rosental. What is known, however, is that the year saw a disintegration of the government and the Russian army. Large numbers of soldiers deserted, many with their weapons, and armed bands roamed the steppe, attacking villages and estates more or less at will.

At the end of October, Lenin and the Bolsheviks managed to topple Kerensky's government and seize power. While the coup in Petrograd was completed relatively quickly and with minimal bloodshed, in Moscow there were ten days of fierce fighting in the streets before the Bolsheviks gained control.[11] For ordinary residents of Moscow, such as Heinrich, it was a fearful and dangerous period.

On December 3rd, 1917, his thirty-fourth birthday, Heinrich wrote to his wife:

Dear Lena,
Greetings! I am in a strange frame of mind. I would like to go away, but where? To you! Yes, to you. For the others are strangers to me, especially now that I have returned to Number 35 [a unit in the *Soyuz* where he had worked in 1915].

I know I must stay, otherwise I would leave. But to persevere to the end is my watchword, and I know it is better for you there, and I prefer that rather than have you starve here. Take each week one or two ¼ of milk for you and the boys, and you too, eat properly and I shall get by somehow and send you some money; it would be better to send coffee, which you can sell.

Today, on December 3rd, I am 34 years old. It is quiet here, but there is enough ferment here. There is some snow and little frost.

Went to divine service in the dormitory after I had written this letter so far. A Russian brother gave the address and we were blessed.

I have to look hard for sugar, it is very scarce. Got a few letters at the post office. Shall inquire at Medinka concerning the parcel from P.R. [possibly Peter Rempel] and to get bread for December for the ration cards.

Greetings and kisses to you and the boys.
Heinrich

After the October revolution, the Bolsheviks sought to consolidate their grip on power. One of their first acts was to seek an end to Russia's participation in the war. Negotiations with Germany got under way early in 1918.

Heinrich's notes record that the orderlies were demobilized on January 23rd, 1918. The advent of war had broken off his career at the wagon plant, and his service on the trains had impaired his health. Now he was able to return to the village where he had grown up.

But life in Rosental was to be very different from the life he had recorded in 1911.

THREE *Civil War, 1918–1920*

Our walks here extend only to the cemetery.
—Letter from a Mennonite woman in Rosental

THE RESIDENTS of the Mennonite colonies and their Russian neighbours survived World War I about as well as could be expected. They had suffered shortages of food and other essentials, together with considerable financial hardship. Yet the actual fighting had taken place beyond most people's horizons, in Poland, Galicia, and other western regions.

This situation began to change near the end of 1917, with the revolution that brought Lenin's Bolsheviks to power. The Bolsheviks' opponents responded by organizing armed resistance. The next three years saw widespread fighting, brutality, and chaos. During 1919, six different armies fought each other in South Russia. By the time the civil war ended in 1920, some seven million lives had been lost through combat and disease—more than during the war with Germany. There were often no fixed fronts, as military operations ranged over a wide area. Alexandrovsk and the Chortiza colony where the Kroeger family lived changed hands nine times.[1]

The Mennonite colonists had shared in many of the hardships experienced by Russians during World War I, and they were also to suffer the violence and devastation that spread across the country during the civil war. But there was an important additional consequence: the civil war was to be the first phase in the destruction of the Mennonite presence in Russia.

In early 1918, the Bolsheviks succeeded in establishing tenuous control in parts of the Ukraine, and then proceeded to set up local administrative structures based on peasant councils, or Soviets. The advent of the Soviets put an end to the system of self-government that had been a basic feature of the Mennonite colonies and villages for well over a hundred years. No time was lost in establishing a harsh new order of things. Decrees were issued expropriating property, and some people were evicted from their homes. The Chortiza soviet took hostages and made their release conditional on the payment of a tribute of two million rubles within three days.[2] Similar actions were taken in parts of the Molochna colony. The Mennonite colonists lived in fear.

The Soviet government's control of the Ukraine was to be of short duration. Under the treaty of Brest Litovsk, Russia withdrew from the war, and most of the Ukraine was ceded to Germany. In April, German and Austrian forces moved in and assumed control.

In contrast with their response to the outbreak of the war four years earlier, in 1918 the Mennonite colonists came to identify with the Germans. The loyalty they had expressed in 1914 with evident sincerity had been to the czar as the embodiment of their adopted homeland. But the czar was gone, and the Russia they had known no longer existed. Their homeland had turned on them. They had suffered anarchy and violence after the March 1917 revolution. Then the advent of the Bolshevik regime in October had brought expropriation and harsh authoritarian rule. The arrival of the German and Austrian armies in the spring of 1918 enabled the colonists to resume something approximating their traditional way of life.

The new occupiers put an end to the anarchy and re-established a semblance of order. Russian landowners and the Mennonite colonists were able to recover much of the property that had been seized from them. In doing so, a number of Russians engaged in harsh reprisals, including some executions of peasants and members of soviets who had been involved in property seizures—actions for which the Russians were to pay a high price some months later, when the German and Austrian armies were withdrawn. The Mennonites were less aggressive in recovering what had been taken from them, but the fact that the recovery of their property was enforced by the foreign occupiers would later be used to justify harsh measures against them.

The breakdown of civil authority and the raids by armed bands that became pervasive in the summer of 1917 led some of the foreign colonists in Russia to organize self-defence units. For groups such as the Volga Germans and the Lutherans, this was a fairly straightforward step. In the Mennonite communities, however, the question of taking up arms created painful divisions and, for some, a crisis of conscience. On the one side were those who vehemently opposed such a step as a violation of the principle of non-resistance that had been a basic tenet for Mennonites for nearly four centuries. On the other side were those, particularly young men, who held that the state had failed in its basic responsibility to afford them elementary protection, and that they should see to their own defence. To the present day, the term, *Selbstschutz*, which was the name given to the self-defence units set up in 1918, can stir divisions among Canadian Mennonites.

The main *Selbstschutz* units created were in the Molochna colony, and the one in Chortiza was apparently quite small. At their peak, the total number of young Mennonite men involved came to a few thousand. During initial engagements, they gave a good account of themselves and beat off several attacks on their communities by bandits and anarchist forces. Inevitably, however, their successes were of short duration.

When the German army withdrew after the armistice in the West, the *Selbstschutz's* situation became untenable. By March of 1919 it had been overwhelmed by greatly superior forces, particularly those of the anarchists, and some of its members were executed in reprisal.

Once the *Selbstschutz* had been crushed, the Mennonite communities were completely defenceless. Heinrich and Helena Kroeger and other families faced a situation in which there was no civil authority capable of protecting them—or indeed interested in doing so.

Heinrich Kroeger returned to Rosental from Moscow after he was demobilized in January 1918. He had rented out the family farm when he left Rosental at the end of 1913 to become a partner in the Olchowatka wagon plant. The house had also been rented, so he and Helena stayed with relatives for a time.

Heinrich made a living by doing carpenter work, as well as miscellaneous tasks. His notebook lists the following:

- from the warehouse 4 boards costing 10 rubles
- repair work on a wagon wheel.
- for taking care of a cow 6 rubles
- repaired wooden barrels 7 rubles
- set two saws and sharpened them
- miscellaneous work for blacksmith 1 ruble
- Lena earned another 5 rubles by working on Saturday for A. Goerz

In 1911, Heinrich had been on friendly terms with Israelski, a Jewish grocer and bookbinder, and his 1911 diary referred to trips the two of them had made together to neighbouring villages. Now, there was a new dimension to their friendship. A 1918 entry reads, "Worked at Israelski's doing sewing 10 rubles."

These were hard times. In June 1918, Heinrich sold the cream separator for 300 rubles, and then in October his summer coat, also for 300 rubles. With winter in prospect, he bought a padded jacket for 65 rubles. On a later occasion he could afford to purchase only half a loaf of bread. The family made its own soap, using fat, oil, and soda.

And then on December 1st and 2nd, 1918, in the immediate aftermath of the German army's withdrawal, came the first reference in the notebook to military operations:

Had [Red Army] soldiers billeted and fed them. 99 rubles and 10 rubles for butter, then for laundry and repairing 5 rubles, 25 rubles for food. Baking and milk 46 rubles equals 211.25 rubles.

A few months later, in March 1919, the Kroegers had a baby daughter and named her Helen after her mother and her deceased sister. The child was born at the beginning of a particularly turbulent and violent period.

In the first months of 1919, the conflict between the Red and White armies spread rapidly, and in the Ukraine the government effectively collapsed. Armed bands roved the country at will, sometimes joining with the Red or White armies when a common objective presented itself. The Mennonites called them all "bandits." Thus, one village resident wrote of "nightly break-ins such as we have become accustomed to during the White Army's regime."[3] Whites, Reds, or others—the Mennonites' experience was not materially different. In later life, Helena Kroeger would tell of hiding her small children under straw in the cellar when bandits came to the village.

Once, bandits appeared at the Kroeger house demanding money. The family had almost persuaded them that they were poor and owned nothing of value, when one of the bandits noticed that Helena was not wearing a wedding ring. He held a gun to Heinrich's head and demanded that she produce it. After hesitating, she pulled from a rat hole a cloth containing the precious ring. The bandits seized it and left. For the Mennonite colonists during the civil war, such experiences were all too common.

As the year 1919 progressed, Heinrich's notebook intermingled entries concerning income and expenditure and the happenings of everyday life with events reflecting the see-saw campaigns of the civil war:

- 10 eggs to Friesens 6 rubles
- Repairing a saddle 20 rubles
- Dug grave with Peter for A. Lehn. Took 100 bricks of pressed manure [commonly used as fuel] as payment.
- Pistol handles—a couple of halves—for Bolsheviks 2 rubles
- 2 piglets 360 rubles May 16 bought
- Tea and bread for Red Army officers 50R July 2
- 10 eggs 20R
- Sabre sheath July 18 15R [ownership unspecified, but not a Mennonite artifact]

- Laundering for soldiers of the White Army August 6 30R
- For cobbling by my wife 15R
- From the Reds for food 50R
- 5 pood of wheat from Penner. had it ground to feed the soldiers

An interesting sidelight of these entries is the evidence they provide that—at least in the Chortiza colony—both the Whites and the Reds paid for the food and services they received from the colonists.

The Mennonites came to dread the anarchist leader, Nestor Makhno. He had grown up in the town of Gulai Pole, near the Molochna and Chortiza colonies, and had worked on some of the large estates in the area. He was imprisoned for anarchist activities in 1908, but was released in 1917 as part of an amnesty declared by Kerensky's government. He was twenty-nine when he returned to his village, where he organized a soviet and began assembling an armed force. Short and slight of build and with boyish features, he became a charismatic figure. He appealed to the peasants' rooted hostility to all forms of authority, and large numbers of them soon began to rally to him. They were joined by army deserters, many of whom brought their weapons with them.

Estimates of the strength of Makhno's forces in 1919 run as high as 35,000 to 50,000. Most of the time their actual strength was probably closer to 15,000, but there is no doubt that Makno's troops were an important factor in the civil war; at times, they controlled large areas of southern Ukraine.[4]

They were also highly independent. Historian Orlando Figes gives the following account of Makhno's operations:

During the civil war Makhno's partisans fought almost everyone: the Rada forces; Kaledin's Cossacks; the Germans; Petliura's Ukrainian Nationalists; the rival bands of Grigoriev and countless other warlords; the Whites; and the Reds. The strength of his guerrilla army lay in the quality and speed of its cavalry, in the support it received from the local peasantry, in its intimate knowledge of the local terrain and in the fierce loyalty of its men.[5]

Makhno was noted for his ruthlessness. In the summer of 1919, he invited Grigoriev, a rival warlord, to a meeting, had him killed, and proceeded to take over his army.[6] In the winter of 1919, the Red Army joined forces with Makhno's anarchists. By spring, the combined force had succeeded in taking control of much of the Ukraine. The Molochna colony came under Makhno's control, with horrific consequences for the colonists. The Chortiza colony's turn would come a few months later. The twelve months of 1919 were to be the worst in the Mennonites' 130 years in Russia.

In the summer of 1919, the White Army under General Denikin launched a major offensive, in which they drove north up the left bank of the Dnieper with the Red Army retreating before them. Alexandrovsk was taken in short order. Makhno and his partisans also retreated and took up positions on the right bank in Chortiza, which was across the river from Alexandrovsk. Heavy fighting ensued, and artillery barrages across the Dnieper destroyed some Mennonite buildings. Eventually, the Whites moved on north towards Moscow, leaving Makhno's forces in control of the Chortiza colony and the surrounding area.

After nearly two years of raids and widespread disorder, the Mennonites of Chortiza were no strangers to violence, looting, rape, and other depredations. What befell them at the hands of Makhno and his anarchists in the fall of 1919, however, made their previous experiences pale by comparison.

During the anarchist occupation, a young Mennonite teacher, Dietrich Neufeld, kept a diary that he later published as *A Russian Dance of Death*. For much of this period he lived across from Heinrich and Helena Kroeger's house on the main street of Rosental. When the Makhno force swept in on September 21st, he wrote of hearing cannon shots, followed by:

horsemen and troikas careening madly into our village. The clouds of dust were so long we couldn't see the end of the column. There is a sense of nameless terror and impending disaster in the air.... The village is overrun with more and more of these gangs. The farmyards are thronged with wagons and mounted troops. They do whatever they please. Our very lives belong to them.

And on September 23rd:

...mounted troops demanding to be quartered.... There was much shouting and cursing; fences were broken down, and there was a hideous clattering of arms.[7]

Another resident of Rosental wrote of "hoof beats, neighing, grinding wagon wheels, and shouts—and soon the main street from Chortiza was over-run with mounted soldiers, armed with rifles, sabres, revolvers, and hand grenades dangling from their belts."[8] On the first day of the anarchist occupation, five residents were killed.

Makhno's troops looted the Mennonites mercilessly, and they were soon joined by peasants from the surrounding Ukrainian villages. There are contemporary accounts of hay racks, day after day, hauling away loads of furniture, bedding, clothes, and other effects.

The number of anarchists occupying Chortiza/Rosental and other villages in the colony was probably in the range of five thousand to ten thousand. There would have been some variation from week to week as Makhno orchestrated sorties to attack the White Army forces from the rear and to disrupt their supply lines. Virtually every house in Chortiza/Rosental was forced to provide billets for his soldiers, in some cases in numbers of ten or more. Impeccably clean linens on beds were soiled by the unwashed and lice-ridden bodies of the anarchist peasant occupiers. Furniture was mindlessly broken and china smashed.

Few of those billeted developed any civil relationship with the inhabitants. The three months of the occupation were dominated by threats, cursing, random beatings, robbery, torture, and casual shootings. Villagers were killed on the slightest provocation, or sometimes with no provocation at all. In one case, three anarchists attempted to shoot a fleeing

Mennonite but were so drunk that they missed. Other intended victims were less fortunate.[9]

Women were constantly at risk. A Canadian Mennonite, Anna Dyck Klassen, recounted an episode from her youth in Rosental:

> At this time, the Reds and the Whites were fighting at the bridge, and we were feeding and housing 30 Reds. Twenty-eight of them slept in the summer house and two slept in our house. Helena and I each went to other houses to sleep and early each morning we would slip back home. One morning as I was coming through our hedges, I was startled to find my mother waiting for me.
>
> That night, while I was gone, bandits had come and demanded the girl with the black hair and dark eyes. They had searched the whole house for me, and the soldiers, hearing the noise, had come to see what was the matter. When they found out, one of the soldiers told them to get out and leave me alone.
>
> "She's only 14," he said, "and anyway, if anyone is going to get her, it will be us."[10]

During the Makhno occupation, many women in the colony were raped. For women raised in such strongly religious communities, the experience was intensely humiliating as well as terrifying. For their husbands, it was traumatic. There are accounts of men being tied to chairs and forced to watch, or being tied to the beds on which their wives were subjected to multiple rapes by men billeted in their homes. After the anarchists had been driven out of the colony by the Red Army at the end of 1919, large numbers of women sought treatment for venereal disease. It was of course never possible to assess how many pregnancies resulted from the occupation.

One of Makhno's lieutenants during this period was Simeon Pravda. In his earlier life he had worked in a mine, where he had lost the lower part of both legs in an accident. Thereafter he walked on the stumps of his legs. Prior to the civil war, he had made a living as a beggar in his home village of Liubimovka, near the Mennonite colonies. Early in 1918, he had made himself the head of a sizeable group of anarchist brigands. When Makhno's forces occupied Chortiza, Pravda established a residence in a house next door to Heinrich and Helena Kroeger. One of Heinrich's notebooks includes a notation, "1 chicken for Pravda 50 rubles."

In the weeks after he had taken up residence, Pravda developed a quasi-civil relationship with a Mennonite teacher, Gerhard Schroeder. In conversation with him one day, Pravda pointed to his pistol and remarked that he had used it to kill fifty-six men. One of them was his brother, whom he had shot in a drunken quarrel. In another conversation with the teacher, Pravda swore that he would never be taken alive, and he proved to be as good as his word. In 1920, when a unit of the Red Army was closing in on him, Pravda used his pistol to take his own life.[11]

During the occupation the anarchists attacked and razed seven of the eighteen villages in the Chortiza colony. One of these, Eichenfeld, had formed a Selbstschutz unit that killed several partisans. On October 26, 1919, the anarchists launched a reprisal. Four hundred horsemen arrived in late morning. Some blocked the streets leading out of the village, others entered houses demanding food. Looting followed, and then the killings began. Some men were shot, others were clubbed to death with rifle butts, still others were hacked to pieces with sabers. Women and girls were raped. When it was over, according to one account, eighty-four men and five women lay dead.[12]

One of the worst events took place in the colony of Zagradovka, some 200 kilometers south-west of Chortiza. Six villages were attacked and one was burned to the ground. Some 220 men, women, and children were shot or cut down and buried in a mass grave.[13] A similar attack took place on November 10 in the Molochna at the village of Blumenort, which was burned to the ground. A few days later, those who had carried out the attack were in turn massacred by a regiment of Cossacks. Such was the chaos in Russia during the civil war.[14]

On October 30th, 1919, Dietrich Neufeld recorded in his diary the first appearance of a new scourge: typhus. Some of the anarchists who had entered the Chortiza colony in September were already suffering from typhus. From them it spread to their fellows and then to the local population. Lice were the carrying agents. Contemporary accounts speak of Makhno's peasant partisans being covered with lice, which could be seen crawling on the sleeves and collars of their clothes. An additional factor was their complete lack of personal hygiene. Because of the crowded quarters resulting from billeting, the Mennonite residents were unable to protect themselves from the disease, and in November it spread rapidly. Local facilities were soon overwhelmed, and the schools were taken over as infirmaries, with students providing care to the patients. The problems were compounded when two Mennonite doctors fell ill and were no longer able to care for other victims.

Contemporary estimates were that 85 to 90 per cent of the residents of Chortiza/Rosental contracted typhus. Many died, but the death rate among Makhno's partisans was much higher, possibly 50 per cent, because of their greater infestation with lice and their unsanitary lifestyle. Makhno himself was reportedly in a coma for a time in January 1920.[15] Because of the very high incidence of the disease, which left its surviving victims in a weakened condition for months, it became difficult to find anyone with the strength to dig graves. Multiple burials in single graves became unavoidable. On February 5th, 1920, Neufeld recorded that twenty coffins were carried past his house on one day, and twelve the next. The typhus epidemic continued into the spring of 1920.

In the winter of 1920, Heinrich Kroeger contracted typhus, as did his parents. In later life he recounted lying in bed with fever and sending his eldest son Nick, age five, into the other room to check on his father. When the boy returned, he said, "Grandpa is very cold." There followed these entries in Heinrich's notebook:

From Aunt Fr. Dyck lumber for two coffins for the parents 800 rubles. We paid with tallow. 2 cross pieces sold. Coffin for father is not yet paid for 500 R. Paid for the coffin later.

Being too weak to dig graves himself for his father and stepmother, he managed to hire someone to do the work:

150R contributed by Fr. and 250R father had in money was spent for digging the grave. Friesen contributed also 150R to the coffin and we gave 350R.

Just before Christmas 1919, residents of the Chortiza colony had the first indications that their ordeal was coming to an end. Artillery fire could be heard from a distance in the north, and then drew closer. On December 25th, large numbers of Makhno's forces began to withdraw from the villages. The Red Army, having broken the White offensive, was now moving to reoccupy the Ukraine. When they entered the Chortiza colony, they were virtually regarded as liberators. Their numbers grew, and Neufeld recorded seeing thousands of them marching through Rosental in the month of February. Although they in their turn had to be billeted and fed from severely depleted food supplies, they were regular troops and thus better disciplined than Makhno's anarchists. There was no more looting, and in relative terms relations with the population of the colony were generally civil. Heinrich recorded being paid 400 rubles for billeting Soviet soldiers from March 23rd to 26th.

The Chortiza colony was in a ravaged state, psychologically as well as physically. According to one estimate, some 1,500 residents had died of typhus, and a further 245 had been murdered.[16] After the nightmare of the Makhno occupation, the well-ordered and peaceful life of the pre-war period seemed like a distant dream.

Before the war, a typical Mennonite farm might have had eight horses, three or four work wagons, a buggy, machinery, five cows, and other livestock. In the three months of Makhno's occupation, the villages of the colony had been stripped bare. There were virtually no draft horses with which to work the land, and fields were becoming overgrown. Before the war, the grain harvest in one village had been 24 tonnes; in the early 1920s it was under 3 tonnes. Between 1917 and 1920, as a result of disease, killings, and flight to other colonies, the population of the Chortiza colony fell from 18,000 to 13,600.[17]

People's homes had been devastated. Anna Dyck Klassen wrote of re-entering her family's house, which was across the street from the

Kroegers, after the anarchists had vacated it: "Filthy people had been living in it, so it took a lot of work to clean it. Dirty soldiers had invaded Mennonite homes, eating all the food, stealing everything they could, and taking all their clothes."[18]

The Molochna colony had remained in control of the Whites during the last half of 1919, and was therefore able to come to the aid of Chortiza. In February, food, clothing, and seed grain began to arrive, together with clean bedding that helped to stem the typhus epidemic. In addition, arrangements were made for several hundred orphaned Chortiza children to be adopted in the Molochna colony.

Fighting continued between the Whites and the Reds for much of 1920. Having been driven back during the winter months, General Denikin resigned his command and was succeeded by Baron Wrangel, who managed to organize a final White offensive. He briefly held Alexandrovsk and Chortiza in September, but his army was then driven to the Black Sea, where it boarded ships to escape the advancing Reds.

The Bolsheviks had gained effective control of the Ukraine, and they turned on their erstwhile ally, Makhno. Some 1,500 of his soldiers were rounded up in Kiev and deported to Siberia. He for his part continued his guerrilla operations, now against the Red Army, until the summer of 1921. Other armed bands also continued their depredations during this period. In the latter part of 1921, with his forces defeated, Makhno took refuge first in Romania and then in Poland. He made his way to Paris, where in the last years of his life he wrote his memoirs and published a series of anarchist pamphlets denouncing the oppressiveness of the Bolshevik regime. He died of tuberculosis in 1934. His ashes are held in the Pere Lachaise cemetery, in a vault purchased by anarchists in New York.[19]

If the civil war yielded dreadful experiences for Heinrich Kroeger, his brothers and sisters fared no better. He received a distressed letter from the wife of his younger brother Peter, dated December 20th, 1920, with a sad catalogue of events. They had sold their effects in Rosental and moved to her home village. Peter was no longer at home. He had been conscripted into the White Army and had died not long after, possibly of typhus. His wife, who had come from a wealthy family, wrote:

> We still have food for the children and myself. But I have to earn it at cobbling. I charge 4 pounds of butter for a pair of shoes. I received word concerning my parents, that they are dead. This is very hard for me. It certainly was dreadful at your place. Have you any food left?

She too died during this period, leaving their children orphaned.

The younger brother Abram, still serving as a medical orderly on a train, wrote to Heinrich on November 18th, 1920:

> I am waiting and waiting with a heavy heart for letters from you, since the Wrangel bandits probably have committed many horrible deeds in your parts. Tell me what has happened during the four years of my absence. Have you been starving there?

Abram spent seven years as a medical orderly, first in the war against Germany/Austria, and then during the civil war. In a letter to Heinrich on Christmas Day, 1920, he described himself as an army conscript, and said:

> On the train, I am the assistant of the manager, the same as in former days. I am afraid they might appoint me manager. I am very tired of the service here, but I cannot leave and furloughs are not granted. Furthermore, is it worthwhile to go somewhere on a passenger train and become infected with typhus? Although I recovered from recrudescent typhus, I have no desire to go down with spotted fever. Our route is Gomel-Kaluga [southwest of Moscow], one trip after another with typhus patients.

The youngest member of the family, Maria, had been a nurse in a mental hospital known as Bethania, which the Mennonites had established in the Chortiza colony in 1911. It was repeatedly looted by bandits in 1918 and in 1919 was nationalized by the Bolsheviks. A letter dated May 17th, 1919, from Abram reported that Bethania was again functioning, and that the patients had returned. But this was only temporary, as matters turned out. When Makhno occupied the colony some four months later, Bethania was again looted; subsequently, it was used as an anarchist headquarters.

Harshly treated though the Mennonites were, there were a good many others who fared as badly or worse. The Jews became the object of repeated attacks by virtually all the contestants in the civil war. Jews were particularly hated by the Whites because some of the prominent Bolsheviks, such as Trotsky and Kaganovich, were Jewish. A number of the commissars were also Jews. For other parties in the civil war such as the Reds, the Ukrainian Nationalist and Polish armies, Makhno's anarchists, and the various armed bands, the strong anti-Semitism that had historically characterized Russia, plus the unfettered violence of the times, motivated an unrelenting series of attacks. A 1920 report by a Jewish organization spoke of "more than 150,000 deaths" among Russia's Jews.[20]

There is no record of what happened during the civil war to Heinrich Kroeger's friend Israelski or the other Jewish residents of Chortiza/Rosental.

By the end of the civil war, Russia's national income had fallen by two thirds, the railways had been destroyed, and Moscow and Petrograd had lost over half of their inhabitants.[21] The country was exhausted.

In March 1921, Lenin declared the New Economic Policy (widely referred to as the NEP), which called a halt to nationalization, relaxed some controls on economic activity, and restored a degree of independence to the peasants, including the ability to sell their produce at markets. A further component of the NEP's proclamation was that emigration would be allowed.

Heinrich and Helena Kroeger, their relatives, and many other Russian Mennonites began to look seriously at far horizons.

FOUR *Hay for Butter, 1920–1924*

A handful of meal in the barrel, and a little oil in the cruse.
—1 KINGS 17:12

FROM 1914 TO 1920, Russia suffered a succession of apocalyptic events: war, revolution, occupation by foreign armies, civil war, and a typhus epidemic that took the lives of millions across the country. The victory of the Red Army late in 1920 brought an end to the civil war, but in the years that followed two further seals of tribulation were to be opened: famine, and hyperinflation, which destroyed the currency and wiped out personal savings.

Heinrich Kroeger continued to suffer from ill health after the war. The notebooks convey a picture of difficult circumstances. He retained possession of the house and the adjoining barn, but not of the fields that had figured in the 1911 diary; they were rented out for rather modest sums, perhaps because his health did not allow him to work them. At most, he seems to have cultivated several small tracts of land and quartered some livestock in the barn. He also worked for a time in the Lepp and Wallman plant, manufacturing agricultural machinery. The money he brought in from carpentry accounted for a good deal of his income, but it had to be supplemented by a range of odd jobs: cobbling, repairing a saddle, driving people to neighbouring villages, digging graves, threshing for a neighbour. Having directed a hired man—sometimes several—on his farm before the war, he was now reduced to acting as hired help for others.

In 1920, food shortages became more severe, partly because of a poor harvest. In November, Heinrich's name was included with 182 other residents of Rosental in an official list of the poorest villagers, who had the right to receive flour. Again in May 1921, he was on a list of villagers authorized to receive foodstuffs. That summer a severe drought devastated crops, and signs of famine emerged.

As food grew more scarce, Helena would go out to search for whatever food might be available. On a good day, she might return with an onion or a few beet greens that could be boiled. When she was unsuccessful, the children—Nick, now six, Henry, four, and Helen, two—would go hungry. A fourth child, Aaron, was born in March 1921, in the early stages of the famine. He died in January 1923. There is no record of the cause, but older members of the family cite diphtheria.

Problems of food shortage had emerged in Russia in the first year of World War I. Millions of men had been conscripted from farms into the army, and this reduced the production of grain. Wartime pressures on the transportation system affected its distribution. In addition, spiralling inflation and shortages of goods made it more attractive for peasants to consume what they produced or to feed their grain to the livestock, rather than exchange food for the rapidly depreciating currency.

The advent of the Bolshevik regime in late 1917 set in train events that several years later would turn food shortage into famine. The chaos and destruction of the civil war severely reduced production in much of the countryside, as did attacks on landowners and seizures of estates by peasants. Production was further affected by initial steps towards the establishment of state and collective farms.[1]

The strategy of seizing grain from well-off farmers, as urged by Lenin in the early post-revolutionary period, did not yield enough to feed the country, and requisitioning was soon extended to the peasantry. The response of the peasants was the same as it had been in czarist times: they reduced their production or hid it from the government. Armed squads sent out by the regime met armed resistance. It was a contest that

Famine victims. (Mennonite Heritage Centre 078.069)

the peasants could not hope to win, and ultimately they were crushed. In the process, the stage was set for a famine that would take five million lives—on the heels of civil war, in which some seven million Russians had already died.[2]

The drought of 1920 to 1922 was devastating. Historically, the peasants had anticipated and prepared for periodic crop failures by keeping some grain in reserve. This time, however, there were no reserves left after the heavy requisitioning. By the spring of 1921, one quarter of the peasants in Russia were starving.

The Mennonite colonies felt the full impact of the famine as it developed. People ate moss, chaff, dried weeds, ground corn cobs, and other fodder. Heinrich and Helena suffered great stress. They suffered prolonged hunger, their small children often went hungry, and death claimed friends and neighbours. By the spring of 1922, the death toll in the villages was climbing.[3]

A resident of Rosental wrote of people being swollen with hunger. He also observed:

We noticed [the hunger] in our church service, especially in the matter of singing.... Singing takes physical strength and this was lacking. So the singing was becoming very weak.[4]

What is most remarkable about this period is the unshakable religious faith displayed by Mennonites through all the tribulations they endured. Individuals displayed a commitment to non-resistance even as they faced death. A book by Gerhard Schroeder dealing with the horrific events in Chortiza/Rosental is entitled *Miracles of Grace and Judgment*. Its chronicle of one catastrophe after another is interspersed with repeated expressions of thanksgiving and passages of religious affirmation. Small wonder that, when Winnipeg author Al Reimer came to write a novel about the civil war period, he chose as its title the words *My Harp is Turned to Mourning*—a passage from the book of Job, whose resilient faith in times of adversity the Mennonites emulated.

The dire conditions in Russia attracted the attention of the outside world. The American Relief Administration (ARA), headed by Herbert Hoover, had been established to provide food to European countries that had been ravaged by the war. It offered to extend its operations to the Soviet Union. Lenin's reaction was one of fury at the humiliation of having to accept food from abroad, but ultimately he had no choice. The Bolshevik government concluded an agreement with the ARA in October 1921. Partly because of obstruction from Soviet officials, it was to take another six months before food supplies began to reach the population. By the summer of 1922, the ARA was feeding ten million people a day in the Soviet Union.[5]

Reports of acute distress in the Mennonite colonies reached their co-religionists in the United States, Canada, and Europe. In the summer of 1920, the Mennonite Central Committee (MCC) was formed in the United States to undertake a relief program. In the same year, Canadian Mennonites organized themselves to provide relief supplies and made a decision to channel them through the MCC, which in turn allied itself with the ARA. Because of the civil war, it proved impossible to deliver any supplies to the Ukraine during 1920, and further delays were caused by Soviet officials in 1921. The first supplies reached the Russian Mennonites in March 1922. Some who lived through this period said later that the food relief arrived just in time to prevent as many as ten thousand deaths in the communities.[6] Nick Kroeger recalls that a shipment of Carnation milk from the United States helped the family survive the famine.

By August of 1922, 140 Mennonite field kitchens had been established and were feeding 40,000 people daily. The kitchens distributed food not only in the colonies but also in the neighbouring villages. From its inception, the MCC practiced a policy of non-discrimination in its relief operations—an approach that continues to the present day. In the region of Halbstadt, one third of the children fed by the MCC in 1922 were Ukrainian.[7]

The arrival of the supplies alleviated, but did not end, the suffering. Priority was given to feeding women and children. Much of the population received only limited rations, and deaths continued into the summer of 1922.

The return of the rains that year provided badly needed relief. Relatively good crops in 1922 and again in 1923 permitted some rebuilding of food supplies. The suspension of grain requisitions under Lenin's New Economic Policy also helped to relieve shortages. However, the relief program continued into the following year.

On September 6th, 1923, Heinrich Kroeger recorded, "Worked on the threshing floor, American grain is being threshed all day long." Thanks to assistance from North America, his family survived the famine.

Difficult as Heinrich's and Helena's situation was, their poverty may have spared them the treatment that the local soviets meted out to those of more substantial means in the 1920s, including confiscations, arrests, deportations, and executions. Representative of what happened to many better-off Mennonites during this period was the experience of Helena's older brother, George Rempel, who owned a flour mill. One day he saw a group of Red Guards and Bolshevik functionaries approaching his mill, evidently with the intention of taking it over. He did not wait for them to arrive, but took to his heels. The Red Guards opened fire when they saw him running away. He was wounded in one leg, but managed to escape.

The notations in Heinrich's internal passport of March 1923 placed him on the acceptable side of the socio/ideological divide:

4. (a) Military status in old army: labourer
6. In what military campaigns participated: - - -
11. Political party: - - -
14. Main occupation: carpenter
15. Other occupation: wheat grower

In a similar innocuous vein were the entries in his application for a passport to emigrate in 1926:

5. Occupation: till 1918 was engaged in agriculture. After 1918 worked as a carpenter.
6. Former status: peasant
7. Was not a member of a trade union.
8. Was not a member of the party.
9. Was not brought to trial.
10. Was not abroad

The other scourge of the early 1920s was hyperinflation. In their struggle to make ends meet as prices spiralled upwards, Heinrich and Helena increasingly sought compensation in kind for their work, rather than in depreciated currency:

- through knitting, 5 rubles and 1 kerchief and shirt for child
- for washing at Heese Lena received 20 rubles and 5 pounds of beans.
- 2 loads of rye chaff from Penner for work on sleigh
- traded chest of drawers for 3 piglets and 10 pood of grain.
- two loads of hay for two pounds of butter

Inflation had begun under the czarist government, which had printed money to finance its war effort. Inflation continued under the Bolsheviks, and then accelerated during the civil war, when government control of much of the country had ceased to exist. In the absence of any means of collecting taxes, the Soviet government had no alternative but to increase the printing of money. The cumulative results are reflected in the notebooks. In the fall of 1918, Heinrich paid 26 rubles for a piglet. In May of the following year, he paid 360 rubles for two piglets and, in August, 500 for one.

The upward spiral of prices did not worry Soviet officials. Bukharin, a member of the Politburo, went so far as to extol extreme inflation as a way of moving to a true communist economy that would function without money.[8]

Extreme inflation did come to pass, even if the true communist economy did not. As money became virtually worthless in the early 1920s, butter came to be used as a medium of exchange. In Rosental, one pound of butter was the equivalent of 25,000 rubles in late 1921; 110,000 rubles in the first part of 1922; and, by the fall of 1922, it was worth 1.8 million rubles.[9]

Heinrich's notebooks reflect the culmination of inflation in early 1924, including "14 billion rubles paid to B. Toews to remit to the financial division for me." In that year, the Soviet government carried out a major currency reform, with the result that for a time there were two kinds of currency in circulation; the new currency was known as "Soviet coupons." On February 21, 1924, Heinrich recorded receiving rent money from Julius Siemens in the amount of 170 billion rubles—in the new currency, this amounted to only 8 rubles.

The currency reform proved successful. From 1924 on, prices were stable.

The political and economic instability in the USSR, and particularly the traumas experienced by the Mennonites since 1917, caused Heinrich and Helena to consider emigration.

The question of the Mennonites' future in Russia was a subject that had been raised from time to time in the colonies. After a major exodus in the 1870s, various families chose to follow their co-religionists to North America in the years up to 1914. Sad to relate, a few, after experiencing the harsh winters of Saskatchewan, made the fateful decision to move back to Russia.[10]

As early as 1911, Heinrich had clipped an advertisement for sailings to Western Europe from Libau in Latvia—Libau would later be the port from which most Mennonite emigrants departed. He also saved a German-language newspaper dated April 1918, containing an article about the prospects for emigration of persons of German descent. The countries discussed included Australia, New Zealand, and Argentina. North America was described as unpromising because of the difficulty of obtaining a block of land sufficient for a large settlement. Also in 1918, non-Mennonite colonists in Russia who were of German origin began discussing a possible mass return to Germany.

The Mennonites' interest in emigration intensified after the civil war. Religion was under attack, the Soviet government was seizing lands and transferring them to Russian peasants, people were being arrested and beaten on trivial grounds, local soviets had superseded village self-government, and the Red Army was conscripting Mennonite young men. The famine of 1920 through 1922, and the hyperinflation that followed, further strengthened the urge to emigrate.

These factors weighed on Heinrich and Helena, but still they had mixed feelings about leaving. She was more favourably disposed to it than he. She had been alienated from her stepmother from an early age, and her father had died in 1915. Several of her brothers and a sister had made up their minds to leave. On Heinrich's side, the civil war had claimed the lives of his father, stepmother, and younger brother Peter, as well as a cousin who was also a close friend. On the other hand, both Heinrich and Helena had deep roots in Russia, where their families had lived for five generations. It was the only society they had ever known. Many family members would be left behind. And perhaps times would get better.

In January 1920, the leaders of the Russian Mennonites sent a *Studienkommission* of four people to explore the prospects for immigration in Western Europe, Canada, and the United States. On February

7th, 1922, a meeting of the Union of Mennonites of South Russia, after considerable debate, arrived at a decision in favour of leaving.

Putting this decision into practice entailed some risks. There was a serious possibility that, if the Mennonites applied to leave the country, they would suffer reprisals from the authorities. Nevertheless, they decided to open negotiations.

While sentiment in the colonies was predominantly in favour of leaving Russia, the decision was not unanimous. The arrival of relief shipments from abroad had alleviated the famine, and the years 1922 and 1923 had seen good harvests. Some flour mills owned by Mennonites were reopening. After a series of meetings with Soviet representatives in the spring of 1922, the Mennonites obtained recognition as a national minority with certain privileges such as independent farming, together with other concessions that granted them significant economic freedom. The New Economic Policy with its provisions for economic liberalization held out the prospect that, over time, things would return to normal.[11]

Only late in the decade, with the brutal imposition of the First Five-Year Plan by Stalin, would it become evident—too late—that the apparently promising situation of the mid-1920s had been a false dawn.

FIVE *Opening the Way*

*Steps should be taken to prevent the entry to Canada of all persons who may
be considered undesirable...owing to their peculiar customs, habits, modes
of living, and methods of holding property...*
            —*Excerpt from Canadian government Order-in-Council*
                                    P.C. 1204 of May 1, 1919

THE THOUSANDS of Mennonites who wanted to leave Russia, including
the Kroegers, faced two big questions: Would they be allowed to go? And
would any country take them in?

When Mennonite leaders opened discussions about emigration with
the authorities in Kharkov, the response was reminiscent of what the
Mennonites had encountered in Prussia some 135 years earlier, when they
sought to accept Catherine the Great's invitation to migrate to her "New
Russia": emigration by the poor and landless could be contemplated, but
there was to be no mass exodus. A complicating factor was the division
of responsibility between the USSR and the Ukraine. The Soviet government in Moscow had lifted its controls on emigration as part of the New
Economic Policy in March 1921. The authorities in Kharkov, on the other
hand, wanted to keep their Mennonite farmers and therefore caused most
of the difficulties.[1]

The Mennonite side was led by B.B. Janz. He had served as a teacher for twenty years before the war, and then in 1914 had, like other Mennonites, entered non-combatant service. During the famine of 1921 to 1922 he negotiated the entry of American relief supplies into the Mennonite colonies. Tall and spare of build, he displayed unlimited patience and energy as he dealt with the authorities on the proposal to emigrate.

Some of the obstacles were simply bureaucratic; others stemmed from the hostility of officials. At one point, Janz's activities attracted the attention of the GPU (as the secret police were known at the time), and he was interrogated at the notorious Lubyanka prison in Moscow.[2] Because of his experiences with Soviet officialdom, he correctly came to the view that the concessions made under the New Economic Policy were only a temporary expedient, and that emigration was the right course for the Mennonites.

In the early stages, the authorities demanded evidence that some country was willing to receive Mennonite immigrants from the USSR. Initially, Paraguay was the only prospect, but in June 1922, the newly elected Liberal government in Canada lifted barriers that its predecessor had put in place three years earlier.

There was also the question of what was to happen in the cases of emigrants who were rejected as immigrants on medical grounds after they had crossed out of the USSR, since the Soviet authorities took the position that these people would not be allowed back in. Eventually, the Weimar government was persuaded by Mennonites in Germany to provide temporary accommodation for medically rejected individuals while they were receiving treatment—most commonly for trachoma, a highly infectious eye disease then prevalent in Russia.

The next big question was how passage was to be financed. Prior to 1914, this would not have been a problem; some Mennonites were wealthy, and most had sufficient means to travel abroad if they chose to do so. In 1914, Heinrich Kroeger's property had a valuation of 9,000 rubles (about $4,500 in Canadian currency) and at that time he could easily have paid for his passage if he had chosen to leave. Now, however, years of looting, confiscations, and vandalism had left the Mennonite colonists destitute.

Those who had been able to hold onto any savings had seen them wiped out by hyperinflation.

Difficult as it was to open the way for emigration from the USSR, it was in Canada that the greatest obstacles had to be overcome in the early 1920s. Principal among them were a legal prohibition on the admission of Mennonites to Canada, and the problem of financing the travel of the Russlaender—as the Mennonites in the USSR came to be called.

Many Mennonites in Canada, together with some in the United States, played an important part in overcoming these and other obstacles. The leading role was played by a Saskatchewan schoolteacher and church elder named David Toews (pronounced "Taves"). A controversial figure in the first years of the immigration program, today he has a near-iconic status among Canadian Mennonites.

Toews emigrated to the United States from Russia with his family in 1884, at the age of fourteen. He was trained as a teacher in Newton, Kansas, and moved to Canada in 1893 when offered a position at the Mennonite Collegiate Institute in Gretna, Manitoba. He subsequently became a school-teacher in the Rosthern area of Saskatchewan, where large numbers of Mennonites had settled in the 1890s. In 1901, he was elected a minister in the Rosenort Mennonite Church; twelve years later, in acknowledge-ment of qualities that had become widely recognized, he was elected a church elder. In 1914, he became Chairman of the Conference of Mennonites in Canada.

Broad-shouldered and heavy-set, he was an imposing figure who con-veyed a sense of strength. His leadership style was characterized by an unshakable determination that ultimately enabled him to overcome formidable obstacles.

In late 1918, Toews and his fellow Mennonites in North America began to hear of attacks on Mennonites in Russia. The reports multiplied during the Makhno period of 1919. In June 1920, Toews chaired a meeting of the Conference of Mennonites in Canada to discuss ways of helping their co-religionists, including the possibility of arranging for them to immigrate to Canada.

A major obstacle to bringing the Russlaender to Canada was an Order-in-Council that Sir Robert Borden's government had passed on May 1st, 1919, prohibiting the entry of Doukhobors, Hutterites, and Mennonites. Members of these groups were described in the Order as "undesirable because, owing to their peculiar customs, habits, modes of living, and methods of holding property, they are not likely to become assimilated or to assume the responsibilities of Canadian citizenship within a reasonable period of time." The order was primarily the result of alarm that Hutterites in the United States might try to come to Canada to avoid military service, but the prohibition was extended to the other two groups for good measure.

In Canada, a number of groups were hostile to the Mennonites, not only because they were German-speaking, but because of their pacifism, which had led them to refuse military service during World War I. In 1916, the Borden government amended *The Elections Act* to disenfranchise all conscientious objectors. As the war dragged on, the Mennonites were harshly criticized at public meetings, some of which were attended by Borden's minister of immigration. The Great War Veterans' Association denounced Mennonites because "they were slackers [during the war], would not learn the language, maintained a distinctive religion, and would not assimilate with other Canadians." The same criticisms were expressed by, among others, the Orange Lodge and the British Citizens' League. In the 1920s, units of the Ku Klux Klan were formed on the prairies, particularly in Saskatchewan. In the absence of a black population, they took up the anti-immigrant chorus with their slogan "One Flag, One Language, One School, One Race, One Religion." The church in Rosthern was vandalized. In Manitoba, where large numbers of Mennonites had lived since the 1870s, the government expressed strong opposition to Mennonite immigration.[3]

Some groups in the United States were equally hostile. In 1921, the American Legion sent letters to the Canadian government describing Mennonites as "very objectionable" and expressing strong opposition to their admission to the United States from Canada. In his reply, the

Secretary of the Department of Immigration and Colonization observed that Canada's Mennonites "are seldom found in our courts of law."[4]

From the vantage point of 21st-century Canada, the 1919 Order-in-Council is notable for its discriminatory approach, but in its time it was regarded as quite normal. The *Immigration Act* passed by Laurier's government in 1910 authorized the government to prohibit landing of immigrants "belonging to any race deemed unsuited to the climate and requirements of Canada, or immigrants of any specified class, occupation, or character." Similar provisions were included in subsequent versions of the Act as late as 1952. Canadian governments explicitly characterized some countries as "preferred" sources of immigrants, with Britain at the top of the list, followed by France and countries in Northern Europe plus Italy. A second category comprised the "non-preferred" countries, which were located in Eastern Europe. Most southern European countries were not on either list, while after World War I immigration from much of Asia and Africa was for all practical purposes prohibited.[5]

Restrictive as it was, the Canadian approach was fairly liberal by comparison with that of the United States, where the House of Representatives in 1920 debated a proposal to ban all immigration in order to keep out the "European horde." In 1923, the American quota for immigrants from Russia was set at 1,500. Emigration to the United States was therefore not an option for the Russlaender.[6]

In the summer of 1921, Mennonites in Western Canada sent a delegation to Ottawa to request the repeal of the 1919 Order-in-Council. Although the passions generated by the war had abated and there had been some softening of views within the Canadian government, the delegation was not given much encouragement by Sir George Foster, the acting prime minister.

During the same visit, however, the delegation also had a meeting with Mackenzie King, who was at that time the Leader of the Opposition, which yielded better results. Mr. King had grown up in the area of Waterloo, Ontario, where a substantial number of Mennonites lived, and he had formed a good opinion of them. He promised that if he became prime minister he would see to it that the Order-in-Council was repealed.[7]

In the election held in late 1921, Mr. King did become prime minister. After a meeting with a Mennonite delegation in March 1922, he was as good as his word, and on June 2nd, the Order was repealed. Toews responded with an emotional letter to the prime minister:

> It is with the deepest feeling of appreciation that all our Mennonite people have read the glad news that the Order-In-Council prohibiting Mennonite immigration has been repealed…We are again on a level with others with whom we will gladly co-operate in service to Canada which we learned to love as our home…You have kept your word, and our people will ever remember this with deepest feelings of gratitude, and I hope that we, our children and others of our stock who may yet settle in this our beloved Canada may ever prove worthy of the confidence you place in us.[8]

Toews' forecast of the Mennonites remembering what Mr. King had done for them was borne out. When the former prime minister died in 1950, the Mennonites sent a wreath to his state funeral.[9]

The admission of the Russlaender was subject to several conditions: the Mennonites in Canada were to provide shelter and support for them, the new immigrants would be settled on land and engage in agriculture, and none was to become a public charge for at least five years.

Removal of the legal barrier was an indispensable step, but other obstacles remained. The most important of these was financing the Russlaender's passage to Canada. Here the Canadian Pacific Railway (CPR) was to play a key role.

Canadian railways had historically been active promoters of immigration to Canada. The CPR had a Colonization Department, which ran advertising campaigns and maintained agents in Europe. There was close collaboration between the CPR and the Canadian government. Once the war was over, the federal department of Immigration and Colonization, as it was called at the time, sought to restore immigration levels to something like their pre-war levels. Between 1918 and 1921, over 100,000 immigrants entered Canada each year.

Colonel J.S. Dennis.
(*Glenbow Alberta Archives* NA–2430–1)

In 1921, the Mennonites in Western Canada sent a delegation to the offices of the CPR in Montreal to explore possibilities. They got a good hearing but, because of the ban on Mennonite immigration, the meeting did not go on to deal with specific measures.

In their dealings with the CPR, the Mennonites benefited from a favourable disposition on the part of three individuals: Colonel John Dennis, the Chief Commissioner of Colonization and Development; Sir Edward Beatty, the President; and Sir Augustus Nanton, who was one of the principal shareholders in the CPR.

Colonel Dennis was a vigorous sixty-six when he was first approached about the possibility of bringing the Russlaender to Canada. As a young man, he had been an employee of a survey company in Manitoba when the first Mennonites arrived in 1874.[10] As a result, Dennis had seen the success with which these new immigrants had established themselves in the Red River valley. He was also aware that the Canadian government had made a loan to them of $96,000, on the basis of securities pledged by Mennonites in Waterloo, Ontario, and that the loan had been repaid with interest by 1892. On the strength of this knowledge, Dennis in 1921 became a strong proponent of bringing the Russian Mennonites to Canada. Many years later, David Toews said in a speech, "When we needed a friend, we found him in the person of Colonel J.S. Dennis."[11]

Key to Dennis's success in this undertaking was that he gained the ear of the CPR's president, Sir Edward Beatty.

Appointed in 1918 at the age of forty-one, Beatty was the youngest president in the CPR's history and was also to be its longest-serving, holding the position until 1942. A complex figure, Beatty combined a dominating presence and an aloof manner with private displays of personal warmth. One of the subjects he pursued aggressively during his long career was immigration, particularly to the under-populated West. This activity brought him into contact with Mennonites, of whom he came to have a high opinion; in a 1923 speech to the CPR's shareholders he described them as "immigrants of the highest type."[12]

The third member of the CPR triumvirate was Sir Augustus Nanton. He had come to Winnipeg at the age of twenty-three as an employee of a mortgage company. During the ensuing years, he traveled the West extensively and became one of its most prominent business figures. The financial firm of Osler, Hammond, and Nanton bore his name, as did a town in southern Alberta and streets in twelve western cities and towns. As a member of the CPR's board and its executive, he was an important source of support for Beatty and Dennis on the subject of assisting Mennonite immigration.[13]

Once the repeal of the Order-in-Council was in sight, Mennonite leaders lost no time in seeking another meeting with the CPR. More meetings followed. The result was that Colonel Dennis agreed to develop a set of arrangements that would permit the Russlaender to immigrate to Canada.

The contract he drafted went well beyond any colonization initiatives the railway had undertaken before that time. Under the proposed contract, the CPR would charter two ships and bring 3,000 Mennonites to Canada at an estimated cost of $400,000 (a 21st-century rough equiv-alent of this amount might be $10 million). Terms of repayment would be 25 per cent in the first ten days after the immigrants had arrived and an invoice had been presented by the CPR, with 25 per cent to follow after three months, and the balance after six months. These obligations were to be assumed by the other party to the contract: "The Mennonite Church of Canada."

Two difficulties stood out: no such body existed, and in any case such a body, if created, would have no financial resources. The CPR's vice pres-ident of finance was appalled, and called the proposed contract "one of Colonel Dennis's crazy ideas." Remarkably, Dennis nevertheless secured the approval of President Beatty and the CPR executive.[14]

The requirement to give the Mennonites a legal identity was met when a charter was issued to the Mennonite Colonization Association of North America on July 26th, 1922—four days *after* the contract with the CPR had been signed. The Association was subsequently renamed the Canadian Mennonite Board of Colonization (CMBC).

Finding the necessary financial resources was a daunting undertaking for Toews and his colleagues. Generous as it was, Dennis's draft caused consternation when it arrived in Rosthern. Toews later said that, "in view of our poverty and the huge responsibility toward the Company and toward our congregations the entire matter was for me a frightening pros-pect." At the same time, the alternative of abandoning the project and leaving the Russlaender to their fate was unthinkable to him. In the end, there was no alternative: a signed contract was essential if Dennis was to get clearance to proceed within the CPR. Toews went to Montreal and handed Dennis the signed contract on July 22nd. In doing so, he explic-itly told him there was no possibility that the stipulated terms of repayment could be met. Dennis was undeterred.[15]

Dennis's willingness to proceed was the more remarkable because the contract caused widespread alarm among Mennonites in the West, who feared that it burdened them with potentially ruinous financial commit-ments. Some American Mennonites feared that it could implicate them as well. A number of groups held protest meetings, passed resolutions, and sent communications to Dennis dissociating themselves from Toews' action in signing the contract. All this could well have caused Dennis to doubt that Toews would be able to raise the money when the time for payment came. But he stood firm, and simply responded to the barrage of communications with assurances that the contract did not commit or put at risk the resources of any individual. Nevertheless, expressions of alarm and opposition continued. For a time Toews and his colleagues were vilified and had the support of only a minority of the Mennonite community.

In addition to their financial concerns, some Mennonites were opposed to helping the Russlaender on religious grounds. The most severe took an Old Testament view, believing that the sufferings of the Russlaender were an expression of divine wrath that had been visited upon them because of their prosperity and worldliness. On a visit to Kansas in quest of funds, Toews was harshly told by one Mennonite, "We should be sending missionaries to Russia. It's their own fault that they are having a hard time of it. In Molochna, modernism has taken over."[16] A more widespread concern derived from reports about the *Selbstschutz*: the fact that Mennonite young men had resorted to arms in defence of their communities was regarded by many as a grave apostasy, and raised strong doubts that they could any longer be regarded as members of the Mennonite congregation.

Toews' determination was unshaken. He and his colleagues continued their communications with Dennis, out of which came a decision that the CPR would charter two ships and send them to pick up the first group of Russlaender in Odessa. Word that Canada was prepared to accept Mennonites evoked a strong response in the colonies, and some families began getting ready to leave by liquidating their property. Then word arrived that transportation would be available for only 3,000 that year (1922). Further setbacks came when an outbreak of cholera in Odessa, and hostilities between Greece and Turkey on the other side of the Black Sea, made it impossible for emigrants to leave by the southern route. The CPR cancelled its arrangements to send the two ships to Odessa, and all departures from the colonies had to be postponed until the following year.

When the emigration arrangements collapsed in 1922, it was a major psychological stumbling block for the Mennonites in the Soviet Union. Some began to have second thoughts about the need for so drastic a step as emigration. Others, including B.B. Janz, remained determined to leave and pursued discussions with the authorities during the winter of 1922/1923, while in Canada Toews and his colleagues continued their dialogues with the Canadian government and the CPR.

Sufficient progress was made that the CPR representative proceeded to arrange for ships to be on hand at ports in Latvia in the spring of 1923 to board Mennonite emigrants. In Canada, the government agreed to waive the requirement for these emigrants to have passports. The Mennonite Board of Colonization for its part gave undertakings that it would assume full responsibility for the Russlaender when they arrived in Canada, and would bear the costs of those whose entry was delayed because of medical problems.

The way had been cleared, and in late June, 1923, the first train bearing Mennonite emigrants would leave the station in Chortiza headed for the Latvian border. Among those on board were Helena Kroeger's sister and her family. Their departure brought to the fore the question of whether Helena and Heinrich should seek to follow them.

What historian Frank Epp aptly termed "the rescue of the 20,000" was achieved through intense efforts by Mennonite leaders in both Russia and Canada. Without the determination and perseverance of those people, the rescue would in all probability have failed. Equally important was the extraordinary co-operation extended to these leaders by the Canadian Pacific Railway. That some 80,000 Mennonites were left to tragic fates in the USSR when the doors finally closed in 1930 is a wrenching part of the story, but the fact that 20,000 were brought to Canada represents an achievement for which there are few parallels.

I have at times reflected on the degree to which the fate of the 20,000 was determined by accidents of timing and the actions of a few individuals. If the election of 1921 had turned out differently, if Colonel Dennis and Sir Edward Beatty had not held senior positions with the CPR in the early 1920s, and if the Mennonites had not had the intensely committed leadership of people such as B.B. Janz and David Toews, my family and I would very likely be living—or, more probably, dead—in the former Soviet Union.

SIX *Even the Strong Wept*

*He shall return no more to his house, neither shall his place know him
any more.*

　—JOB 7:10

HEINRICH KROEGER'S FINAL NOTEBOOK dealing with his life in Russia
begins on March 17th 1925 and ends in the summer of 1926. On the inside
back cover is written:

G.G. Rempel
Monitor, Alta
Canada

George Rempel was Helena's older brother, and Heinrich's partner
in the wagon plant at Olchowatka before the war; he had emigrated to
Canada in November 1925. Helena's younger sister, Tina, had left with her
family two years earlier. Heinrich's uncle Abram had also emigrated and
was living in Saskatchewan.

Heinrich and Helena knew that, to follow George, Tina, and Abram,
they would have to pull up deep roots. Their families had lived in Russia
for 120 years. Whatever the religious stresses and social inequalities within
their villages, the Mennonites had enjoyed stability, comfortable homes,

religious fellowship, self-government, and a strong sense of community there. Now, in scarcely half a decade, their world had been shattered by the cataclysmic events since 1917.

Some members of the colonies remained strongly opposed to the notion of leaving, convinced that better times lay ahead if they stayed. In the spring of 1923, a Mennonite leader passionately implored a colleague to "Think of our mission here in Russia, our Mennonite ideals, our beautiful villages, the fertile soil! Our task is and remains in Russia."[1] Many others, however, had concluded that their communities could not be re-established and that they would have to seek new lives elsewhere. In the summer of 1922, some 17,000 Mennonites applied to leave.

By early May 1923, negotiations with governments in Kharkov, Moscow, and Ottawa had opened the way to emigration. The authorities in Moscow had agreed to authorize special trains to transport those leaving the Mennonite colonies; the Canadian Pacific Railway had committed to finance the passage of an initial group of 3,000.

On June 22nd, a train of 28 boxcars came to a stop at the station in Chortiza. The first departures were at hand. The cars were not large, but each had to accommodate some twenty-five passengers, adults and children. The cars had no windows; they were unheated, which could explain why the annual movements of Mennonites took place in the summer and early fall (even though the port of Libau, from which they were to sail, is ice-free all year long).

Before the passengers could board, the train had to be made ready to accommodate them. The cars were cleaned with boiling water and soap, and rough boards were nailed together to create bunks and benches. Water tanks were installed in each car. There is no record of how sanitary requirements were met, but it could not have been easy.

The travellers had to take with them food for a journey of uncertain duration. While some families brought meat and other foods, the fare of most emigrants was a Mennonite staple known as *zwieback*, a crusty bun made with generous portions of butter. Some families brought several hundred-pound bags to see them through the 1,700-kilometre trip from

Chortiza to Riga in Latvia. Some roasted the *zwieback* to keep it from going stale during the trip.

Each group of emigrants elected a train committee of five, one member of which was then chosen to act as the car leader. Every car had its own leader and an assistant. People agreed on certain rules and complied with them.

Heinrich and Helena Kroeger were living in Chortiza/Rosental when some of their friends and neighbours boarded that first train in June 1923, and they joined the crowds of Mennonites at the station.

There are many moving accounts of these departures. One deals with Dietrich Epp, who was born in Chortiza, educated at the elementary and the *Zentralschule* there, and then became a teacher in the village. He was also the conductor of the male choir, which he conducted one last time at his farewell party. The evening before his departure, he walked once more along the streets of Chortiza and Rosental, taking leave of old friends, buildings, and places dear to his memory. The following is an account of the departure of his train the next day:

> The train was scheduled to leave at 6:00 PM. Never had so many people been assembled at the Chortiza station. An extremely depressing mood prevailed. Those who departed and those who remained looked at one another probably for the last time. Here and there a burst of sobs, tears in the eyes of everyone. A last parting handshake, the emigrants boarded the cars, and the train began to move.[2]

This train, bearing 738 colonists, left Chortiza on June 22nd. A second train left on July 2nd, a third on July 13th, and a fourth on July 24th. As the trains prepared to leave, the Mennonites sang a favourite hymn, perhaps *Nun ade mein liebe Heimatland* (Now farewell, my beloved homeland) or "God be with you until we meet again."

But for many, there was to be no such meeting in the future. There was an air of finality in the departures. Many of those leaving and many of those remaining knew that they would never see each other again.

Mennonite emigrants holding a service of thanksgiving upon their arrival in Riga.
(Mennonite Heritage Centre 062.018)

The first train took ten days to reach the Latvian border, partly because it was frequently shunted onto the siding. Sometimes officials came on board and bribes had to be paid.

At the border between the USSR and Latvia, a high arch had been erected over the railway tracks. In czarist times, the arch had been a fairly simple monument, but the Bolsheviks had replaced it with an elaborate iron structure that bore a large red star. This came to be known as the Red Gate. The side that greeted people leaving Latvia welcomed visitors to the "workers' paradise" with the inscription, in Russian, "Workers of the World, Unite!" The Mennonites were thankful to be proceeding in the opposite direction.

The first stop inside Latvia was at Rezekne, where there was a major medical and quarantine centre. Here the migrants were given medical examinations. Of those who crossed into Latvia in 1923, individuals found medically unfit were diverted to Lechfeld in Germany and held there until their medical condition had been successfully treated. (The eye disease trachoma was common in south Russia; it was highly infectious and had therefore become widespread in the Mennonite colonies.)[3]

When the train crossed the border, a Latvian official from the Ministry of the Interior boarded the train, and accompanied the emigrants to Riga. The Mennonites expressed gratitude for his helpful approach, which stood in contrast to what they had become accustomed to at the hands of Soviet officials. At Riga, the emigrants left their boxcars and transferred to a narrow gauge railway for the final leg of the journey to the port of Libau. A local newspaper reported that, since the group left Chortiza, thirteen babies had been born.[4]

Following is an excerpt from the report filed by the Canadian immigration officer who met them at Libau:

> This party arrived in Libau on the 5th inst. and was put on board S.S. "Bruton" for Southampton...I examined all this party as it came aboard the steamer and the examination was over by about 2 o'clock P.M....
>
> This party...appeared to be of a very good class of emigrants, great numbers of them were children, and I have no doubt that, if the balance, which is coming forward, is like this first party, they will prove very good immigrants for Canada.[5]

On July 11, a Canadian immigration official's report about the second group from Chortiza included the comment that "the train arrived in extraordinarily clean condition."[6]

The emigrants crossed the Baltic, sailed along the Kiel Canal, and landed in Southampton. After a short stay, they boarded the CPR's *Empress of France* for Canada.

The group landed in Canada at last, at Quebec City's port, where most immigrants entered the country during that period. On hand when the Russlaender arrived were two members of the Canadian Mennonite

Arrival of the first group of Russlaender at Rosthern, Saskatchewan, July 1923.
(Glenbow Alberta Archives NA 4497–1)

Board of Colonization (CMBC), together with German- and Russian-speaking representatives of the CPR.

After completing immigration formalities, the Russlaender boarded a special train. The CPR supplied them with blankets that were on long-term loan from the Department of National Defence. The immigrants no longer needed to carry food with them, as part of the CPR's undertaking was that it would provide each immigrant with two meals a day at a cost of 25 cents each.[7]

The train then set off on the five-day trip to Rosthern, Saskatchewan, the centre of a heavily Mennonite part of the province and the location of the CMBC. Word of their progress across the country had preceded them and excitement was growing in the area.

Late on the afternoon of July 21st, the long train bearing the first group of Russlaender came into sight and pulled to a stop at the station in Rosthern. Their 6,000-mile migration was at an end. It had been one month less a day since they left Chortiza. Residents of the surrounding area had poured into Rosthern throughout the day, and a throng was gathered at the station. As the first Russlaender disembarked, a surge of emotion ran through the crowd. There were tears and expressions of thanksgiving.

When all the new arrivals were gathered beside the train, David Toews mounted a small platform and welcomed them to Canada. After five days in a strange land, they again heard their own Low German language.

Gerald Brown, a reporter for the *Saskatoon Star Phoenix*, described the religious service that followed:

> A great hush fell upon the assembled thousands and to the ears of the Canadians came a soft, slow chant, "*Lobe den Herrn den machtigen Konig der Ehren,*" which is the German equivalent of our own "Praise God From Whom All Blessings Flow." Besides being a favourite hymn of the Mennonites, it is their nearest approach to a national anthem. Softly the chant rose and fell, seeming to be a musical expression of the great tragedy and heartbreak of the Mennonites. Then the Canadian Mennonites took up the song, and the tone increased in volume, growing deeper and fuller, until the melody was pouring forth from several thousand throats.
>
> When the first note of the song burst upon the air, every Mennonite removed his hat, and the others paid like tribute. There were many in the crowd who had sprung from other races, but the significance of the song was manifest to them when they saw their Mennonite friends bare their heads and when they saw grown men, whom they had known for years, burst into tears.[8]

At the end of the day, the immigrants and their effects were taken to, and welcomed in, the homes of Mennonites who lived in the area surrounding Rosthern, with whom they would be billeted. Their new life was about to begin.

The principal constraint on the numbers of Mennonites who could be moved each year was a financial one. Since most of the emigrants were poor, the CPR knew that its loan for their transportation was risky. Experience with the first group would determine what, if anything, the company might agree to do in future years.

The first invoice presented to the CMBC by the CPR was for $165,000, of which $68,000 was due on October 23rd. Near-desperate appeals for funds were sent to Mennonites in other provinces and in the United States, but the results fell far short. Toews sent $22,500 to Colonel Dennis on the 23rd, and a further $3,500 the next day.

It then came to light that Toews and the Board had overlooked a late modification to the repayment terms. The first amount due was only $17,186.98—the first payment had been made on time and was several thousand more than the payment due.

In future, all the payments would be late and they would often be short of the amount due. Nevertheless, the initial impression had been made, and Colonel Dennis had evidence he could use to persuade the CPR executive to continue the program. On the basis of the company's experience in 1923, President Beatty agreed to the movement of 5,000 Mennonites in 1924. He also eased some of the terms of repayment.

A further component of the post-1923 arrangements was that, in addition to financing the movement of the Russlaender on credit, the CPR agreed to undertake the movement of individuals who were able, by one means or another, to finance their own passage. As a result of this decision, a number of Mennonites in addition to those brought out on credit were able to find refuge in Canada.

But most Russlaender were too poor to pay for their passage. Illustrative of the change in their fortunes was the case of Heinrich Sudermann, whose family before 1914 had farmed some 4,000 hectares. Upon arrival in Canada, he obtained employment as a section hand maintaining tracks for the Canadian National Railway. Similarly, Isaac Zacharias, a multilingual university graduate whose family had once had a net worth of $500,000 was employed in the offices of the CMBC at $40 per month.[9]

In 1924, the CMBC continued to experience difficulties in raising funds to meet its obligations to the CPR. By the end of 1924, the total debt incurred had reached $825,238.65, against which the Board had managed to pay only $183,000—of which $60,000 had been loans obtained from other sources. Nevertheless, President Beatty agreed to further concessions that enabled the 1925 movement to take place.

The saga was to continue through to the end of 1930, with the CPR continuing to ease its terms to accommodate the straitened circumstances of the CMBC. Expenditures by the CPR in bringing Mennonites from Russia to Canada eventually totalled $2.4 million[10]—the 21st-century equivalent might be $100 million to $200 million.

There was unquestionably an element of self-interest in the CPR's actions. It was, after all, a commercial entity. In bringing the Mennonites from the USSR, the company was providing passengers for its ships, potential settlers for the lands it held on the prairies, and future customers for its railway, particularly in Western Canada.

There is more to the story than that, however. In providing credit transportation to destitute people sponsored by an organization that had no financial resources, the Canadian Pacific Railway went far beyond the terms on which it normally brought immigrants to Canada. It is hard to visualize a 21st-century chief executive matching the compassion and extraordinarily enlightened corporate self-interest displayed by Sir Edward Beatty over more than two decades.

And, in the end, Beatty and Dennis's actions were vindicated, even though neither of them would live to see the final outcome in 1946, when the last of the debt was finally paid.

In 1923, it was the Russlaender of Chortiza who emigrated. In 1924 came the turn of the Molochna colony. Trains had been arranged for, and the necessary exit permits issued by the authorities. When the first train prepared to leave the station in Lichtenau, the scene was comparable to that witnessed in Chortiza by Heinrich and Helena Kroeger the year before. One of the emigrants described the sadness of the farewells:

Departure of Mennonite emigrants from Lichtenau in the Molochna colony, 1925.
(Mennonite Heritage Centre 044.309)

The evening shadows lengthened, the sun was about to set. We loved the soil of our homeland. Now it was time to bid adieu and leave one's hearth, village, customs, relatives, and friends. People took leave of one another. Even the strong wept, some sobbed…. The bell sounded once, then again. Everyone knew only a few minutes remained…. Here a firm handshake, there the last embrace, tears flow…. The third bell, the train begins to move. "Goodbye. Come after us." "Reunion in eternity," shouted one emigrant…. Gradually those remaining behind fade into the distance.[11]

The 1924 emigrants followed the same route as their predecessors from Chortiza the year before. When they arrived in Quebec City, an immigration official reported of one group that "the entire party was very well behaved while in this building, and physically they were a very good group of people."

This group included the future parents of Jake Epp, who in 1979 would become the first Mennonite appointed a federal cabinet minister; of Gordon Thiessen, who served as Governor of the Bank of Canada from 1994 to 2001; of Peter Harder, who was appointed deputy minister of foreign affairs in 2003; and of Henry Friesen, who served as president of the Medical Research Council of Canada from 1991 to 2000.

In 1925, 3,772 Russlaender came to Canada. They included the future parents of Vic Toews, who in 2006 became Attorney General of Canada.

The last year of large-scale movement was 1926, involving nearly 6,000 emigrants.

Among the 1926 group was B.B. Janz, who had tirelessly negotiated with the Soviet authorities over the previous four years to secure the emigration of the Mennonites from the USSR. Shortly after his train had left, the secret police came looking for him.[12] B.B. Janz's granddaughter Edith Wiens, who was born in Canada in 1950, later became an internationally renowned soprano.

Life in Rosental continued to be difficult for the Kroeger family in the mid-1920s. Heinrich's notebooks indicate that he owned some livestock, but give no indication that he farmed any land, possibly because it had by this time been expropriated by the state. In March 1925, he rented to tenants half his stable and barn, together with several rooms in the house. In June, he was able to buy material to make suits for the two boys. The following May, the tenants were unable to pay their rent in cash, and Heinrich had to accept payment in corn stalks.

Despite these difficulties, Heinrich had been disposed to remain in Rosental, and came to a decision in favour of emigration only in response to pressure from his wife. He eventually applied to leave, but there was no certainty as to what the result would be.

Getting permits from the authorities for emigration was a lengthy process, even though some of the paperwork was handled by local Mennonite leaders. Would-be emigrants had to get clearance from the finance department concerning tax liabilities, then from the military authorities concerning any outstanding service obligations, then from the police, and finally from the chairman of the regional soviet. Often, these officials were located in centres far removed from the colonies, and a failure in one step of the process could make it necessary for the applicant to start over.

After the Kroegers had submitted their application, life in the spring of 1926 went on as it had in the past. Heinrich noted on March 8th that he had "bought old boots from J. Siemens for 2.50 rubles." As spring advanced, he planted potatoes on May 5th, ploughed the garden a week later, and hatched twelve chicks in mid-June. If their application were to be refused, they would need food to live on.

A particular source of uncertainty for those who applied to emigrate was whether they would be able pass the mandatory medical examination. Dr. E.W. Drury was the Chief Medical Inspector for the CPR and had been delegated authority by the Canadian government to examine prospective immigrants. In June 1926, his work took him first to the Molochna and then to the Chortiza colony. In each village, he examined passengers who had been selected for emigration and stopped when the quota for that village had been filled.

One such village was Rosental, and among those he examined were Heinrich and Helena Kroeger and their children.[13] On the identification cards issued to the Kroeger family is stamped:

Canadian Pacific
16 June 1926
Passed
Dr. E.W. Drury

The registration cards issued by the Russian-Canadian Passenger Agency based in Moscow, which handled the movement of the Mennonite emigrants, bore a note saying they were to be presented during application for passports for foreign travel. They were also to be presented upon

The passport with which Heinrich Kroeger travelled from Russia to Canada in 1926.

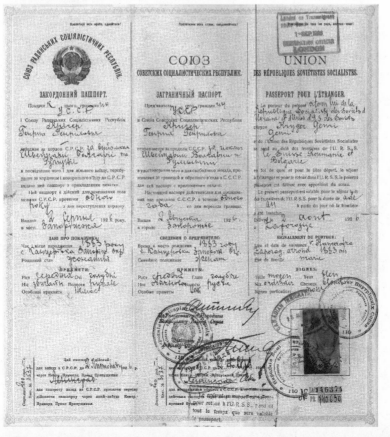

crossing the border of the USSR. On June 22nd, the local authorities made an official record of the family's application to go abroad.

Heinrich and Helena Kroegers' period of waiting came to an end on August 2nd, when their passports were issued in Zaporozhe. The passports were valid for three months. The passports were printed in Russian, Ukrainian, and French (the international language of the time). In the Latin script used in the French section, Heinrich's name was rendered as "Kriger," Helena's as "Kryger." Fortunately, when the passports were eventually presented in Quebec, Canadian immigration officials ignored the capricious spellings and rendered the name as it has been ever since—Kroeger.

Heinrich paid 200 rubles for each passport. Helena's brother George had managed to send money from Canada to help the Kroegers meet these and other costs. In addition, Heinrich recorded that he had borrowed 41 rubles "from P. Klassen for the expensive immigration papers." He also had to find funds for the family's rail trip from Chortiza to Latvia, after which transportation would become the responsibility of the CPR.

Heinrich could not sell the land he had been working because, under the New Economic Policy, land sales were forbidden. What was left to him and others, therefore, was the sale of their buildings, farm equipment, and such livestock as they still possessed—usually sold at a steep discount because of uncertainty about the future on the part of the prospective buyers.

Since the cost of the Kroeger family's passage to Canada was to be $675, it was clear that they were not among those able to pay cash when they left. Before leaving, Heinrich held a sale of the "belongings of our late parents," and listed each item with the price obtained.

1 chest of drawers 50 *rubles*
1 table 10 *rubles*
1 old chair 1 ruble 1 large tin bowl 1.50 *rubles*

And on a second list:

1 iron stove 10 *rubles*
1 bedstead 15 *rubles*
1 cow 20 *rubles*
2 pigs 35 *rubles*
22 chickens 7.85 *rubles*
10 forks and knives 3 *rubles*
1 saw 5 *rubles*

On a third list:

scales and weights, barrel 10 *rubles*
flour box 5 *rubles*
clothes lines, pins 2 *rubles*

The items were quite basic, and the returns modest. The respective totals on the three lists were 139 rubles, 171.60, and 101.75. A note indicates that some of the returns from the sale were shared with Heinrich's siblings.

Heinrich must have been depressed at how little money his sales yielded. However, the neighbour who purchased his buildings and livestock eventually fared even worse. Several years after the family's departure, the property was seized by the state, and the purchaser, together with others from the Chortiza colony, was deported to Siberia.

When Heinrich's younger brother Abram learned that the family was seeking to emigrate, he was very angry and reproached Heinrich for his decision. When the emigration movement began, he was among those who believed that things were getting better and so chose to remain in the USSR.

Abram defied tradition. He was energetic, ambitious, and perhaps the most intelligent of the four siblings. Heinrich used to say that Abram "had modern ideas," "drove a hard bargain," and was "proud" (by which he apparently meant self-confident). Abram eschewed agricultural life; as the youngest son, he could not in any case inherit the farm under Russian law. Instead, he had taken training in accounting and found a white-collar job working for a Mennonite manufacturer of farm machinery.

The pre-emigration photo of the Kroeger family taken in Moscow, August 1926. Back row (left to right): Henry, Heinrich, Nick; front row: Anne, Helen, Helena with George on her lap.

During his war service as a medical orderly, he had met and married not a Mennonite but a Latvian nurse—another unconventional act.

On August 15th, 1926, the Kroeger family boarded one of the boxcars at the Chortiza station. There were seven in the family: Heinrich, age forty-two; Helena, thirty-nine; Nick, eleven; Henry, nine; Helen, seven; Anne three; and George, a baby of seven months. As was by now established practice among emigrating Mennonites, Helena had roasted a substantial quantity of *zwieback* as their staple fare for the trip.

Because of space limitations in the boxcars, the emigrants could take little else with them. The Kroeger family took the carpentry tools Heinrich had purchased when he joined his brothers-in-law at the Olchowatka wagon plant, the polished wooden box he had inherited from his maternal grandmother, and the family's Kroeger clock. Among the papers that Heinrich kept until the end of his life was a parting gift: a small booklet

A view of the Red Gate from the Latvian side of the border.
(Latgale Cultural History Museum, Rezekne, Latvia)

of stories in German. On the inside cover was written, "To remember Jakob M. Neufeld, Rosental, August 15."

The first stage of the journey took the family from Chortiza to Moscow. When they arrived on August 17th, they were photographed for their travel documents and issued "nominated immigrant" cards by the CPR. While they were in Moscow, two mishaps occurred: Heinrich's trousers were stolen during the night (when I once asked him who had done it, he replied, "No address"), and Henry fell down a flight of stairs, with the result that in one photograph he has a bandage on his head.

Once the paperwork in Moscow had been completed, the final phase of the family's departure was at hand. Together with other Mennonite emigrants, they boarded the train for the Red Gate at the Latvian border.

The Gate was a landmark engraved on the memories of those who passed through it. Each passage was a time of tension for the emigrants.

The T.S.S. Baltara, *on which the Kroegers sailed from Libau in 1926.* (Marine Museum, Liepaja, Latvia)

The CPR offices in
Riga, Latvia. (CPR A 15403)

They were questioned, sometimes aggressively, by the border guards. All baggage was unloaded. Officials examined travel documents and searched personal effects, even small packages, while the emigrants watched with growing apprehension.

Finally, the baggage was reloaded, the guards disembarked, and the train slowly started to move again, passing through the Red Gate. Then: "as the last car passed through, as with one voice, the song, 'Now thank we all our God' could be heard from all the cars."[14] For the first time in years, people were able to breathe freely. Whatever the future might bring, the fears and oppression they had experienced in the USSR were behind them.

Once the Mennonites had crossed into Latvia, the CPR took over the management of their travel. The Kroeger family's passports were stamped at the town of Zilupe inside the Latvian border on August 22nd. While many Mennonite emigrants were processed at the nearby medical and quarantine centre at Rezekne, others, including the Kroegers, went on to Riga.

It was customary for the Mennonites to hold a religious service immediately after disembarking at the station in Riga. They were then taken to an "Emigrants' House" operated by the CPR, where they underwent a process that carried the unvarnished title, "de-lousing and disinfection." Clothes were fumigated, steam baths were taken, and sulphur was applied to disinfect the baggage. The smell of antiseptic filled the air.

On August 25th, Canadian immigration officials examined the Kroeger family and stamped their passports. On the night of the 27th, they and other Mennonites who had arrived in the past few days were placed on a train to Libau, where they arrived the next morning. Their ship was waiting for them.

Abram Martens, a member of the group with whom the Kroeger family traveled, later wrote an account of the departure:

That same evening we boarded the ship *Baltara* and left for England. We had barely left port when the ship began to rock so much that many of our people became ill. But the rocking soon subsided… The rest of the trip…was beautiful…we arrived at Kiel…The high

The Atlantic Park immigrant transit centre near Southampton, England, in the 1920s.
(Jeff Pain, Southampton, UK)

bridges over the Canal opened to let the ships go through… On September 1, at seven in the morning we arrived in London. In 83 hours we had arrived…From the Port we were taken by bus to the train station…An electric train with three cars took us…to Southampton.[15]

During the late stages of World War I, the U.S. Air Force had established an air base, including a set of hangars, some ten miles north of Southampton. At the end of the war, the complex was sold to a consortium of shipping companies, White Star, Cunard, and Canadian Pacific. The consortium converted the air base to a transit centre for immigrants en route from Europe to North America. Named Atlantic Park, the centre opened in 1921. It could accommodate up to 3,500 transients at any one time, and in total some 20,000 passed through it in 1928, the peak year. In 1931, the depression effectively brought North American immigration to a halt, and the centre ceased to function.

A mid-1920s description of Atlantic Park published by the consortium said that it

> provides a cosy temporary home for people in transit…where they can obtain comfortable sleeping quarters and meals at a moderate cost and where such amusements are given which help to pass the time pleasantly. Sympathy is the prevailing note and every person is treated with the utmost consideration. Special attention is paid to Jewish passengers, for whose benefit there is a Kosher cook, Kosher supplies, a special dining room and a rabbi on staff who acts as an interpreter and holds special services for his co-religionists.[16]

Judging by the Mennonites' experiences there, Atlantic Park did not entirely live up to this description. The hangars were cold, usually no more than 15 degrees Celsius, and the living facilities rudimentary. Men and women were segregated, although families ate together in a large hall.

What the immigrants particularly resented was that they were again medically examined, despite having already passed medical examinations once or twice en route. Like others, Heinrich and Helena faced the prospect that, if they or any of their children did not pass the medical examination, they could be detained for many months. At one point there were over 700 detainees at Atlantic Park.

However, the Kroegers were among the lucky ones. Their CPR identification cards, on which Dr. Drury declared them to have passed his medical examination of June 16th, were stamped "Atlantic Park Hostel—September 1, 1926—Disinfected"[again]. A second stamp read "Atlantic Park Hostel—Medically Examined—September 2, 1926."

That same day, Heinrich, Helena, and their five children boarded the S.S. *Marloch* and were assigned two rooms in third class. Their route took them first to Cherbourg, France, where another group of immigrants was taken on board, and then the ship proceeded to Quebec City, Canada. The passenger manifest shows that, of some one thousand passengers who travelled in third class, only about 130 were Mennonites. The balance included Czechs, Yugoslavs, Poles, Lithuanians, Russians, and Austrians.

During the crossing, members of the family recall that a minor collision occurred. No details are available today, but for whatever reason the passage from Southampton to Quebec took seventeen days in all rather than the normal six, thus prolonging the seasickness and other discomforts of the people in third class. The *S.S. Marloch* docked in Quebec on September 19th, and the passengers disembarked the following day. The Kroegers' life in their new, strange land was about to begin.

Wherever possible, the Canadian Mennonite Board of Colonization arranged for new arrivals from Russia to stay with relatives who had come to Canada in previous years.

When the Kroeger family left Quebec, therefore, their destination was Monitor, a small town in eastern Alberta, near which the CMBC had settled George Rempel on a farm. It was George's address that Heinrich had entered in his notebook. The trip from Quebec to Monitor took six days, with several changes of train en route. The CPR provided the family with blankets and meals, and there were sleeping accommodations on the train—but not enough for everyone.

By the time their train arrived in Monitor, the Kroegers and their children had been travelling for six weeks: by rail from Chortiza to Moscow and then Libau, by ship to London, by rail to Atlantic Park, by ship to Cherbourg and then Quebec, and finally 2,500 miles by rail to Alberta.

George Rempel was unable to meet them in Monitor, as his farm was fifteen miles to the south and he did not have a car. Instead, the Kroegers were met by George's neighbours, the Liknesses, a Norwegian family with whom Heinrich and Helena were to develop a lifelong friendship. The Liknesses delivered them to George's farm, where the two families would live together for the next two months.

Heinrich's notes about 1925 and 1926 come to an end with the family's departure for Canada, halfway through his notebook. The remaining eigh-

"After darkness, light." The harbour gates of Libau (now Liepaja) in the distance are the ones through which the Kroegers and most Russian Mennonites sailed in the 1920s. (Alix Kroeger)

Monitor, Alberta in the 1920s. The railway station where the Kroeger family disembarked in September 1926 is at the bottom of the street. (Glenbow Alberta Archives NA 1644–101)

teen pages were later used in Canada by his son Henry for school exercises because there was not enough money to buy scribblers.

In October 2003, I visited Latvia to see the route the Mennonites had taken. The Red Gate is no longer standing, which did not particularly surprise me. After Latvia was incorporated into the Soviet Union in 1940, there was no longer any reason to have a major border portal there. Probably more to the point, after Hitler's armies occupied the region in the summer of 1941, the inscription urging workers of the world to unite would have been an adequate incentive for them to dismantle the gate. Today, only two low obelisks and a broad white line painted across the railway tracks mark the border between Russia and independent Latvia.

In Libau (today's Liepaja), substantial brick facilities bespeak a past that includes large-scale emigration. The twenty thousand Mennonites who crossed through Latvia were only a small fraction of the total. Between 1917 and 1929, up to three million people left Russia for Western Europe and North America. In the early 1920s, Berlin had over half a million Russian residents who had fled the revolution.[17] Many of these émigrés passed through Latvia and the quarantine complex in Rezekne. In Libau (Liepaja), there was a set of large brick hostels to accommodate transient emigrants. During World War II, these buildings would serve as barracks for the German army, and then in the post-war period for the Red Army. Today they sit vacant, in a state of decay.

In the twilight at the end of our tour of the harbour, my daughter Alix took a photo. In the foreground the waters were dark. The western sky was overcast, but the golden rays of the low sun behind the clouds illuminated the sea beyond the harbour gate. The image in her photo, of light beyond darkness, captured what the Mennonites must have felt as they sailed through the harbour gate and into their new future.

PART II *Canada*

SEVEN *The Great Lone Land*

THE CANADA in which the Kroeger family arrived in the fall of 1926 bore only a distant resemblance to the Canada of the twenty-first century.

Canadians today hold social programs, the *Charter of Rights and Freedoms*, and the multicultural society to be among the hallmarks of their country. In the early twentieth century, none of these existed. Most of the Canadian social safety net was put in place during the 1950s and 1960s; the racial diversity of today's Canadian cities stems from a major change in immigration policy in the late 1960s; and the Charter was legislated in 1982.

If asked in the 1920s to name the distinguishing feature of their country, most Canadians outside Quebec would have cited membership in the British Empire, as reflected in the title of the Constitution, *The British North America Act*. They would have acknowledged that, because of the need to populate the country, immigrants from Europe and the United States were also needed—but there was a clear expectation that these newcomers would adhere to British values and norms.

The prairies, particularly Saskatchewan and Alberta, were a new, raw society. Hence the title of Sir William Butler's nineteenth century book about the Canadian prairies—*The Great Lone Land*.

At the beginning of the twentieth century, rapid settlement got under way. In 1901, Alberta's population was only 73,000; twenty years later, it had reached nearly 600,000. In 1921, sixteen years after the creation of the province, nearly half of the farmers had been on their land for less than four years. There were few tractors; horses were commonly used to work the land.[1]

Distance had a different significance in those years. In 1929, a community farewell party was held in Consort for a local resident, Carl Leaf, who was leaving to open a business in Monitor, eight miles to the east. Edmonton and Calgary were not much more than good-sized towns, and no trunk road connected them in 1920.[2] No road in the province was surfaced with gravel, much less pavement, and rains could make highways, as well as streets in towns, impassable. Each year the rural roads were choked with snow from about November to March, and the population travelled mostly in horse-drawn sleighs. Among the election promises that the Bennett government had to shelve because of the depression of the 1930s was the construction of a Trans-Canada Highway.[3]

In the late nineteenth and early twentieth centuries, the government survey program divided the prairies into one-square-mile tracts of land known as sections. Thirty-six sections made up a township. Settlers commonly described the location of their farms by using the coordinates established by the surveys, and identified the locations of their neighbours by the same means. Thus, a strictly accurate description of where I was born would be SE3–32–6–W4: the southeast quarter of Section 3, Township 32, Range 6, west of the Fourth Meridian (that is, the Saskatchewan border). However, I have always found it expedient when completing passport applications to use the less precise locator of Naco, Alberta, even though that town no longer exists.

As more and more people settled in the prairies, the railways rapidly expanded their networks of branch lines, to carry supplies to the new settlers and to haul away the grain they produced. The branch lines ran parallel to each other, approximately twenty miles apart, in an east-west direction. Along each line at eight-mile intervals were small towns, consisting of one or more grain elevators and, at a minimum, a grocery store, a post office, and a dealer in motor fuel. The purpose of this configuration was to enable any farmer to reach a grain elevator with a horse-drawn wagonload of wheat and be able to return home in time to milk his cows that night.

Finding names for hundreds of new small towns taxed the imagination of community leaders and railway executives, but they rose to the challenge. To name the prairie towns they borrowed names from, among others, the British Indian Empire (Midnapore), Austrian aristocrats (Esterhazy), aboriginal words (Wetaskiwin), a British battleship that had taken part in the battle of Jutland (Warspite), an Italian marquis (Bassano), composers (Handel, Mozart), a French Field Marshal from World War I (Joffre), ecclesiastical titles (Prelate), Napoleonic battles (Marengo), parts of the body (Elbow), an aide to a governor general (De Winton), political philosophies (Liberal), adjectives (Superb), and exhortations (Onward).

In 1911, the CPR began construction of a branch line eastward from Castor, Alberta towards the Saskatchewan border. King George V had recently been crowned, and the divisional point on the new line was called Coronation. The naming of the first four towns east of Coronation also reflected monarchism and service to the crown: they were called Throne, Veteran, Loyalist, and Consort. The next town east was Monitor, where the Kroeger family disembarked from their train in 1926.

The Kroeger family, and most of the Mennonites who arrived in the region during the mid-1920s, settled along the Canadian National Railways (CNR) line some twenty miles to the south of Monitor. The towns on the CNR line, running from east to west, included New Brigden (named after Brigden, Ontario, where some of the early settlers had originated), Sedalia (after Sedalia, Missouri), Naco (named by a settler who had lived near a town of the same name on the Arizona/Mexico border), Little Gem, and Hemaruka (composed from the names of a railway official's four daughters—Helen, Mary, Ruth, and Katherine). Because of the primitive state of the roads, virtually all supplies were brought in to the communities by rail, and trains were commonly used to reach even towns that were only a short distance apart.

There was no social safety net to speak of in Canada during the 1920s and 1930s. The prevailing view of welfare—"relief," as it was called—was not materially different than in the era of the industrial revolution in nineteenth-century Britain. Payments in support of individuals were considered a misuse of public funds: they rewarded irresponsible conduct, and should therefore be made only in the most dire of circumstances. The accepted role of government was very circumscribed and budgets were small; the federal and provincial governments combined spent only $630 million in 1929/1930.[4] Governments acknowledged some responsibility for education, but scarcely any for the support of the needy, unemployed, disabled, elderly, or sick. To the extent that any relief payments were made, they were the responsibility of municipalities; the provincial and national governments initially acknowledged no role for themselves.

So far as civil liberties were concerned, immigrants could be—and were—deported if they became a public charge. Political activities of the wrong kind could also have this result. Between 1930 and 1934, some 2,500 immigrant residents of Alberta were deported.[5]

It was not a welcoming environment for a newly arrived family such as the Kroegers, with five children, no knowledge of English, minimal financial resources, and a father in poor health.

EIGHT *To Be at Home Somewhere, 1926–1930*

THE CLASSIC CANADIAN IMMIGRANT STORY is of the man who arrives with little more than his bare hands and achieves success through hard work. The Kroeger family's life in Canada did not follow this pattern. For them, success did not begin to unfold until half a generation later, when the two eldest sons, Nick and Henry, came to maturity and began to make their way in the new world.

Heinrich had been permanently weakened by rheumatic fever during the war. He then lived through the traumas of revolution and civil war, followed by typhus, famine, and finally emigration. The stresses of trying to settle in a strange country undermined his health still further. He developed an ulcer, and at one point it appeared that he might not live.

He was no stranger to hard work, but he was not by nature an aggressive person. Soft-spoken and slightly below average in height, he was of a gentle disposition and had a quiet sense of humour. Throughout his life, he had a special fondness for small children. Had he been able to pass his life in the well-ordered and familiar environment of his village in pre-war Russia, his story would have been that of a happily settled family man making a moderately good living as a carpenter. It was not to be.

His wife was the stronger personality of the two, and perforce came to play an important part in the family's affairs during the difficult years that followed their arrival in Canada. However, much of her time and attention were taken up looking after the five children, two of whom were under three when the family arrived in Canada.

One of the challenges faced by the Canadian Mennonite Board of Colonization (CMBC) was placing the new arrivals when they arrived in Canada. The Board had to find agricultural land, because the Canadian government had made it a condition of the Russlaender's admission that they become farmers. However, the normal terms for purchasing farms in the 1920s required a down payment of 50 per cent, with the balance payable over a period of two to five years. It was out of the question for the largely destitute Russlaender to meet such terms.

The solution to this problem emerged from a body known as the Canadian Colonization Association (CCA), which had been formed in 1921 to promote immigration to Canada, and particularly to the prairies. Its members initially included the railways, an association of mortgage companies, and the federal department of immigration. The Canadian Pacific Railway was a particularly active member of the Association and eventually took over its operation from the other parties.

At the suggestion of the CPR, the CMBC formed a separate Land Settlement Board to work with the CCA in finding farms for the Russlaender. David Toews added the leadership of this body to his other responsibilities. The joint efforts of the CCA and the Land Settlement Board brought about what came to be known as The Mennonite Contract, under which the Board, on behalf of newly arrived individuals, would enter into trust agreements with farmers and others who had land for sale. Under these agreements the Board was able to acquire fully equipped farms, including buildings, equipment, and livestock, with no down payment and with provision for the new owner to retire the debt over a fifteen-year period through 50/50 crop sharing arrangements with the vendor.[1]

Financing the purchase of farms was one problem; finding farms to purchase was another. The Land Settlement Board acquired land owned by the CPR, and also entered into trust agreements with various farmers who were ready to transfer their land to the Russlaender. In addition, a substantial number of the newly arrived Mennonites were settled on abandoned farmsteads in an area of the West known as the Palliser Triangle.

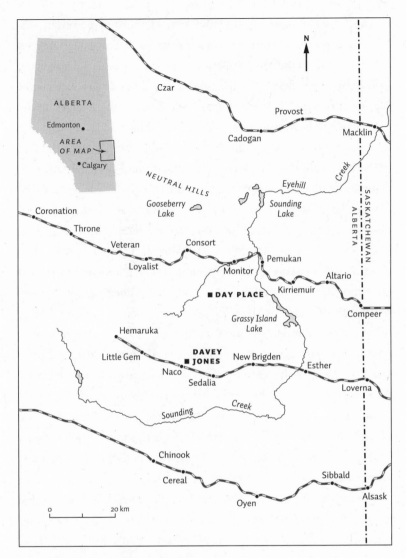

Map of the area where the Kroegers settled in 1926.

The Palliser Triangle is a geographic entity familiar to prairie farmers, but few people elsewhere in the country have ever heard of it. Those who have encountered the name at all would most likely associate it with the Palliser Hotel in Calgary. The Triangle takes its name from a nineteenth-century survey that had found much of the West suitable for agriculture, but excluded a large, roughly triangular area in the middle of the prairie that was characterized by thin topsoil and low rainfall. With the U.S. border as its base, the triangle (which is actually more of an irregular pentagon) extends from Brandon, Manitoba to the Rocky Mountains. The area on a line running from Moose Jaw to Calgary, and the land lying immediately to the north of this line, was found to be especially arid and alkaline. The apex of the Palliser Triangle is approximately at Monitor, Alberta.

In the early years of the twentieth century, influential figures persuaded governments that the Palliser expedition's conclusions had been unduly pessimistic. In 1909, the Triangle was opened to homesteaders. A surge of settlement followed, and soon the area was dotted with farms, rural schools, small towns, and grain elevators. Good harvests in the initial years seemed to bear out the optimistic forecasts that had been made, but after the bumper crop of 1915 harsh reality began to reassert itself.

Much has been written about the impact on the prairies of the drought and depression of the 1930s. What is less widely known is that the period from the latter part of World War I until the mid-1920s was equally harsh.

In southeastern Alberta, grain harvests plummeted from an average of 35 bushels per acre in 1915 to 4.9 in 1918, and to 1.4 in 1919.[2] Then grain prices collapsed. There was widespread personal hardship. In some areas, there were reports of children unable to attend school for want of winter clothing, and a 1921 survey by the Red Cross in southeastern Alberta found that nearly two thirds of the children were suffering from malnutrition.[3]

Farmers were unable to meet their debt obligations, and many had no choice but to abandon the land and buildings in which they had invested years of effort—they were "droughted out," as the expression of the times put it. By 1926, when the Kroeger family arrived in Canada, there were over 2,700 abandoned farms in Census Division 5 where they settled.[4]

The existence of a large number of abandoned farms in the Palliser Triangle offered an opportunity of sorts to the Mennonite Land Settlement Board. Settling the Russlaender on farms that had been unable to support their predecessors was something less than a guarantee of future prosperity, but it was at least a way of giving the new arrivals a start. In the area south of Monitor, and particularly around the small towns of New Brigden, Sedalia, and Naco, some thirty Mennonite families were settled between 1924 and 1926.

Upon their arrival in Canada, the Kroeger family lived with Helena's brother George and his family on their farm south of Monitor. Nick and Henry, who had no knowledge of English, began attending the local school.

In mid-November 1926, the family moved to a farm north of New Brigden that the Board had obtained for them from a bachelor named Joe Smith. Part of the transaction was that Heinrich made a loan of $50 to Smith, for which he received a promissory note (there is no record of the reason for the loan, or of how Heinrich came to have this amount of money). Some household provisions came with the farm, but not enough to carry the family through the winter, so they had to seek help from the Mennonite Colonization Board in Rosthern. Part of their problem, which they had in common with other families who had arrived late in the fall, was that the harvest was over and there were no longer opportunities to earn wages by working on farms in the area. In early January, the Board arranged for them to receive a shipment of clothing and provided financial assistance to enable them to purchase groceries and coal.

During the latter part of the winter, a kindly local schoolteacher began giving Heinrich and Helena lessons in English. One of Heinrich's notebooks contains phrases he had copied during their lessons, such as "I am a cabinet maker from Russia."

When spring arrived, Smith returned to the farm—and forced the Kroeger family off the property. It is impossible after this many years to reconstruct exactly what happened. The records of the Mennonite Land Settlement Board show that the land was transferred to Heinrich Kroeger, but there is no comparable entry in the land title records of the province. However, the standard Mennonite contract included a provision giving the owner of a property the right to manage it until the new occupants had settled in.[5] It is possible that Smith developed second thoughts about the transfer he had agreed to and used this clause to evict the Kroegers and take back his farm.

According to older members of the family who have some recollection of the affair, Heinrich and Helena reacted strongly to Smith's attempts to displace them. Smith invoked the local Justice of the Peace, who also happened to be the agent who had arranged the original transaction. The RCMP were also called in, and at one point Helena threw a barrel hoop at the constable who came to enforce the family's eviction. But in the end, the Kroegers' resistance proved unsuccessful, and on May 20th the family was forced to move. It brought to an abrupt end Heinrich and Helena's plans to start a new life in Canada.

Smith resumed farming the property that he had once given up. As of early 1928, he had still not repaid Heinrich's loan, and the records do not show whether he ever did.

The family's first relocation was to an abandoned building—not much more than a granary—south of New Brigden, where Heinrich was able to find temporary employment with some of the local farmers.

In the archives of the Mennonite Land Settlement Board is a series of letters in German from Heinrich to the Board about finding another farm for him.[6] On July 31, 1927, he wrote:

We would like to take up a farm of half a section [half a square mile] in the fall… My wife is sick and I have to work away from home, that is not very good…but I have to go back to work because winter is coming.

He followed up on August 8th:

The house is leaky and it is still leaking a day after the rain stops… We cannot stay much longer with our children when it gets colder.

A third letter on August 29th had a tone of urgency:

> We cannot stay in this old ramshackle house…our boys are too
> small to be of much help, they have to go to school, that comes first.

He concluded:

> We would like to be at home somewhere.

Heinrich expressed particular concern in his letters about his daughter
Helen, who was badly cross-eyed. Although eight years old, she was unable
to begin school because of her condition, and Smith's failure to repay the
$50-dollar loan made it impossible for Heinrich to pay for the surgery
she required.

The solution to this problem was provided by the Alberta Red Cross,
which sometimes arranged for medical care in particularly difficult cases.
In response to an appeal from Heinrich, the Red Cross in June 1928 agreed
to pay for surgery to deal with Helen's condition. They did not, however,
have funds for transportation. A solution to this problem was provided
by Jim Doolan, the local storekeeper in Naco, who knew of a truck driver
in Hemaruka (a hamlet a few miles west of Naco) who would be going to
Calgary with a load of cattle. Helen, by then nine years old, travelled alone
with him, and the surgery was performed at the Holy Cross Hospital. At
last, she would be able to begin school.

Heinrich had been reluctant to leave Rosental, and from time to time
he spoke of going back. His inclinations were strengthened by a letter he
received in November 1927 from Helena's sister Susanna Rempel, who
had remained in the Chortiza colony:

> We have a nice building made of brick with a stable and barn; it is
> better than the one we had in Kitschkas…we have worked in the
> fields and with the threshing machine all summer. Thank God, we

have enough to eat and drink…I know for a fact that if you were to see all the changes here, you would not find your way. Well, how are you doing far away—better?…if that is not the case, what did it help that you have sought and found another home? Give our regards to [brother] George when you visit one another.

Helena, on the other hand, was adamantly opposed to the idea of returning to Rosental. In any case, there was no practical prospect of them doing so, since they had no money to finance such a trip.

The family finally managed to move in late 1927, before the onset of winter, but only to another vacant farm building, this one in the Sedalia area. For the fourth time in a little over a year, Nick and Henry changed schools. By this time, they had developed a working knowledge of English.

The Mennonite Land Settlement Board was sympathetic to the family's problems but unable to help. Its staff was small, and the need to find land for recent arrivals considerably exceeded what was available. On January 9th, 1928, Heinrich received a letter from a representative of the Board, which read in part "Your difficult situation is well known to us… Mr. Klassen has sent you a parcel with clothing and I have…contacted Elder David Toews in Rosthern…I hope you will receive some help from there."

In March 1928, Peter Kroeger was born. Heinrich walked several miles through the snow to Sedalia, where he mailed a form registering his son's birth. He also applied his carpenter's skills and made a cradle for him.

Between 1928 and 1930, the family moved twice more, each time to an empty farm house. The settlers who had built the houses had in most cases concentrated their efforts and resources on acquiring equipment and breaking land, with the result that the houses they built were generally quite rudimentary. The only insulation against prairie winters was tarpaper over which the siding had been nailed, and the roofs invariably leaked.

In August 1929, Heinrich was informed by the Land Settlement Board that something might be available after harvest. In mid-November he wrote again:

I just want to ask you on the Board how things are with our farm deal now ...again there are those who pressure us to move out of the house in the winter...please do not forget us in the future. I have work in Naco and Sedalia at 30 cents per hour and do not have to worry about that for the time being but the *Reiseschuldt* [travel debt] remains, yes it grows [the family's debt for its passage from the USSR was increasing because of interest charges].

In November, he wrote again, reporting that the family was being pressed to move out of the building it was occupying.

Conditions continued to deteriorate for the Kroegers. On December 20th, the Board's local representative sent a letter to Rosthern:

We have just received word...that the Kroeker (sic) and Pauls families who are residing in the Sedalia district have nothing to eat and are in dire straits economically. We hope that we will be able in spring to do something for these families. We are now dealing with a need for immediate help, otherwise we would probably have difficulties with the municipality...the harvest in that district was so poor that these families could not earn enough money to get through the winter.[7]

The Board was unable to reply in time for the Kroeger's Christmas, but on December 30th they sent their local representative a cheque for $50 to meet the immediate needs of the two families.

Many of the Mennonite families who arrived from the USSR in the 1920s faced situations similar to that of the Kroegers. They could not apply to their municipalities for assistance because a condition of their admission to Canada was that they would not become a public charge for at least five years. As a result, the Colonization Board had to deal with the most pressing cases as best it could within its limited resources. In 1927, the Board was making carefully rationed payments to needy families, sometimes for food, sometimes for fuel in winter, sometimes for medical care.[8]

Compounding the difficulties of the Mennonites who arrived in the Palliser Triangle was the state of the local farm economy. Over the longer term, residents of the Triangle who had survived the crop failures and depressed prices that followed World War I saw their fortunes improve, with good crops in the latter part of the 1920s. They were however far from well off. Usually, their farm buildings were no more than basic, cash was in short supply and, even in the good years, many had trouble keeping up their mortgage and tax payments. When they engaged individuals such as Heinrich to help them with farm work, they could afford to pay only minimal wages, and often payment was made in kind.

All of these problems were to become more acute when the drought and depression of the 1930s arrived. In 1930, Heinrich saw himself at a dead end. Despite four years of correspondence with the Board, he had been unable to obtain a farm. His health had deteriorated, and when he engaged in heavy physical labour he experienced acute internal pain. His family had often gone hungry, and he saw nothing in the future that offered a better prospect. In 1930, he had one more exchange with the Board on the question of acquiring a farm, but again it proved unproductive.

The cumulative effect was to break his morale, and he gave up the effort. Heinrich's resigned mental state became a source of tension between him and Helena. Repeatedly, she urged him to take action of one kind or another, to which he would reply that it was useless to go on trying. From time to time, she would shake her head and say to their children, "Your father was not always like this." Her efforts were to no avail. Heinrich continued to do his best to support his family, and took whatever work became available, but he was unable to muster the inner drive that could have enabled him to identify and seize opportunities.

In August 1930, Helena wrote to the Board herself. This was an extraordinary step for her. She was of limited education and, while sufficiently literate to be able to read, she almost never attempted to write. The fact that she took it upon herself to write pressing the family's need for a farm bespoke the desperation she felt about the need to do something about the family's situation.

The Board's response was sympathetic but did not advance matters:

> I hope that several farms will become available in the fall. We will certainly consider your application at that time. Until then, we can only recommend that your sons as well as Mr. Kroeger will make use of all job opportunities in order to earn as much as possible.

The fact that this exchange took place at the beginning of the 1930s did not augur well for the family's future.

NINE *Boiled Apple Peels, 1930–1934*

IN 1930, the Kroeger family moved to a farmstead some two miles northeast of Naco, Alberta. Naco was one of the small towns that sprang up in 1925 when the Canadian National Railway extended its branch line westwards from Loverna, Saskatchewan, across the Saskatchewan/Alberta border. Sedalia, Alberta had been in existence for a few years, and Naco was established eight miles west of it. Still further west, Little Gem and Hemaruka came into being. Within a few years, Naco could boast of two grain elevators, a post office, a blacksmith shop, a hardware store, a restaurant, a livery stable, a bank, a bulk motor fuel depot, a garage, a grocery store, a community hall that doubled as a church, and a municipal office. Children living on farms in the surrounding area attended Naco's primary school and high school. For six years, it was the Kroegers' nearest town.

When the Kroeger family moved, the economic downturn that had begun the year before was spreading across Canada and around the world. On the prairies, the effects were compounded by a severe drought that was to go on for nearly a decade.

Difficult as the times were, the first years of the 1930s marked the beginning of a modest improvement in the circumstances of the family. After having to move from one abandoned farmstead to another in the late 1920s, in 1930 they were able to settle down. In addition, the two eldest sons were now old enough that they could begin to help support the family.

*Davey Jones and
George Kroeger, 1934.*

View of Naco, 1938.

The farmstead near Naco on which the Kroeger family settled was owned by Davey Jones, a bachelor in his sixties.

On the Canadian prairies, the term "bachelor" had acquired a particular connotation during the early twentieth century. As settlement of the prairies proceeded, those who took up tracts of land and began farming included a number of men who were single and would remain so all their lives. They typically lived in crude shacks and, as the stereotype had it, ate a diet consisting mostly of canned beans. Their clothes, and in some cases their persons, were washed only infrequently. Protracted isolation, particularly during harsh prairie winters, had turned some of them into harmless eccentrics.

Davey only partially matched the stereotype. He lived in a one-room building furnished with a stove, a table, and a bed. In one corner was a pile of coal. His overalls were often shiny with grime. However, he was also soft-spoken and was never heard to use coarse language. Those who knew him thought he might have been well educated in his earlier years.

Originally from Wales, Davey had come to Canada from the United States, specifically, from Nome, Alaska. During the 1898 Yukon gold rush, he had walked much of the way from the B.C. coast to Dawson City. Boxing was a popular form of entertainment in Dawson City, and Davey made his living at it, even though he was of modest height and build.

After the gold rush petered out, Davey decided to move to Alberta and seek a farm. To qualify for a homestead, it was necessary to either be a British subject or to intend to become one. Davey duly applied for naturalization, and it was granted on September 3rd, 1908. He next paid the $10 homestead fee and thus acquired 160 acres of land (one quarter of a square mile, or a quarter-section) northeast of Naco. By a process known as pre-emption, he was also able to purchase an adjoining 160 acres.

He took up residence in May 1909. The following year he acquired the two quarter-sections adjoining his from a veteran of the Boer War living in Montreal, who had been given prairie land rights by the government in recompense for military service. Davey thus obtained ownership of an entire section, which he then proceeded to develop. Despite periods of drought, the land was sufficiently productive in the 1920s that he was able to purchase a tractor on credit. He also acquired a telephone when the Alberta system was extended to the Naco area.

On his property, Davey erected the usual farm buildings and a corral for livestock, together with two frame houses. The property records show that one was 8 feet by 16 feet in size and in 1913 was valued at $100. It was in this building that Davey lived during the years that we knew him. The reasons he built the second house are lost, but it was 14 feet by 18 feet, had two rooms, and was valued at $300. It was sitting empty when the Kroeger family moved into it, with Davey's approval, in 1930.

A kind of loose collaboration developed between Davey and the family. Heinrich and his eldest sons helped Davey with seeding, haying, and harvesting, in return for a share of the crop. Living on his property, the family was able to keep cows, chickens, and geese to meet its own needs for food and also to produce items they could sell locally; there are frequent entries in Heinrich's notebooks about the sale of butter and eggs, albeit for very low prices. Helena also planted a large garden every year. Periodically she would do Davey's laundry, and from time to time she would send him some baking or a cooked meal.

In addition to his collaboration with Davey, Heinrich worked for neighbouring farmers. The work was intermittent, partly because of his health. His pay averaged a dollar a day. Sometimes he was paid in kind, and it was in this manner that the family acquired its first milk cows. The calves from these cows added to the family's modest herd. As it had done in Russia, the family made its own soap, using caustic soda and tallow. Heinrich managed to acquire a sewing machine; clothes were mended, patched, and then patched again.

Excerpts in Heinrich's notebooks dealing with earnings and expenditures for the period provide the flavour of the family's life. A number of the entries record part of a day's work, probably reflecting Heinrich's impaired health. In April 1931, Heinrich recorded, "Bought an old buggy on the 13th, $5.00, down payment $2.50." With this purchase the family acquired a means of mobility that it was to use for the next fifteen years.

April 14 [1931]—arranged with D. Jones that one of us would be
　helping to seed 45 acres.
April 23–4 Bible study Sedalia.
Hauled stones [from fields being cultivated] 29–30. Fencing
　D. Bair.
May 8–9 seeded wheat for us 25 acres.
July 29–31 Gathered [dried] cow dung at D. Bair for cookstove.
September 3 helped half a day with threshing at Hedges—75¢
　Plus $1.50 = $2.25
April 23 buggy repair. $5.15 to be paid at the blacksmith shop Naco
On the 23rd the horses ran away on Henry because the shaft
　broke, he injured his face in several places [an accident that left
　him with something of a Roman nose because the bones did
　not set properly]

In the fall of 1931, Heinrich built a house for a German settler and was paid $58.25 for eight weeks' work. Helena also worked during this period, sewing for others and doing laundry. In addition, she cleaned the school in Naco and the houses of some residents. The returns from their combined efforts were sparse. At the end of 1931, Heinrich recorded a total income for the year of $203.34—about half the amount a rural teacher would have been paid at the time.

During the depression, access to medical care was haphazard. People had recourse to doctors and hospitals only in extreme circumstances. Each family maintained a stock of ointments, cough syrup, and a few other medications. Heinrich Kroeger's papers included a number of hand-written recipes for home remedies that he had brought from Russia. After the successive crop failures of the early 1920s, the hospital in Consort published a notice that, because of its financial situation, it could no longer accept patients who were unable to pay cash.

Many prairie communities found themselves in such straits. In these cases, the only option for residents was to apply to the municipality for relief in the form of hospital care. The results sometimes depended upon whether the municipality itself had any funds left.

During this period, doctors became accustomed to providing medical care first and addressing the question of payment afterwards. One such physician was Dr. Arthur M. Day—a widely revered figure. Based in Consort, he was the only doctor within a radius of thirty-five to forty miles. Endowed as he was with a generous disposition and a good sense of humour, he often received payment in kind in the form of a calf or a young pig, and sometimes, when very needy patients were involved, he received no payment at all. He supplemented his income by operating a large cattle farm.

In the winter of 1934, Helena had a severe attack of gallstones. Word was sent to Dr. Day, who hired a driver with a covered sleigh, bundled himself in a buffalo robe, and made the twenty-mile trip to the farm where we were living. When he had attended to Helena, all the family could offer him was some tomato soup. In another case, when a two-year-old boy developed life-threatening pneumonia in winter, Dr. Day boarded the local mixed freight and passenger train in Consort and rode it some sixteen miles east to Pemukan, where the boy's father met him and took him by sleigh the five miles to his farm. Long-term residents of the Consort area have a limitless supply of such stories about Dr. Day.

During these years, both Nick and Henry became fully involved in the struggle for survival. Like many boys of the era, they attended school only in the winter months. During harvest in the fall and seeding in the spring, they were able to obtain work on neighbouring farms. Again in common with the normal practice of the era, they quit school as soon as they could do so legally, at age fourteen. Nick did so in 1929, Henry in 1931. Thereafter, they took work wherever they could find it. Residents of the area remember the boys working in stubble fields at harvest time in their bare feet.

Their earnings helped support the family. Usually these earnings were in small amounts of cash, but they were sometimes in kind, because the drought and depression had left many farmers very short of money. At the age of thirteen, Nick worked for a neighbour and was paid in milk. For the first job he took, Henry was paid in vegetables.

Nick and Henry both put out trap lines in the winters. The sale of weasel pelts (technically ermine, but everyone called them weasels) enabled them to buy themselves .22 calibre single-shot rifles, which gave them access to yet another source of income. During the 1920s and 1930s, the prairies were overrun with rabbits, and groups of farmers would periodically hold rabbit drives, in which six hundred or more would be killed in a single day. The drives had the dual benefit of reducing the numbers of rabbits and providing the farmers with income from selling the pelts. One winter day in 1935 when Nick was walking across a field, he paused at the edge of a slough, steadied himself by leaning against a tree, and shot 25 rabbits that were sheltering in snow burrows. Over the course of that winter, he shot approximately 1,600. The pelts were sold for seven cents each, yielding the very considerable sum, for the times, of $112.

By these and other means, the two oldest boys helped support the family. One of Heinrich's notebooks includes a representative entry: "From Henry received $10 on October 17th. Paid the store in Naco."

Most of the formerly abandoned houses in which the Kroeger family lived in had only one or two rooms. The parents and their children slept in wooden beds that Heinrich made. The pillows were former flour sacks filled with down and feathers from geese that had been killed for food. (Helena commented disparagingly about the practice of "the English" of using chicken feathers.) The mattresses were denim covers stuffed with straw. So long as the children were small, they were able to sleep three or four in a bed, but this ceased to be possible as Nick and Henry grew to maturity. During the 1930s, when they came home they usually slept in Davey's granary.

With the onset of cold weather, a supply of coal had to be laid in. In 1931 Heinrich recorded, "November 4th–7th, Nick [age 16 at the time] went to the coal mines, 2½ tons." To save paying shipping costs, many residents of Naco/Sedalia hauled coal for themselves in horse-drawn wagons from the mines at Sheerness, some seventy miles away. Sometimes the wagons travelled in convoy. The coal was not of very good quality, but it was affordable. The round trip to the mine took three days. The travellers carried blankets, and a supply of oats for their horses and dry bread for themselves. At night, they would sleep in farm buildings or under their wagons.

Prairie winters are harsh. Temperatures of -30° C were common, and more extreme cold was not rare. On one occasion, a blizzard swept in during the middle of the day. Heinrich put on a heavy coat and walked to the school that his children were attending, some three miles distant. He led them home, walking ahead to shelter them from the wind and to break trail through the snow. On Christmas 1935, Henry arrived home on foot from the farm where he had been working. He was wearing a pair of 49-cent canvas shoes and no socks. His feet were so badly frozen that his mother feared he would lose some of his toes, but he made a full recovery and went back to work.

Heinrich Kroeger's diary for 1911 had recorded rainfall every few days during the summer months in Rosental. The conditions he encountered in Alberta were very different. Among the afflictions endured by residents of the prairies during the 1930s were dust storms. In part, they were a product of the drought, but a dust blanket was also encouraged by prevailing agricultural doctrine. Experts advised farmers that the best way to prevent sub-surface moisture from evaporating was to keep "an insulating layer of dust" on the surface by working the land continuously. However, strong winds are a normal feature of prairie weather and, when they blew during the summertime, they produced what were known as black blizzards. Only in the latter part of the 1930s did practicing farmers come to realize that the best way to conserve moisture was in fact to disturb the surface soil as little as possible, and to leave it covered with cut vegetation.[9]

After the dust storms subsided, the banks of topsoil were often large enough that it was possible to walk over fences rather than climbing through them. In the houses, the floors, counters, and tables would be covered with a layer of gritty soil.

The weather in the 1930s was violent in other ways as well. One hot summer afternoon, when the Kroeger family was returning from Naco, Peter and George stood in the back of the wagon. The sky was dark, and suddenly there was a loud bang as lightning struck the ground nearby. The strike produced a large cloud of dust, and the horses bolted.

All members of the Kroeger family remember Davey Jones with affection. Although a lifelong loner, he was kindly by nature and took a particular interest in the children, who were at his house virtually every day. In July 1931, Heinrich recorded that "the boys and D. Jones went to pick Saskatoon berries [in a distant coulee and] stayed there for the night." Sometimes Davey would make bannock for them. Other times, he would put on his old gloves and show the boys how to box, getting down on his knees with the younger ones to match their height. He taught them numbers and the alphabet before they started school, drawing pictures to illustrate each letter.

He kept leaf tobacco under his bed to dip in molasses and chew. Occasionally he would get quietly drunk by himself at nights, using moonshine that he had brewed from raisins.

I was born in the farmhouse on Davey's place in September 1932, when my mother was 46. At the time, births in hospital were the exception rather than the rule. Roads were primitive, few rural residents had cars, and there was no Medicare to cover the costs of doctors and hospitals. In the Naco/Sedalia area, there were perhaps half a dozen women who regularly served as midwives. Two of them, Mrs. Holmen and Mrs. Cross, attended when I was born.

When my mother's labour pains began, most of the children were at school, and Peter, age four, was taken to a neighbour's. He recalls that when he was brought back hours later, he saw me lying on a little table, covered with a flour sack, being spoon-fed sugar and water by Mrs. Holmen. My father was pleased and excited. That afternoon, when Helen, Anne, and George came home from school, they were surprised to find a new baby in the house. They had not known that their mother was pregnant.

In the days that followed, I inherited the small cradle that my father had made for Peter four years earlier.

In December 1932, Heinrich made the following entry in his notebook: "Received for Christmas from D. Jones $7.00." This was a very substan-

Arthur (18 months) and
Peter Kroeger (6) at Davey
Jones' home, April 1934.

tial sum, and Davey was by no means well off. His generosity expressed his compassion for an indigent immigrant family with a new baby.

Even with the additional money that Nick and Henry were able to earn in the early 1930s, food for the family was sometimes in short supply. One of my earliest recollections is of eating boiled wheat for supper, which our family did quite often in those days. Sometimes a meal would be made of beet peels. Reviving a practice that had been common in Rosental when food was scarce, Heinrich and Helena roasted rye kernels as a substitute for coffee. They also roasted oat seeds to make them more palatable when there was nothing else in the house.

On one occasion, our mother walked the two miles into Naco in quest of food. A shipment of relief supplies in the form of a carload of apples had arrived by rail. Because the apples had arrived badly bruised, they were unloaded with scoop shovels and had to be processed at once. Helena asked for and was given the peels and cores, which she brought home and boiled. For the next two days, the family lived on apple sauce.

Jim Doolan in front of his store with his neice Mary and another Naco businessman,
Mr. Huston.

Sometimes privation could be compounded by human action. Anne recalls taking a sandwich of lard on bread to school for her lunch one day when she was perhaps eight years old. A local farm boy knocked the sandwich off her desk and then, as a joke, stomped on it with his boots. One night, the same farm boy and some of his young friends gathered outside our house at Davey's and shouted threats about "foreigners."

For Heinrich and Helena, the taunts brought back terrifying memories of what they had experienced during the Russian civil war. They drew the blinds and huddled inside, waiting for the intruders to leave. The next day Helena went to Jim Norton, the secretary of the municipality, to complain about the incident. Nothing of the sort happened again.

Community leaders in Naco and Sedalia always treated the Kroeger family with kindness and compassion. Like many small prairie towns, Naco benefited from the presence of a few exceptional individuals.

One such figure was Jim Doolan. When Naco was created in 1925, he moved there from Sedalia and opened a grocery store. He also established a board of trade, and then became chairman of the school board, coach of the baseball team, and captain of the broomball team, as well as participating in many other community activities.

Genial and generous by nature, Jim Doolan had the reputation of never refusing credit to needy families, and there were many who benefited from his open-handedness. In the absence of a local bank, he regularly cashed grain cheques received by local farmers. He also provided financial assistance to some young people who wished to pursue their education outside the Naco area. On exceptionally cold winter nights, Jim and his wife invited the local teacher to spend the night with them, the neighbouring teacherage being uninsulated and equipped with an inadequate heater. The Doolans were among those in Naco who periodically donated used clothing to needy families.

Jim Doolan was a consistent benefactor of the Kroeger family. He arranged for Helena to have employment cleaning his house—probably more often than was strictly required—and the local schools. Sometimes he would find himself with more bread in stock than he was able to sell, and would give Helena the surplus. When necessary, she would trim the mouldy edges before the bread was eaten. Credit was never withheld when the family needed to purchase food.

One year, just before Christmas, a large quantity of sugar was accidentally spilled on the floor of Doolan's store. After asking for and receiving permission, Helena swept it up, bagged it, and took it home. She dissolved the sugar in water, strained out the dirt, and then used the sweet solution to make cookies. It was the only special food the family had that Christmas.

A second notable resident of Naco was Jim Norton. As secretary-treasurer of the municipality, he was responsible for administering the local welfare system, known as "relief." During the 1930s, much of the population was on relief—including at times the Kroegers—and the funds available were severely restricted by the provincial and federal governments. Nevertheless, those who lived through this period still speak warmly of the humane manner in which Jim Norton tried to discharge his responsibilities.

Henry Jack was a unique individual. After serving in World War I, he settled in the Sedalia area, where he was appointed manager of the Union Bank that opened there. Later, he took up farming near Naco, and eventually conducted his operations from his residence in town. He conducted the Naco choir, as well as being an accomplished gardener and a frequent tennis player. The farmhouse he had vacated was occupied for a time by the Kroeger family, and Heinrich did farm work for him.

The 1930s were hard times, and yet people who lived through the period, when asked today, reply that they never really thought of themselves as poor. Members of my family say the same thing. Things simply were as they were.

Within the family, there was warmth and mutual support. On one occasion, when our parents were painting a house in Naco, sixteen-year-old Henry arrived home to find the house dark and the five younger children hungry. He lit the kerosene lamp, found some bread dough in a stone crock, and built a fire in the stove. Then, as the dough was frying, he put one foot on the open oven door and, holding me (then age one) on his knee, proceeded to tap out music with two forks. Soon he had everyone laughing. Eventually our parents came home from Naco bearing a few groceries. Mother punched two holes in a can of Carnation condensed milk and gave the smaller children a drink directly from it.

Outside the family, too, the small communities in the area made the best of the situation, despite the grinding depression. The success of local residents in creating their own diversions in hard times was impressive by any standard. Naco, with a population that never exceeded 85, boasted a set of tennis courts and a ski club (the latter was a remarkable accomplishment, given the flatness of the surrounding countryside). The swimming club used a nearby slough. The baseball team, soccer team, and girls' basketball team all regularly played against teams from other towns. (The basketball team played on clay courts, since there were no gymnasia anywhere in the region.) Teas, sewing bees, and other social events were regularly organized by the local chapters of the United Farm Women of Alberta, the Women's Institute, and the Women's Christian Temperance Union.

A dramatic society organized by Henry Jack regularly performed locally and in the neighbouring towns. In February 1930, their chosen play was George Bernard Shaw's *An Intelligent Woman's Guide to Socialism and Capitalism*. Other events included a Burns' Night Supper in Little Gem, a Dickens' Night in Naco, and a debate by the Naco High School Students' Literary Society. In June 1932, a program featuring duets, recitations, and readings was held at Naco school to mark the end of the school year. Included in the program was a talk on patriotism by Miss Sorenson, one of the teachers. Her theme was that "the law of kindness...[was] one of the laws of patriotism."

During the late 1920s and early 1930s, the *Consort Enterprise* carried a steady flow of reports about skating parties, dances with music provided by local musicians, curling matches, and broomball. In February 1930, young people from Naco took the local train to a dance in Little Gem, eight miles to the west. Little Gem had a band, as did Monitor. In February 1932, the Monitor band was scheduled to perform in Consort, eight miles to the west. A snowstorm made part of the road impassable, and the band had to walk the last few miles into Consort to put on their concert. Almost any occasion was sufficient reason to put on a dance. In April 1934, a dance was held to commemorate Vimy Ridge. Proceeds from such events were usually donated to the Red Cross.

The principal winter sport was hockey, which was played on outdoor rinks. The creation of the Naco rink in 1927 took some effort and ingenuity. Strips of tough prairie sod were cut and stacked around the perimeter. Later, when finances permitted, boards were put in their place. Creating an ice surface was also a problem, because the Naco townsite had only a limited water supply. Heinrich Kroeger was among those who hauled water from sloughs in barrels on horse-drawn sledges. In 1930, the acquisition of a diesel generator permitted the rink to be outfitted with electric lights.[10]

Despite the problem of roads frequently being choked by snowstorms, ways were found to hold regular games between teams from towns in the area. Nick and Henry played for the Naco team, wearing skate blades strapped to their boots. For shin guards, they wore lengths of canvas ribbed with wooden slats from a binder harvester.

Similar ingenuity was displayed when skis were needed. Nick and Henry took a set of boards four inches wide and six feet long, and cut a point at one end of each. Next they boiled the pointed ends for several hours to soften the wood, after which these ends were bent upwards and tied in position until they dried. Short strips of harness leather were then nailed across the middle of each board to create loops into which the skier's feet were inserted.

Although a substantial number of Mennonite families were settled in the Naco/Sedalia-New Brigden area during the 1920s, they didn't establish their own church. One factor was the distance between the farms where the various families lived; another was the fact that, after a few years, a number of the Mennonites moved to other parts of the province to seek a more rewarding life than was offered by farming in the Palliser Triangle. Those who remained held religious services in each others' homes, with leadership from an individual who in Russia had been a church elder. Once a year, they held a Bible conference, and at Christmas they held special services at which they sang traditional Mennonite hymns.

They also participated in services at the local churches of other religions. Heinrich's notebook tells of his attendance at a religious service in the home of Jack Thornton, an English neighbour. There is also an entry from 1935 about "the English minister" coming to visit the family.

During the summer months, it was common practice on the prairies to hold religious services outdoors in the beds of sloughs that had dried out. These sites were pleasantly green, in contrast with the brown grass that characterized much of the prairie, and they were usually surrounded by trees that provided shade. On July 21, 1935, Heinrich recorded attending an "English service in the slough."

Although many Canadians of Anglo-Saxon origin had very reserved attitudes towards "foreigners" (that is, immigrants from Europe, and particularly from the Slavic countries), the Mennonites were generally well accepted. When the first families arrived in the area, the *Consort Enterprise* carried the following editorial on May 7th, 1925:

> The Mennonites are a class of people who have suffered much priva-
> tion and abuse on account of their religious and other beliefs; they
> are absolutely honest, steady, and working people...while they have
> little money, they deal and live entirely within their means.

Nevertheless, the Mennonites generally kept to themselves during the early years, and concentrated their efforts on making a living in their new country. Integrating into society and its various organizations was something for the future. Local businesses, social groups, and political organizations were solely in the hands of people of British descent; there is no record of "ethnics" playing a role in any of them during the early years.

However, the files of the *Enterprise* also record a striking instance of how the community could reach out to its new neighbours. On June 26th, 1930, it reported, "The service of Sunday, 22nd was given by the Mennonite choir and their minister, Mr. George Harder." Local residents remarked on what good singers the Mennonites were.

Some Mennonite families who came to Canada were determined from the outset to become Canadian, and the parents insisted that their children learn and speak English. The majority of parents, however, sought to preserve the language and culture they had known in Russia. The Kroeger family fell in this category, and in the early years only the Low German language was spoken at home. As a result, when Helen and Anne began school in 1929, they knew scarcely a word of English. The three younger sons had an easier time of it because our older siblings, notwithstanding their parents' concerns, increasingly brought English into the household.

In the files of the *Consort Enterprise*, a Mennonite name appears for the first time in a report of Irene Epp's receipt of a prize in the 1934 school festival—nine years after the first Mennonite families arrived in the area. The following year, Anne Kroeger was cited as having won a prize for recitation.

On June 8th, 1933, Heinrich received a letter from his younger brother, Abram, who had remained in the USSR and had reproached Heinrich for leaving. Its message was in stark contrast to the cheerful letter the family had received from Helena's sister Susanna Rempel in 1927:

Today I received a letter from [sister] Maria, which was full of tears and grief. I sent her some money. We are not doing well ourselves. We both work, I in the office, my wife in the bureau. There is a lack of food. The summer was practically rainless, hence a crop failure… Elsa, our only daughter was buried in 1930. We are very sad. Hermann attends school the second year and does very well. We often regret the fact that we did not follow you in 1926… Give me a detailed account of your way of life. We think of dying.

Heinrich kept this letter to the end of his life, and from time to time referred to it in conversation with us. He did so in tones of resignation, clearly wishing that what it said was not so, wishing that he could regain the life he had known before the war.

TEN *Russian Thistle and Relief, 1934–1939*

The years that the locust hath eaten.
—JOEL 2:25

FORMER SASKATCHEWAN PREMIER Tommy Douglas once said of the drought and depression of the 1930s on the prairies, "Only those who lived through that period can fully understand what it meant in human terms."[1]

During their first years in Canada, the Kroeger family had periodically benefited from the support of private charitable organizations as well as from the Mennonite Colonization Board. As winter approached in November 1931, Heinrich recorded, "clothes from the Board" and "received clothing from the English society" (unspecified, but possibly the Red Cross).

Once his application for naturalization as a British subject was approved in 1933, he became eligible to apply for relief. He hesitated to do so. He and Helena were apprehensive about the unknowable consequences that might follow such a step. After their experiences in czarist Russia and then the USSR, they regarded contact with government as something to be avoided whenever possible. But eventually they had no choice. At the end of 1933, the family began receiving relief, in kind and in the form of subsistence vouchers. In doing so, they joined about one third of the residents of the municipality.

Among the papers that Heinrich saved were a number of bills from Jim Doolan's store in Naco. Interspersed with the listed purchases are entries in the credit column that say "By voucher." The value of these vouchers for a couple with a family—in the Kroegers' case, there were by now seven children—was $8 per month. During this period, a rural schoolteacher in the area was typically paid $35 to $40 per month.

Recipients of relief were required to acknowledge in writing an obligation to repay the government for the benefits they received. This was normally to be done by working. A directive from the Alberta government stated, "Any man refusing to work for the Municipality when requested to report for duty is to be cut off relief forthwith."[2]

The work obligation imposed on recipients of relief in rural areas usually took the form of road construction. When the prairies were surveyed during the late nineteenth and early twentieth centuries, road allowances were provided at one-mile intervals running north and south, and at two-mile intervals running east and west. However, the actual construction of the roads was governed by the availability of resources. To encourage development, municipalities allowed farmers to liquidate their tax obligations and relief recipients to liquidate their debt to the province by working on road construction.

Heinrich's first notations about road work were for June 11th to 18th and 20th to 22nd, in 1934. He was fifty-one and still in poor health. A document issued by the municipality in September of that year showed the status of his relief account: a credit of $28.80 for work he had done, and a remaining balance owing of $139.92. In October, he made further entries about "relief work."

Dirt roads were constructed using ploughs and large scoops, known as fresnos, that were drawn by horses or mules. Peter recalls travelling by buggy with his mother when he was about six to take lunch to Heinrich at a road construction project. The men doing relief work on the project were a sorry lot, dressed in ragged clothes, unshaven, and eating the most basic of food. Their work was credited against their relief accounts at a rate of 15 cents per hour.

As the drought and depression ground on, Davey Jones began to run into financial trouble. His tractor was repossessed by the machinery company. Next, his unpaid phone bills caught up with him. One day, as he and Peter were returning with a team of horses from one of his fields, they saw a man wearing a suit and hat leave Davey's house and drive off in a car. Davey commented, "You see how they kick a man when he's down." The man had let himself into the house, unscrewed the telephone from the wall, and carried it off. In March 1932, an Alberta Government Telephones crew removed forty miles of telephone lines from the area because so many residents had lost their phones.

What prairie residents commonly spoke of as "the drouth" was particularly harsh in the Palliser Triangle. The period from 1933 to the end of 1937 came to be known as "the five terrible years."

In 1934, crops in southeastern Alberta averaged 2 to 6 bushels per acre, compared with 15 to 20 in many previous years and over 30 when there was a bumper crop. Wheat prices in Edmonton stood at $1.20 per bushel in 1930; one year later they had fallen to 36 cents, and in December 1932 the *Consort Enterprise* reported that they had reached a low of 22.5 cents—prompting the editor to observe, "and Christmas is only ten days away." During the summers, there were clouds of grasshoppers, little rain, and violent storms. In 1936, temperatures frequently approached 40 degrees Celsius, and in 1937 a number of lakes dried up. Tests by agriculture officials in some years found 2,000 grasshopper eggs below the surface of a single square foot of soil.[3]

Most farmers had only limited resources to fall back on when the bad years came. They had few savings and many carried substantial debt loads from earlier purchases of machinery when times had been better. Consequently, when one crop failure followed another, they had to turn to governments for assistance.[4]

Historically, relief had been the responsibility of municipalities. However, the crop failures that followed World War I had given the United Farmers of Alberta government in Edmonton the unwelcome experience of dealing with rural distress so widespread that the province had found it had no

Teams and wagons lined up for government relief, Acadia Valley, February 1938.
(Glenbow Alberta Archives NA–2296–9)

choice but to provide assistance to municipalities. When severe droughts returned in the early 1930s, the government knew it would not be able to stay uninvolved. It responded by creating a Charity and Relief Branch in the Department of Municipal Affairs.

Ottawa was determined that the depression was not its problem. Prime Minister Mackenzie King famously declared that his government would not provide "even a five cent piece…for these alleged unemployment purposes." When R.B. Bennett succeeded King as prime minister in July of 1930, he was initially of a similar disposition, but soon came to the view that action was unavoidable. He acknowledged that the problem had become so serious as to be a "national concern," and his government in its first months allocated $20 million for public works and the sharing of relief costs with the provinces.

The opposition of governments to providing relief had some support in the public opinion of the times. In 1924, "economy clubs" were formed in various parts of the country in response to the perceived "extravagance" of governments before the war. In 1932, as the depression deepened, the question debated in various forums was "Are we over-governed?" The editor of the *Consort Enterprise* contributed a series of four thoughtful editorials on this subject.[5]

The prevailing view in the first decades of the twentieth century was that welfare payments usually created more problems than they solved. This view was not limited to the wealthy and the major political parties. In an annual report prepared before World Was I, the Associated Charities of Winnipeg had stated:

> Unfortunately, the large majority of applications for relief are caused by thriftlessness, mismanagement, unemployment due to incompetence, intemperance, immorality, desertion of the family, and domestic quarrels. In such cases the mere giving of relief tends rather to induce pauperism than to reduce poverty.[6]

The predisposition of governments against relief was sometimes reinforced by the expert advice they received. In 1932, Prime Minister Bennett hired Charlotte Whitton, a professional social worker and a future mayor of Ottawa, to investigate the situation on the prairies. After a four-month tour, she reported that almost 40 per cent of those receiving relief did not need it, and that what was really required was more social workers.[7]

Governments were also strongly influenced by fiscal considerations. Their budgets were small, and the federal government's principal source of revenue was the customs tariff.[8] The downturn in the economy had substantially reduced the revenues of both federal and provincial governments. Alarmed at the prospect of rising expenditures for relief, they made strenuous efforts to limit the cost. Relief was provided, not in cash, but in the form of vouchers that could be submitted to purchase the bare necessities of life. A circular from the Alberta government directed that only such items as cheap flour, ground meal, and boiling beef were to be eligible for purchase by voucher.[9]

An interesting sidelight on Jim Doolan's records of purchases by the Kroeger family is that, while they provided specific descriptions of some of the items purchased, most entries simply read "goods." His purpose may have been to preclude objections from zealous government officials about what kinds of food he was letting his customers buy with their relief vouchers.

During this period, anyone wishing to purchase spirits had to have a permit issued by the provincial government. As a safeguard to ensure that assistance was provided only to the truly deserving, one of the questions on the relief application form was "Do you possess a liquor permit?"[10]

Farmers' operating needs were also met with assistance in kind: seed grain, harvest binder twine, coal, machinery repairs, and tractor fuel (but only in cases where the farmer could demonstrate that he did not possess sufficient horses to work his land).[11] To qualify for relief, farmers were required to sell off any "surplus" livestock. There were long line-ups of farmers in their wagons whenever rail shipments of relief feed grain arrived in a town.

One measure used by governments to limit costs was to restrict relief to British subjects, and to deport "indigents" who were not naturalized. On June 1, 1931, the Relief Committee of the Alberta Department of Municipal Affairs received a report that stated in part:

> Aliens in this province are receiving relief on the same basis as Canadians. This is the only country where such consideration would be given...some drastic action should be taken, destitute cases should be given the privilege of transportation to their own country, and those remaining advised that no relief would be granted.[12]

R.B. Bennett's minister of labour strongly supported this approach.[13] Between 1930 and 1935, 28,000 indigents were deported from Canada.[14]

To prevent such a fate befalling the Russlaender it had brought to Canada, the Mennonite Board of Colonization provided families with such support as it could from its own limited resources.

The Kroeger family, in common with many others in the area, continued to draw relief in one form or another during most of the 1930s. Life continued to be a struggle for survival until nearly the end of the decade, when the rains returned and there were finally crops to be harvested.

Heinrich's notebooks provide a sense of how the family lived during those years, including the earnings contributed by the two eldest sons:

1934

On the 19th potatoes and apples (relief shipment) arrive
in Naco

December 13

56 rabbit skins. 7 cents a piece.

1935

February 18–19

Bible conference

April 6

Sharpening saws for P. Durksen. Received chicken feed for
the job.

May 31

Planted 9 ½ acres oats

June 12

Road work all day

September 2

from Nick $5

November 7

700 pounds of coal. Paid in Sedalia $2.00

December 6

33 bushels oats Sedalia relief

1936

February 11

    Nick to work for Redels

March 7–9

    2 ½ days harrowing for H. Durksen $1.75

March 31

    D. Epp gave us 1 load of straw

April 3

    Received 6 bales of hay Sedalia relief

May 15

    6 sacks potatoes. Relief

May 18

    Work (Duerksons) (Received one pair of shoes)

May 24

    Set the geese for brooding 20 eggs

November 13

    Oats Relief 25 bushels 10 lbs

December 8

    Henry brought 1 team of horses home [payment in kind from
the farmer for whom he had been working]

As late as November 5th, 1938, an entry says "got apples from New Brigden
9 boxes." And on December 31, "road work on relief $8.04." This proved
to be last year in which the family received relief. From 1939 on—thirteen
years after arriving in Canada—the Kroeger family was able to live on its
own income.

In response to the drought in the Palliser Triangle, some people moved
to regions where there was better land. The federal and provincial governments paid for such moves as a means of reducing relief costs. The railways
also provided concessional rates to those who decided to relocate. By
January 1934, governments had assisted in the relocation of 3,148 Alberta
families. Through most of the 1930s, the *Consort Enterprise* carried reports
every few weeks along these lines:

October 28th, 1933

Eight [rail] car loads of livestock, machinery, and household goods left Consort on Monday night belonging to people moving out of the dried out area south of us.

February 28th, 1935

A family from Sibbald passed through Monitor, their household effects loaded on a hay rack and a wagon. Their destination is Killam, and they expect it will take them three days to get there.

June 1st, 1939

Many people have moved out of the country south and east of Sedalia, and occupied homes are few and far between.

By 1936, there were 3 million acres of abandoned farmland, spanning the three prairie provinces, in the Palliser Triangle.

In parallel with the migration from dried out farms, the population of some towns began to shrink. In the spring of 1938, the community hall in Monitor was dismantled and the lumber shipped to Barrhead, a good-sized town northwest of Edmonton.

Moving was not an option for the Kroeger family. Having virtually no money, the only avenue through which they could acquire, equip, and operate a farm was the Mennonite Land Settlement Board, and the Board's efforts to find them a farm had been fruitless.

Many of those who elected to stay on their farms had increasing difficulty making ends meet. On June 30th, 1932, Jim Norton, Secretary-Treasurer of the Municipality of Stewart, had the unpleasant task of publishing this notice: "Owing to the financial condition of the Municipal District, crops on all lands in arrears will be seized for taxes this year."

Properties in towns such as Monitor and Consort were also seized for tax arrears. In September 1936, the *Enterprise* published a list of some 2,500 quarter sections of land, representing over 600 square miles, that had been taken over by the government because of tax arrears and were being offered for sale. The following month it was reported that there had been no takers.

Soil drifting on an abandoned farm during the 1920s.
(*Glenbow Alberta Archives NA–4357–1*)

Those who remained on their farms sometimes had to take unusual measures. The summer of 1937 saw an almost total crop failure; the fields were covered with Russian thistle (called tumbleweed elsewhere). Severe drought left pastures brown and devoid of grass and, in August, the Alberta department of Agriculture published guidance on how Russian thistle could be cut, stored, and used to feed livestock.[15] One of my early recollections is of the disagreeable, rather bitter taste of milk from cows fed Russian thistle.

The plight of the drought-stricken farmers on the prairies attracted nation-wide attention. Churches and other charitable organizations collected used clothing and raised funds to purchase relief supplies. Apples were sent from British Columbia, blankets and quilts from Ontario, vegetables from different parts of the country. In November 1933, Mennonites in Ontario shipped four railway carloads of vegetables and clothing to needy co-religionists in Saskatchewan. During these years, the railways hauled hundreds of cars of relief shipments, free of charge, to the dried-out areas in the west. Some shipments also came from places in Alberta that had been less severely afflicted by the drought. Relief supplies were sent to Consort from Stettler, a hundred miles to the west, and Viking, a hundred miles to the north.

Individuals also contributed. In 1931, Arthur M. Day, a well-loved, archetypal country doctor who was based in Consort, had a load of wheat from his farm ground and distributed locally. In his words, it was worth little on the market, he had lots of it, and no one should go hungry.

Members of the Kroeger family recall receiving bags of beans and potatoes, rounds of Ontario cheese, apples and plums from British Columbia, and salt cod from Atlantic Canada. The cod came to be called "horse blankets" by the locals; it had the consistency of leather and had to be soaked for days before it could be eaten.

Despite the severe economic conditions, mechanization of farm work and transportation continued during the 1930s, albeit at a slow pace, with horses being progressively displaced by equipment. In May 1939, the *Consort Enterprise* reported:

Complying with the Department of Health regulations, the hitching posts have all been removed from in front of the stores. One rack is now placed south of Mike Covlin's garage and the others back of the Pioneer Store and the Crown Lumber Yard.

During these years, the Red Cross emerged as a life-saving organization. There is no twenty-first-century parallel in Canada for the revered status the Red Cross acquired in the eyes of drought-stricken residents of the prairies.[16]

The Canadian Red Cross was founded in 1909 and came into prominence during World War I. After the war, it took on health promotion as its main role, but was drawn into distributing relief supplies in rural areas as a result of the succession of crop failures that struck the prairies in the early 1920s. The Red Cross continued to claim that it was not a relief agency but, with the return of the drought and the depression of the 1930s, this role came to dominate its activities.

The provincial government, having no regional welfare staff of its own, used the Red Cross and its extensive network of volunteers and staff to deliver clothing and other supplies to those in need. Determining who was truly in need was a matter for the municipalities, assisted in some cases by the RCMP. On December 28th, 1933, the Kroeger family received a parcel containing shoes, stockings, combs, 3 pounds of wool, and 25 yards of flannelette. A subsequent shipment included some ill-fitting canvas running shoes, which the Kroeger children wore to church as well as to school.

The Red Cross was often enlisted to receive and manage the distribution of supplies coming in from many quarters. In 1930, the Alberta Division was supplied with 26,000 articles of military clothing and blankets by the federal Department of Militia and Defence. In 1933, the Red Cross distributed clothing on behalf of the government to over 35,000 needy families in Alberta. On one occasion the Red Cross received donations of toothbrushes from two manufacturers, while on another fabric was donated by textile factories in Ontario and Quebec.

The Red Cross also collected or purchased and distributed some items that were not necessities of life but were important in other ways. One year just before Christmas, a Red Cross shipment of toys arrived in Naco and was distributed to needy families. Helen and Anne Kroeger each received a china doll from the shipment—a wonderful gift for them. Lacking funds to buy toys for his children, Heinrich would sometimes make them toy houses, wagons, and wheelbarrows out of apple boxes. For the two china dolls, he made small wooden beds. The beds and the dolls are still in the family.

At the annual Christmas concerts held in the one-room rural schools, the culminating event was the arrival of a local man dressed as Santa Claus, who would distribute small presents provided by the parents, and sometimes by the teachers. Some Christmases, the only presents some

Red Cross hospital, Altario, Alberta, c.1921 (Glenbow Alberta Archives NA–2903–57)

The dolls Helen and Anne received from the Red Cross, Christmas 1928. The doll bed was made by their father, Heinrich Kroeger.

of the children, including the Kroeger children, received were paper dolls provided by the Red Cross.

An important initiative of the Red Cross was the creation of the Junior Red Cross (JRC) to engage school children. The JRC was hugely successful and came to have members in virtually every school in Alberta. The charge for membership was 25 cents per year, which many children raised from the one cent bounty the province paid for gopher tails. In 1926, membership reached 20,000. The stated objectives of the JRC were promotion of health, citizenship, and service to others. Health Game record charts were distributed in all schools to promote personal hygiene. Every rural student of my generation remembers the green JRC membership buttons with the red cross in the centre.

Just as the Red Cross had arranged for Helen Kroeger to have corrective surgery on her eyes in 1928, so in the depression of the 1930s it provided medical care to those in need. One of the principal activities of the Junior Red Cross was raising funds to support a children's hospital operated by the Red Cross in Calgary. The hospital had thirty-five beds and provided treatment for children from needy families who had been crippled by polio. To raise funds for the hospital, the Juniors organized tag days, candy sales, teas, dances, and sales of Christmas seals. They were also encouraged "to sew and knit...[and] to make toys and collect gifts... for other children less happy than themselves." A school in the Consort area raised enough funds for a local boy to have an operation for club foot.

As the depression deepened, the Alberta Red Cross experienced increasing financial difficulty. Staff was cut, and services curtailed. The nursing service in rural districts was terminated. Membership in the JRC, which had peaked in 1929 at 37,801, had by 1933 fallen to half that number. The 25 cent per year fee was reduced to 5 cents, and later waived altogether, because many school children could no longer afford it. Some functions at the Children's Hospital had to be eliminated. Nevertheless, the Red Cross soldiered on, distributing clothing, drugs, dressings, and other necessities. In 1934, it assisted ten Alberta families whose houses and possessions had been destroyed by fire.

It is difficult from the vantage point of the twenty-first century to grasp the scale of distress on the prairies during those years. In 1937, the Rowell-Sirois Commission on Dominion-Provincial Relations estimated that two thirds of the farmers in Saskatchewan were destitute, and concluded that the requirement for relief was hopelessly in excess of what provincial and municipal governments were able to afford.[17]

Difficult as the circumstances of most people on the prairies were, they continued to donate to the Red Cross to the extent that their limited means permitted. Benefit dances were held regularly in rural schools and small towns; the amount raised was typically around thirty dollars. Arrangements were made for farmers to pledge contributions in grain, with the proceeds to be forwarded to the Red Cross when the grain was sold. A donation of 900 bushels of wheat was milled into flour and distributed to the needy. On March 23rd, 1933, the Naco United Farm Women of Alberta held a "ten cent tea," which raised $8.00 for the Red Cross. Events were also held in people's homes. Following is a report that appeared in the *Consort Enterprise*:

> About 20 folks gathered at the C.E. Gould home to raise money for the Red Cross. Games were played and supper was served by Mrs. F. Campbell and Mrs. Art Redel. The sum of two dollars and forty-five cents was donated to the Red Cross.

In the annual reports of the Alberta Red Cross, the lists of donations go on for pages. While a few donations reported from towns and districts were a hundred dollars or more, most were for much smaller amounts, and some donations from individuals were as small as fifty cents.

In its report for 1935, the Alberta Red Cross reported that "some of the letters received were most pathetic." Following is one such letter quoted in its report for that year—just one case of many that the Alberta Red Cross dealt with during the depression:

Dear Red Cross,

This family consists of three boys, 10, 7, and 4 years with the mother very sick on roughly constructed bed with two baby boys (twins) three days old. The one room farm house, roughly constructed of logs, draughty floors, keep the children shivering, and very sick mother on bed with no bedding of any kind nor clothes, no shoes or caps nor stockings. The children's clothes made of old sacks and patched finally played out and no clothes of any kind for the baby boy twins. The father of these children can not get work of any kind to help them. Can you help them please.

Many municipalities were overwhelmed by the scale of the requirement for relief that they faced. For some, cost-sharing arrangements with the federal and provincial governments became irrelevant when they no longer had funds for any purpose. In August 1932, the Secretary-Treasurer of the Naco School Board informed the Department of Education in Edmonton that matters had reached the point where the district was unable to collect *any* taxes. In Hemaruka the school closed for want of funds, and others operated for a reduced number of months to save money.

In June 1934, the village of Oyen, on the railway line south of Naco, wrote to the Supervisor of Charity and Relief in the Department of Municipal Affairs, advising that "We have had to stay giving relief here as our finances are such that we have no more money to supply it." The department replied that under existing legislation relief was a municipal responsibility.[18] It was not a tenable position.

As early as October 1933, thirteen municipal districts in the Palliser Triangle had been declared indigent by the province. Among them was the municipality of Stewart, with its offices in Naco. More of the financial burden therefore shifted to the province, which intensified its efforts to contain the costs of relief. In April 1935, a circular was sent to all munici-palities instructing them that, with the coming of spring weather, single men on relief in rural districts were to be informed that it would cease on May 1st. The obligation of recipients to perform work for municipalities was re-affirmed. Maladministration of relief in the Goose Lake region, south of Naco, resulted in the province taking over the program.

In 1938, the province cut the minimum salary for teachers to $620 per year. This was not in itself a particularly adverse step, as many municipalities had for some time been able to pay their teachers perhaps only half this amount.[19]

The actions taken by Alberta and other governments were not simply ideological or mean-spirited. Despite strenuous efforts to control costs, government expenditures for relief went from 1 per cent of Gross Domestic Product in the late 1920s to 4.3 per cent in 1934 and 5.6 per cent in 1939.[20] In Saskatchewan between 1930 and 1937, relief consumed 60 per cent of the revenues of the provincial and municipal governments.

Such costs were a growing threat to the solvency of prairie governments. During this period, Alberta was as poor as Saskatchewan and smaller in population. By 1934, Alberta's borrowings meant that interest payments absorbed nearly half of revenues.[21]

The federal government for its part was convinced that the need for relief had been exaggerated and that insufficient emphasis was being placed on the responsibility of the individual. It also believed that bad management was a major part of the problem.

At a meeting with the premiers in January 1934, Prime Minister Bennett berated them for "extravagance and sloppiness." He in turn was attacked by Mackenzie King, who had become Leader of the Opposition, for allowing the provinces to waste vast sums and engage in "an orgy of public expenditure" on behalf of relief recipients.

In early 1935, Bennett, perhaps influenced by the New Deal in the United States, came to believe that a radical change of approach was called for. He introduced a series of sweeping measures to address the problems caused by the depression—but it was too late.

After the election later that year, Mackenzie King returned to power. The change of government produced no improvement for those afflicted by the depression, as King pursued the hard-line approach he had expressed in his earlier statements. In 1937, when conditions on the prairies hit bottom because of the prolonged drought, his government cut grants-in-aid to the provinces from $29 million to $19 million.[22]

As the provinces' financial difficulties deepened, they turned to the federal government, which had no choice but to act on their requests for assistance because of the risk that Canada's credit rating could be damaged if the provinces were to default on their debentures. However, the federal government made it a condition of assistance that each province accept oversight by a loan council. This condition was rejected by Social Credit Premier William Aberhart, with the result that between 1936 and 1939, Alberta defaulted on six sets of debentures.

King's response to the depression stood in some contrast to that of President Roosevelt's administration in the United States. After the passage of New Deal initiatives such as social security legislation, the United States in the late 1930s had considerably more of a social safety net than Canada.

By 1934, the Kroeger family had seven children, and the older ones were fully grown. The family had outgrown the house at Davey's, so in October the Kroegers moved a mile northeast, to what was known as the Monsees place.

Ben Monsees had come to Canada from Sedalia, Missouri before World War I, when southeastern Alberta was opened for settlement. Certain that the area had great potential, he invested heavily in farm equipment, including two Caterpillar tractors, a fourteen-bottom plough, and a steam-driven tractor to operate threshing equipment. He also strung a telephone line from his farm to connect with the line passing through Monitor some twenty miles to the northeast. Like many in the area, he at first had good crops, but then after the war came a succession of droughts. He was forced into bankruptcy. In 1921, his farm was repossessed by the Canada Life Insurance Company. In the mid-1920s, three Mennonite families had moved into the buildings on the Monsees place, but in 1934 they gave up the struggle of trying to make a living there and left for a part of the province where better land was available.

Their departure brought the Kroeger family an opportunity to move into larger accommodation, which they did in October of that year. Although the house on the Monsees place offered more space, it was in other respects similar to the ones the family had occupied in the preceding years: unpainted, drafty, difficult to heat, and it had a leaky roof. The barn was equally marginal, and in February 1936, had to be shored up to ensure it would not collapse during a storm.

They did not farm the land on the Monsees place, having neither animals nor equipment with which to do so. Although the Kroegers no longer lived next to Davey, their relationship with him continued, including sharecropping in return for helping him to put in his crops in the spring and to harvest them in the fall. Thus, on August 23, 1934 Heinrich noted, "One load of wheat. The fourth load is always ours from D. Jones," and elsewhere, "Haying for Davey—we got a ⅓ share."

In November 1936, the family moved again, this time to a property that Henry had found well to the north of the Monsees place. This took them out of the orbit of Naco and Sedalia; their closest towns were now Monitor and Consort. Their household effects, including the Kroeger clock that had moved from house to house with them, were transported on a hay rack. Anne, age thirteen, and George, ten, were given the task of driving the family's small herd of cows, on foot, the twelve miles to the new farm.

The property to which the family was moving was, like many others in the area, held by a mortgage company, and two sections of land were available for rent at $200 per year. After moving seven times during their ten years in Canada, the Kroegers finally had land that they could farm for themselves.

ELEVEN *The Door Closes*

And shut the gates of mercy on mankind.
        —THOMAS GRAY, *Elegy Written in a Country Churchyard*

ONE EFFECT OF THE DEPRESSION was that it brought to an end the immigration of Mennonites to Canada from the USSR.

In 1926, nearly 6,000 Russlaender, including the Kroeger family, reached Canada. Despite difficulties the Mennonite Colonization Board was experiencing in meeting the repayment schedule for those who had been brought over in previous years, the Canadian Pacific Railway was unflagging in its readiness to extend credit to Mennonites. In 1927, the CPR contracted to move a record 20,000.

However, changing times brought about a much different outcome. In the last half of the 1920s, Canadian opinion about immigration shifted, and support for a more restrictive approach rapidly gained ground. In 1926, the Southern Alberta Board of Trade objected to the "Mennonite and Hutterite...invasion," declaring, "If we cannot obtain British and good northern European settlers, it would be better to have no new immigrants at all."[1] This view was to spread across the country in the last years of the decade, as economic conditions deteriorated. In 1930, an editorial observed that, while in past years there had been widespread enthusiasm for immigration, "Now all this has changed, and from all parts of the country there is an insistent demand that immigration be restricted if not altogether stopped."[2]

But it was the Soviet Union that was the main cause of the sharp drop in Mennonite immigration. By 1926, Lenin was dead and his New Economic Policy was about to be superseded by the First Five-Year Plan. As Stalin consolidated his power, conditions grew increasingly difficult for the 80,000 Mennonites still in the USSR. The government sharply curtailed religious observances, turning church buildings into clubhouses, stables, and granaries. In Rosental, the Mennonite farm machinery plants were taken over by the local soviet, as was the facility that manufactured the Kroeger clocks.

In 1927, Stalin launched a campaign against "kulaks" (farmers who had modest land holdings and a few animals). Their property was confiscated and in that year some 850,000 were deported to Siberia.[3]

A number of Mennonites were among those sent to Siberia. Many of those who resisted military service on religious grounds found themselves facing imprisonment, exile, or a firing squad. Mennonite newspapers were forced to cease publication.

Not surprisingly, many Mennonites made strenuous efforts to emigrate, but the Soviet regime was obstructive. In 1926, the organization led by B.B. Janz, which the Mennonites had formed in 1923 to negotiate with the authorities, was disbanded, and those of its leaders who had not yet managed to leave for Canada were later exiled to Siberia.[4] Canadian immigration medical inspectors stationed in the USSR found their freedom to travel curtailed.

The timing of the Kroeger family's departure, in 1926, proved to be fortunate. The following year, 1927, only 847 Russlaender reached Canada. Among them were the future parents of tenor Ben Heppner.

In 1928, the number of immigrants was smaller still, at only 511.

In 1929, a group of Mennonites made their way to Moscow and managed to obtain passports and exit permits on their own initiative (a surprising turn of events, but consistency was not an attribute of the Soviet administration during those years). Word of their success rapidly got back to the colonies. Large numbers of would-be emigrants sold their property and flooded into Moscow. By the fall of 1929, there were 10,000 Mennonites and 3,000 other German-origin colonists in the city, all desperately seeking permission to leave. The Soviet authorities were ready to accede to their requests, but required that Canada confirm it was ready to accept them.

In Canada, President Beatty of the CPR had agreed to provide transportation on credit for all 10,000 of the Mennonites. On November 25th, the Canadian government's response arrived in Moscow. It was negative. Because of rising unemployment in Canada, no Russlaender could be accepted before the following spring.[5]

Prime Minister King remained well disposed towards the Mennonites, but the deterioration of the economy generated rising public resistance to immigration. In 1929, the Toronto Labour Council declared itself "absolutely opposed" to the admission of the Mennonite refugees.[6] Groups such as the Orange Lodge regarded immigration from Europe as a Catholic and French-Canadian plot against Canada's British institutions.

Under the Canadian constitution, immigration is a shared federal/provincial responsibility. The stance of the provinces regarding immigration was negative, with the newly elected Anderson government in Saskatchewan being particularly hostile. Facing an election in the coming months, King deferred to the provinces. Then, in 1930, R.B. Bennett succeeded King as prime minister, and immigration to Canada from Europe came to an end.

After the Canadian government refused to accept the Mennonite refugees then in Moscow, the Soviets deported some 8,000 of them, mostly to Siberia. The refugees were loaded into unheated boxcars. Travelling in December and January, many froze to death along the way, while others died of exposure after they were left in the Siberian countryside.

The Weimar government in Germany granted temporary admission to a fortunate 5,700 refugees; most subsequently found their way to Mennonite colonies in Brazil and Paraguay. Despite all the obstacles to emigration to Canada, 1,123 of these refugees managed to gain admission to Canada in 1930, through the efforts of friends and relatives. This group included the future parents of novelist Rudy Wiebe.

In February 1930, Heinrich Kroeger wrote to the Mennonite Board of Colonization about the possibility of bringing his relatives to Canada.

Undoubtedly he had in mind his sister Maria, his younger brother Abram, and their families. The Board replied that it had been unable to secure the approval of the Canadian government for further immigration from the colonies in the USSR.

This negative response may not have come as a surprise at this stage, but it was still a blow. Heinrich was left to contemplate the likely fate that awaited his relatives.

After the door to Canada closed, the Canadian Mennonite Colonization Board shifted its attention to problems within Canada. Its chairman, David Toews, countered various false allegations that had been spread by groups hostile to immigration in general and to Mennonites in particular. Toews and the Board also responded as best they could to requests for assistance from families who were in need of clothing, food, and medical care. Because of the Board's very limited financial resources, Toews often went without his salary of $100 per month.[7]

It would be difficult to overestimate the importance of David Toews as a leader of the Mennonite community in Canada. B.B. Janz, who himself had played the leading role in negotiating the Mennonites' departure from the USSR, described Toews as "the greatest Good Samaritan and philanthropist of his time." In his dealings with governments, the Canadian Pacific Railway, and other parties, Toews acquired a stature and came to inspire a degree of confidence that were to be among the Mennonites' greatest assets.

Starting in the early 1920s, Toews and Prime Minister Mackenzie King developed a high regard for one another. Toews customarily began his letters to the prime minister with the salutation "Dear Friend." During one of Toews' visits to Ottawa, King invited him to dinner. In 1927, King said to his minister of immigration, "Grant to the Mennonites everything allowable on the basis of our laws. Mennonites are the best citizens we have in Canada." During the royal tour of 1939, the prime minister arranged for Toews to be among those presented to the king and queen when the royal train stopped in Saskatoon.[8]

Equally important was the relationship that Toews developed with the leadership of the Canadian Pacific Railway. Although his regular dealings were with Colonel Dennis, the Chief Commissioner of Colonization, Toews also came to be known and respected by the company's president and senior executives. Such was the regard in which Toews came to be held that, when in 1937 his house in Rosthern burned down, causing the death of one of his children, the CPR sent him $1,000 to help him build a new house.[9]

Toews' greatest preoccupation through the latter part of his life was the debt that the Board had incurred for the transportation of the Russlaender to Canada. For Toews and many of his colleagues it was a debt of honour, and the obligation to repay the CPR for the assistance it had provided hung over them. When from time to time the CPR executives became impatient with the Mennonites' difficulties in making payments against the debt with the company, Toews' personal stature helped Colonel Dennis's case as he persuaded his superiors to continue the program.

As of January 1931, nearly $700,000 had been repaid. The onset of the drought and depression threatened further progress, and led Toews and his colleagues to intensify their efforts. Year after year, they wrote letters and paid visits to those who had not yet paid their *Reiseschuldt*. The responses varied widely. Some debts proved to be simply impossible to collect because of illness or poverty (both, in the case of the Kroeger family), or death. There were also recalcitrants, who refused to recognize their obligations or took the position that "the CPR can wait." At the other end of the spectrum were those who, having paid their own share, went on to contribute more when the Board launched special appeals to retire the remaining debt.

The CPR for its part mitigated the burden by waiving interest charges after 1930—a concession it had made for various other client groups as the depression deepened.[10] By the end of 1938, in spite of severely adverse economic conditions, a further $400,000 had been paid. Toews and his colleagues kept up their efforts. The Mennonites continued to make payments on the principal through the 1930s and into the 1940s.

By the end of World War II, David Toews' health was beginning to fail. His forty-four years of service had taken their toll. He was diabetic, suffered from kidney problems, and was increasingly deaf. In April 1946, he resigned chairmanship of the Board.

In November of the same year, his successor, J.J. Thiessen, came to visit the ailing Toews. He brought the news that the last of the debt had been retired. Toews at first refused to believe him. Then, when the realization sank in that the huge moral burden had finally been lifted from his shoulders, Toews wept uncontrollably.[11] On December 1st, a service of thanksgiving was held in Saskatchewan, the province hardest hit by the drought and depression and therefore the last in which the *Reiseschuldt* was retired.

Three months later David Toews died at his home. He was seventy-six. His funeral in the small town of Rosthern was attended by over a thousand people, many of whom came from outside the province. His successor delivered a sermon based on a passage from the Old Testament: "Do you not know that a prince and a great man has fallen this day in Israel?"[12]

When in 1922 the CPR first began corresponding with David Toews, it had addressed its letters to "Bishop Toews." Toews had protested against this designation, explaining that the Mennonite church had no hierarchy. The CPR persisted, and eventually Toews let the matter drop.[13] More recently, Toews' co-religionists apparently came to adopt the CPR's respectful designation. In the Mennonite Museum in Rosthern, there is a well-worn old desk that bears a card identifying it as having belonged to "Bishop Toews."

TWELVE *British Subjects and Aliens*

"A fit and proper person to receive a Certificate of Naturalization."

UNTIL 1947, there was no Canadian citizenship *per se*. People who were born in the United Kingdom or one of the five dominions—Canada, Australia, New Zealand, South Africa, and Newfoundland—were British subjects. Those who immigrated to these countries from other parts of the world were formally classed as "aliens." They could acquire the status of British subjects by applying for naturalization after meeting a residence requirement of five years.

From Confederation onwards, it was considered a given that Canada needed immigrants. It was also assumed that the immigrants would come from Britain, but the number of Britons who came fell far short of the numbers needed. It became clear that Canada would have to choose between remaining purely British and populating its open spaces.

The decision of Laurier's government to embark on an aggressive program of recruiting immigrants from continental Europe, including the Slavic countries, produced the hoped-for numbers, but proved controversial in some quarters.

The Calgary *Herald* spoke of Canada "becoming the dumping ground for the refuse of civilization."[1] In 1905, the Manitoba *Free Press* deplored admitting "those of serf-ridden Russia, the stiletto-carrying Dago, and the degenerate central European."[2] The Anglican Bishop of Saskatchewan, George Exton Lloyd, after whom Lloydminster was named, denounced "these dirty, ignorant, garlic-smelling...continentals," and wrote disparagingly about "mongrel Canada," which he contrasted with "British Australia."[3]

Some of the 6,500 Chinese labourers brought to Canada to help build the railways also settled on the prairies. After the completion of the main rail lines, these labourers spread across the prairies. Some opened laundries, but most opened restaurants. In a few years, virtually every small prairie town had a Chinese-operated café. Not all residents welcomed this development. When Consort was founded in 1912, a local man opened an eatery named "White Man's Restaurant." In 1915, an accidental fire destroyed the building. The business was not re-established.[4]

However, the main debate on the prairies was about continental Europeans. Not all residents spoke of them in the harsh language of Bishop Lloyd, but many people preferred an arms-length relationship. In 1924, someone who had travelled across the Atlantic in third class on the *Empress of Scotland*, wrote to the Canadian Pacific Railway commending the amenities of that section of the ship. Third class was also the section in which most immigrants travelled, concerning which the writer observed: "The deck space is ample, and a very thoughtful arrangement is the separate accommodation for Continental passengers at one end of the ship, and British, Canadian, and American at the other."[5] Even among those well-disposed towards non-British immigration, there was unease about how such large numbers could be assimilated into the existing thin population.[6]

European immigrants were also regarded by some as politically suspect. After the Winnipeg General Strike of 1919, the federal minister of justice, ignoring the fact that most of the principal organizers had been Anglo Saxons, deplored the "bad habits, notions, and vicious practices" of non-British immigrants, and declared them to be "thorough-paced Bolsheviks, disciples of the torch and bomb."[7] In 1931, an internal Alberta government memo stated that "[aliens] provide our agitators with a following in making unreasonable demands on the municipal and provincial governments. They do not hesitate to express their desire to institute Soviet rule."[8] The Mennonites stayed clear of political activity (*Die Stillen im land,* as they had called themselves in Russia), and welfare provided by the CMBC saved them from deportation as indigents.

In 1934, the Bennett government, unsettled by depression-era displays of support for the Communist Party of Canada, passed new gun control legislation. Nick Kroeger had recently managed to purchase a .22 calibre rifle, which he used for shooting rabbits and other game. He therefore sent an inquiry about the legislation to the local RCMP detachment in Coronation. The response read:

> The New Act regarding Permits requires EVERYONE in Possession of a REVOLVER or PISTOL to register same with the proper authorities...
>
> There are also regulations in effect which make it compulsory for ALL ALIENS to have a permit to have firearms in their possession.
>
> If you are not naturalized you can obtain this permit from a Magistrate for shotgun—rifle etc.
>
> Permits to CARRY REVOLVERS will NOT BE granted [to aliens].
>
> (*Capitalization and underlining in original.*)

Since by this time the Kroeger family had been naturalized, Nick was spared having to get a permit for his .22 rifle.

Notwithstanding the doubts and apprehensions about aliens in various quarters, the overriding consensus was that Canada had to be populated, even if this meant drawing immigrants from less than ideal sources. Typical was a 1923 editorial in the *Consort Enterprise*: "There can be no salvation for the West or Canada save bringing great tracts of land into production." In the 1920s, municipalities and small towns, including Monitor, Consort, and Veteran, formed "colonization committees," and applied annually to have immigrants sent to their areas.[9]

In general, settlers from Northern Europe were fairly well accepted. The same was generally true of the Mennonites who arrived in the 1920s, although there were exceptions. Nativist groups such as the Orange Lodge were hostile, and Bob Edwards of the Calgary *Eye Opener* referred to Mennonites as "German cattle."[10] When in the post-war period they encountered anti-German sentiment, Mennonites often protested that they were actually of Dutch origin.

Heinrich Kroeger applied for naturalization in the spring of 1932, five years and six months after the family's arrival in Canada.[11] It was not a simple process. The first step was for Heinrich to complete an "Application for a decision," formally stating his intention to apply for naturalization. In March 1932, he filled out the form and forwarded it to the Canadian Colonization Association (CCA), through which the Canadian Pacific Railway provided assistance with naturalization procedures to immigrants it had brought to Canada. The CCA forwarded Heinrich's application to the citizenship authorities on April 22nd, 1932, with its standard affirmation that "This party is well known to us and we are therefore recommending him as a good citizen." The naturalization authorities then consulted the Department of Immigration, which confirmed that the family had legally landed in Canada.

An RCMP investigation was part of the process. An officer interviewed Heinrich at Davey Jones' farm, where the family was living at the time. On July 8th, the officer filed the following report:

Speaks fair English, reads a little, does not write.

Applicant was personally interviewed at his home near Naco. Character references were also personally interviewed at Naco. Mr. Doolan spoke well of the applicant: has known him for the past four years. He considered him to be a fit and proper person to become a Canadian Citizen. Mr. Huston also expressed the same views having known the applicant for the past 4 years & been in constant contact with him during that period. Both references signed the usual certificate in substantiation of their statements.

At the end of the summer, Heinrich submitted a "Petition for Naturalization" and was duly summoned to Coronation "to be examined by the presiding Judge" on October 13th, 1932. Making the 55-mile trip was not easy. Not owning a car, Heinrich would have had to find someone to give him a ride to Consort, and then take the train to Coronation. In the course of his appearance before the judge, Heinrich was required to sign his petition, and "to make an affidavit in proof thereof." He also had to submit a form signed by Jim Norton, the Secretary of Stewart Municipality, stating that the family "never has received relief from the municipality"—which was true up to that time.

On June 8th, 1933, the Judge of the District Court in Coronation affirmed that the "Applicant was examined by me and has satisfied me that he possesses the required character and is a fit and proper person to receive a Certificate of Naturalization." Heinrich then made a second trip to Coronation on June 27th, and swore an affidavit before the Clerk of the Court that he was the person who had applied for naturalization and that he intended "to reside in His Majesty's Dominions."

The final step was the Oath of Allegiance. Using the prescribed form, Heinrich laboriously copied (as reproduced verbatim below) the text that had been developed by the government's lawyers and officials, while understanding scarcely a word of it:

Heinrich Kroeger do solemnly declear that I will be faithful and bear thru Allegiance to His Majesty King George the Fifth his Heirs and Successors accornd to law.

And I make this solemn declaration solnlmly beleiving to sam to be true and knowing that it is of the sam force and effect as if made under oath and by artu of Canada Evidens Act.

Heinrich Kroeger

The taking of the oath was duly attested to by Jim Norton and the text was forwarded to Ottawa. The Naturalization Certificate was issued on October 16th, 1933, some eighteen months after Heinrich had begun the process. The *Canada Gazette*, the official publication of the Canadian government, then formally listed him as one of a number of aliens to whom certificates of naturalization had been issued that month.

At the time of Heinrich's naturalization, and for most of the twentieth century, children received their citizenship through their father. Accordingly, the Kroeger children's names (other than Peter's and mine, since we were born in Canada) were included with Heinrich's application, and their naturalization came with his.

Helena's status was dealt with later, when the Kroegers could afford the $1 fee. It was a much shorter process than Heinrich's had been. On June 24th, 1935, Helena completed a "Declaration of a Married Woman under the…Naturalization Act," declaring that she was the wife of Heinrich Kroeger and that she desired to be naturalized. She also copied and signed an abbreviated version of the Oath of Allegiance. Her certificate of naturalization was sent to her three weeks later.

There were substantial differences between the rights of British subjects and the rights of aliens. Voting, standing for public office, and holding positions on bodies such as school boards all required the status of British subject. An applicant for a homestead had to either be a British subject or commit to becoming one. Of more immediate importance to the Kroeger family during the depression was the fact that with the status of British subject came eligibility for government relief programs. A severely worded Alberta government circular ordered that, in the administration of relief, discrimination among British subjects would not be tolerated.

The identification of Canada with Britain lasted through the two world wars and well into the mid-twentieth century. In 1911, when the CPR divisional point of Coronation was created, its streets were given the names of members of the royal family—Albert, Edward, George, Mary, Victoria, and Arthur. The following year, when the railway reached Veteran, sixteen miles to the east, the names given to the streets in the new town included Redan, Lucknow, Balaclava, Delhi, and Waterloo—all famous battles fought by the British army. To the present day, George and Peter Kroeger recall that our family's move to a new farm took place in the year that King George V died. When King George VI was crowned, there were celebrations and parades in small towns across the prairies. Local stores sold cheap plates and cups bearing the faces of the two young princesses, Elizabeth and Margaret Rose.

The royal visit to Edmonton, 1939. (PAA BL473/4a)

In 1939, King George VI and Queen Elizabeth travelled across Canada by rail. Their stop in Edmonton was a momentous event. The week before the tour, the *Consort Enterprise* reported that "George Pringle left by bicycle for Edmonton, intending to be there to see the King and Queen."[12] The trip would have taken him at least four days. The CPR laid on a special train, which left Monitor at 4:30 AM on June 2nd and headed west, picking up passengers in small towns along the way. It took the train nine hours to reach Edmonton.

One of those on board was George Kroeger. George joined the large crowds in the grandstands and was able to see the royal motorcade as it passed along a major street. That street had been re-named "Kingsway"— a name it has borne ever since. At 7:30 that evening, the train returned by the route it had taken, arriving in Monitor at dawn the following morning.

Anne Kroeger, who was fifteen years old at the time, joined a group of students and adults who rode the 250 miles to Edmonton in the back of a truck, over mostly gravelled roads. The $8 charged each passenger by the truck's owner was paid by Anne's employer in Consort, who did not wish her to miss the once-in-a-lifetime experience. Anne was in the crowd who saw the royal couple when they appeared on a decorated balcony at Edmonton's premier hotel, the chateau-like MacDonald. That night in Edmonton, the travellers slept on the floors of acquaintances' homes, and the next day the truck took them back to Consort.

Nick and Henry and their wives, together with Peter and a friend, drove sixty miles north from Consort to be in Wainwright when the royal train came through. They had the bad luck to arrive twenty minutes too late, and consoled themselves with a picnic in the nearby Buffalo Park.

I have a personal recollection of the degree to which Canada identified with Britain in these years. In the fall of 1940, I was eight years old and starting grade three in our local one-room country school. Hitler's armies had swept through Western Europe in the preceding months and were poised at the English Channel. I remember asking my teacher whether, if Britain fell, Canada would also come under German rule.

While gaining status as a British subject had important legal consequences, it did not confer social equality. Even in areas such as northeastern Alberta, where most people were immigrants, the local businesses, medical and legal professions, municipal councils, and service clubs were for many years almost entirely in the hands of British-origin residents.[13] Immigrants who came from other countries generally had little or no role in these bodies, although those from Northern Europe were fairly well accepted socially.

Well below them on the ladder were Slav immigrants from Eastern Europe. These people were generally drawn from rough peasant societies, and many of their personal habits were not those of British North America. The 1921 census found that 25 per cent of Ukrainian-origin males, and 39 per cent of females, were illiterate. Those who were not farmers worked as manual labourers, often on the railways as section hands, maintaining the tracks, replacing ties, and cutting weeds. Their children came to school in the mornings with garlic on their breath.

An aloof view of Eastern Europeans was not limited to residents of British origin. In Consort, Suey Sang, a Chinese man who operated a grocery store and café, grew exasperated with Ukrainian and Polish farmers who would come into his store and carry on conversations in their native languages. Eventually he posted a prominent sign that read: "Speak English or Chinese."

More broad-minded views were also held. The editor of the *Consort Enterprise* anticipated Canadian multiculturalism by some sixty years when he wrote:

> Treat them as people, not Bohunks or dirty Galicians or narrow bigoted Mennonites. Diverse people have a distinct contribution to make to Canada.

The erosion of social barriers took quite a few decades, but eventually it came about. In Consort, an important milestone was passed in the 1950s when James Letniak, a respected local Ukrainian farmer, became chairman of the school board.

It was one of many signs that Canada was changing. In June 2001, I joined a friend for lunch at the *Cercle Universitaire* in Ottawa. I noticed that at a nearby table were Supreme Court Justice John Sopinka and former Governor General Ramon Hnatyshyn, so I stopped to chat for a few minutes. I had come to know John Sopinka quite well some twenty years earlier when I was deputy minister of transport and he was Counsel to an inquiry dealing with civil aviation. I also knew the former Governor General, but not quite well enough to voice the quip that came to my mind: "It gives a Mennonite boy's heart a lift to meet a couple of Ukrainians who made good."

Among the many ethnic groups who immigrated to Canada during the 1920s and 1930s, none was more conscious of their good fortune than the Mennonites. In their correspondence and public statements, David Toews and other Mennonite leaders regularly expressed gratitude to Canada and a determination that their co-religionists would become good citizens.

The Mennonites also recognized how they had benefited from the liberal approach of the Canadian Pacific Railway. In September 1937, a special service of thanksgiving attended by over 800 was held in Coaldale, the largest Mennonite community in Alberta, to mark the fifteenth anniversary of the signing of the first contract with the CPR. The proceedings were led by the two individuals who had played key roles in bringing about the immigration of the Russlaender—B.B. Janz, who had negotiated their exit with the Soviet authorities; and David Toews, who had led the successful effort to secure their admission to Canada. The guests of honour were Sir Edward Beatty, President of the CPR, and Colonel John Dennis, who had been the CPR's Chief Commissioner of Colonization.

Following is an excerpt from an account of the event written afterwards by one of the organizers:

> Reverend Janz, speaking in English, greeted the guests and cordially thanked first Sir Edward, because he, in the capacity of President of the Canadian Pacific Railway, had granted credit 15 years ago, and then Colonel Dennis, because he, as a friend of the Mennonites had stood sponsor for and had arranged credit for an utterly unknown people, who had been made destitute by the Red Terror in Russia... Reverend Janz referred to the great service which David Toews had rendered, for which we owe him a debt of gratitude, and then thanked him in the name of all for his labours. At this point 12 girls (aged 9–12) all born in Russia came forward with bouquets and laid them at the feet of Sir Edward Beatty and Colonel J.S. Dennis with the simple words: "You saved our lives. We thank you." Deeply affected as were the honored guests by the sincere, hearty words of Reverend Janz, this unaffected scene brought tears to the eyes of many and a noticeable quiver to the chin of Colonel Dennis.[14]

Illuminated scrolls had been prepared for both men. Colonel Dennis, who was then eighty-one and had retired seven years earlier, was particularly moved by the occasion. The scroll presented to him read in part:

> More than 20,000 of our people who were rescued from spiritual and moral disaster remember gratefully that 15 years ago there sat in the councils of the Canadian Pacific Railway a man who had the

B.B. Janz presenting a scroll to Colonel Dennis. (CMBS NP052–0110)

Girls presenting Sir Edward Beatty and Col. Dennis with flowers. (CMBS NP052–0112)

vision and faith to save a whole people—total strangers to him—
who were financially crushed and ruined...

Your great confidence in us, noble Colonel Dennis, as well as
that of the Canadian Pacific Railway, the government and people of
Canada, will not be dishonored by us. Our people, strong in faith
and faithfulness, will vouch for that. Your confidence in us stands
out as one of the most glorious pages in our history. Never shall
we forget.[15]

The following year, Colonel Dennis died in Victoria.

The national consensus that Canada's need for population required it
to draw immigrants from many countries and not just from Britain
carried an important expectation—that the "foreign" immigrants should
adopt Canadian (British) values and standards at the earliest possible time.

An organization that was particularly active in promoting this objective was the Imperial Order of the Daughters of the Empire (IODE). Today
the Empire is no more, and the IODE largely belongs to the pages of
history, but in its time it was a considerable force. It described itself as an
"organization whose main purpose is to maintain British standards of
citizenship in a British country." It had an extensive membership across
Canada, with chapters in every province. The national convenor was
based in Quebec.[16] An important program of the IODE was the provision of scholarships to enable Canadian students to study in Britain.

During the 1920s, the Alberta Chapter held regular meetings at which
a range of subjects was addressed: the provision of assistance to British
settlers; the need for immigrants to be subjected to more rigorous medical
examinations at ports of entry; the desirability of IODE representation
on provincial censorship boards; the possibility of banning Hearst newspapers; and the need to investigate the extent to which Communist
propaganda was being spread in the province. On some subjects, voices
of moderation made themselves heard; in January 1927, a resolution from
the Calgary Municipal Chapter protesting the admission of German
settlers to Alberta was denied approval, as was another resolution, again
from Calgary, calling for the elimination of "foreign" publications from

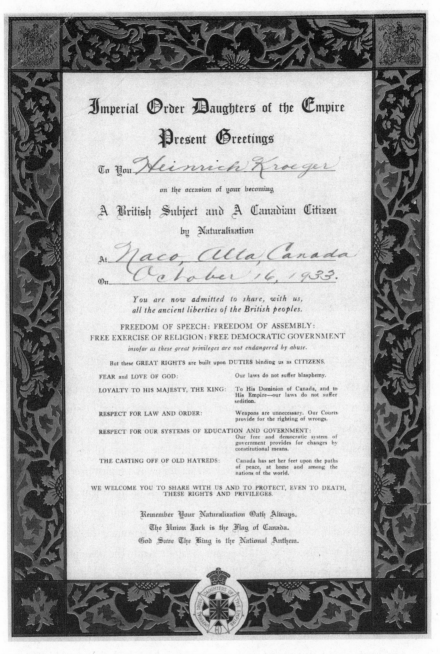

Imperial Order Daughters of the Empire

Present Greetings

To You *Heinrich Kroeger*

on the occasion of your becoming

A British Subject and A Canadian Citizen

by Naturalization

At *Naco, Alta, Canada*

On *October 16, 1933.*

You are now admitted to share, with us,
all the ancient liberties of the British peoples.

FREEDOM OF SPEECH: FREEDOM OF ASSEMBLY:
FREE EXERCISE OF RELIGION: FREE DEMOCRATIC GOVERNMENT
insofar as these great privileges are not endangered by abuse.

But these GREAT RIGHTS are built upon DUTIES binding us as CITIZENS.

FEAR and LOVE OF GOD:	Our laws do not suffer blasphemy.
LOYALTY TO HIS MAJESTY, THE KING:	To His Dominion of Canada, and to His Empire—our laws do not suffer sedition.
RESPECT FOR LAW AND ORDER:	Weapons are unnecessary. Our Courts provide for the righting of wrongs.
RESPECT FOR OUR SYSTEMS OF EDUCATION AND GOVERNMENT:	Our free and democratic system of government provides for changes by constitutional means.
THE CASTING OFF OF OLD HATREDS:	Canada has set her feet upon the paths of peace, at home and among the nations of the world.

WE WELCOME YOU TO SHARE WITH US AND TO PROTECT, EVEN TO DEATH,
THESE RIGHTS AND PRIVILEGES.

Remember Your Naturalization Oath Always.

The Union Jack is the Flag of Canada.

God Save The King is the National Anthem.

The IODE certificate sent to Heinrich Kroeger upon his naturalization.

A meeting of the IODE in Calgary, 1920. (PAA 77.248/44)

schools. On the latter point, the provincial chapter did however express concern at the excessive use of American materials. Women's issues were also addressed. In March 1926, the Alberta IODE took the position that the disposition of homesteads should require the consent of wives.

The growing presence of non-British settlers was a major preoccupation, and there was a public debate as to whether the acquisition of British subject status by such settlers was too easy; many held that it was. The IODE believed that more effort should be made to assimilate these settlers, and in April 1926 discussed sending representatives into the "foreign settlements" of the province "to instill in the foreign born some idea of the conditions under which they are living and our line of thinking."

Out of this concern came a decision in the early 1930s to launch a new way of disseminating the IODE's message. An 8" x 12" certificate bearing a message about citizenship and an ornate border in red and royal blue, was prepared at national headquarters. Copies were printed and distributed to chapters across the country. The local IODE then arranged to attend citizenship ceremonies and present newly naturalized Canadians with the cards. Two hundred cards were distributed at a Dominion Day ceremony in Edmonton on July 1, 1933, that was presided over by William Legh Walsh, lieutenant governor of the province. He commended the IODE for "clothing with dignity and significance the act of signing the oath of allegiance."

The lieutenant governor's expression of approval was echoed in many quarters. The editor of the *Consort Enterprise* wrote on February 12th, 1931: "Administration of the oath of citizenship should impress upon the applicant a clear realization of what he is doing, the meaning of the pledges he gives, and the responsibility he thereby assumes."

Because the name and town of each newly naturalized Canadian were regularly published in the *Canada Gazette*, the IODE was able to distribute its certificates by mail to those who did not attend citizenship ceremonies. It was by this means that Heinrich Kroeger received his certificate shortly after he was naturalized. It was sent to him by the IODE's "Provincial Convenor, Immigration and Assimilation" in Edmonton.

The certificate presented greetings to him on becoming a British subject by naturalization, pointing out that this step admitted him to share "with us, all the ancient liberties of the British peoples: Freedom of Speech: Freedom of Assembly: Free Exercise of Religion: Free Democratic Government." Then came the "however": "these GREAT RIGHTS are built upon DUTIES on us as CITIZENS," [capitals are in the original] which the certificate went on to enumerate: Fear and Love of God, Loyalty to his Majesty the King, Respect for Law and Order, and so on.

When I first found the certificate among my father's papers, my reaction was one of mild irritation at what I regarded as its patronizing tone. In later years, however, I had second thoughts. The good members of the IODE had a point when, for example, they pointed out to new immigrants that "Weapons are unnecessary. Our Courts provide for the righting of wrongs."

I also had occasion to reflect on the IODE's enjoinder about "the casting off of old hatreds" after Air India flight 182 was bombed in 1985 with loss of 329 lives, apparently because of a conflict between Sikh militants in

Canada and the government of India. Eventually I took the certificate out and had it framed. When I became deputy minister of immigration in 1988, I quietly hung it in a corner of my office.

THIRTEEN *Farms, Schools, and Neighbours*

IN NOVEMBER 1936, our family moved twelve miles north of Naco to what was known as "the Day place," after the original settlers of the property. We would live there for the next ten years, during which our circumstances slowly improved. I have always thought of the Day place, if not as home, then as "where I came from."

When we moved to the Day place, it reduced our connections with the Naco/Sedalia area, where we had lived for ten years. From time to time, Heinrich and Helena would go to visit other Mennonites who had remained in the area, but this involved travelling a considerable distance by horse and buggy in summer or by sleigh in winter.

The Day property consisted of two sections (square miles) of land— part pasture, part cultivated fields—together with a house large enough to accommodate a family of seven children whose older members were rapidly becoming adults. There was a large hip-roofed barn that leaned dangerously to the south, evidence of deficiencies in the original construction plus years of the northwest winds that are a hallmark of the prairies. There were also several granaries. We had a modest herd of milk cows, a few horses, chickens, and geese. During the 1930s, only 2 per cent of farms in Eastern Alberta had running water, and just over 5 per cent had electric lights; we had neither.

Water for the livestock was pumped from a well in the farmyard. In winter, it was often necessary to chop away the ice that had accumulated

The house on the Day place that accommodated Heinrich and Helena Kroeger and their seven children. On the right is the barn that the family built to replace the one that collapsed in a windstorm in 1940.

in the trough. Because water from the wells in the area had a high mineral content, soft water for washing was provided by melted snow in winter and rainwater in summer. A single outdoor toilet served everyone, winter and summer; the universal practice of farm families on the prairies, and indeed elsewhere in rural Canada, was to use the previous year's Eaton's catalogue as toilet paper. Baths were taken from time to time by filling a galvanized tub with hot water. All laundry was done by hand and hung on an outdoor line; on very cold winter days, clothes brought in from the line had the consistency of iron. My sister Helen once broke a leg off a suit of frozen long underwear.

Saturday was the day for scrubbing the floors and subjecting the house to a thorough cleaning, so that Sunday could be observed as the biblically-prescribed day of rest.

Glass kerosene lamps were used for lighting in most parts of the house; a pressure kerosene lamp with mantles was bright enough to illuminate the living room. During the winter darkness, kerosene lanterns were also used for milking the cows in the barn. One of my sister Anne's duties was to polish the brass weights and pendulum on the family's Kroeger clock every few days.

Coal was the fuel used for heating and cooking. In summer, it was supplemented by cow dung that we collected in the pastures where it had been dried by the prairie sun. It ignited quickly, producing an acrid smell and providing a hot flame that was excellent for certain kinds of cooking. Heinrich and Helena Kroeger were no strangers to this use of manure; in the Mennonite colonies of Russia, fresh manure had been mixed with straw, dried, and cut into bricks for use as a year-round fuel. A different purpose was served in summer by manure that was still partially damp. When ignited, it could provide a heavy smudge to keep the mosquitoes at bay while we milked the cows in the farmyard.

Notwithstanding the undignified use of the previous year's Eaton's catalogues, the current year's catalogue was a publication of the first importance. The contents were carefully perused by my parents with a view to reconciling the most pressingly needed items with available income. The arrival of the fall order from Eaton's in Winnipeg was a major event. Boots, jackets, mittens, winter socks, long underwear—the distribution of these items was an event akin to Christmas.

When the snow melted in the spring of our first year on the Day place, the family found a number of empty bottles in the hedge, and one that was partially filled with a liquid that smelled of apples. This was not a particularly surprising discovery. From time to time, local residents were fined for "possessing equipment suitable for the production of moonshine." Not everyone could afford the prices charged at the provincial liquor store during the depression years. Heinrich's notebooks annually included entries during the summers such as "made wild berry wine," and "poured wine into the storage crock."

At the time of the family's move, Nick was twenty-one and Henry nineteen. Having each quit school at fourteen, they had by this time gained considerable experience in farm operations. They were increasingly striking

*Heinrich and Helena
Kroeger in front of their
farm house, 1937.*

out on their own, but also proceeded to take on the management of the
property they had rented, making decisions about which fields should be
planted, and with what crops.

In the summer of 1940, a violent storm caused our precariously leaning
barn to crash to the ground. It was an event that the family had foreseen,
and we had for several years kept our cows in another building. Heinrich,
assisted by his sons, used the lumber from the collapsed barn to build a
smaller, more structurally sound, replacement.

Heinrich Kroeger was still in ill health, and after the move to the Day
place he had a mild heart attack which left him unable to work for some
months. It was a further setback for him, psychologically as well as physically. Helena for her part was heavily occupied with their seven children,
cooking, managing the house, washing, and repeatedly mending clothes
to make them last longer. Her husband's heart attack filled her with alarm.
She had always been vigilant in overseeing what he ate and did, lest it
impair his already frail health. Now she felt even greater stress.

Helena was below average height, but energetic and physically strong. Possibly due to a metabolic disorder, she became somewhat stout during the family's years in Canada even though she ate very sparingly. She was outspoken and forthright in her personal relationships. As the family disciplinarian, she would not tolerate disobedience, laziness, or misbehaviour. She would have subscribed to the rule of another Mennonite mother: *"Twee mol sage, daun haue,"* (Tell them twice, then whack.)

She had a quick temper and a tongue to be feared, but when an incident was over it was over, and everything would quickly revert to normal. Her love for her family was always evident. She combined a warm personality with a generous nature. Meagre as the family's resources often were, she was always ready to respond when a friend, neighbour, or stranger needed food or shelter.

The Kroeger family's first year on the Day place, 1937, brought the worst of the 1930s drought. Crops were totally blighted, and the dust blew. It became clear by July that there would be no crop to harvest, and on July 8th Heinrich wrote: "Allowed the cattle to graze in the grain field."

It was also a year of violent storms. One summer day, dark clouds formed to the northwest of our farm, the temperature dropped suddenly, and then the house was hit by huge gusts of wind. When the storm had passed, the doors in the house were difficult to open—the wind had shifted the house on its foundation. Heinrich had to take the doors off their hinges and plane them to make them fit again.

On the Canadian prairies, the decade known as "the Thirties" actually began in 1929 and first showed signs of coming to an end in 1938. A wry saying among farmers as one crop failure followed another was: "We know of two great crops: 1915, and next year."[1]

In 1938, next year finally arrived. The rains returned, and good crops were harvested even in the Palliser Triangle, although grain prices remained well below the levels that had been known in the 1920s. In 1939 there was another good crop, and in 1940 the harvest was the second largest in Alberta's history.

Before the combine harvester came into widespread use, harvesting a crop on a prairie farm was a major operation. In August, the ripened grain would be cut with a binder, which tied the stalks into bundles. Next came stooking, an activity for which most members of the family—including me—were recruited when harvest time arrived. The bundles were stood on end in clusters known as stooks, with the grain heads uppermost to give them a final ripening in the sun. The next stage, a few weeks later, was the arrival at our farm of the threshing crew, which was an awesome sight. A tractor pulled the threshing machine to the middle of a field of stooks. Following it was the crew: ten to fifteen local farmers or their sons, each driving a rack drawn by two horses.

A steel-wheeled bunkhouse provided sleeping accommodation for the crew. Operations began at dawn and continued until twilight. The threshing machine was driven by a large belt running from a pulley on the tractor. To shorten the time required to complete threshing, some crews included "field pitchers," who helped load the bundles on the racks, and "spike pitchers," who helped toss the bundles into the maw of the machine. As threshing proceeded, a huge pile of straw would build up beyond the blower pipe on the machine.

Feeding a threshing crew was a major operation, and at harvest time the daughters of farm families stayed home from school to help their mothers. Preparations for the arrival of the crew went on for days, and sometimes involved the slaughter of an animal to provide meat for the voracious appetites for which the crews were known. Helena Kroeger and her daughters had to prepare three large meals a day; in addition, they would drive a buggy to the site of the thresher mid-morning and again mid-afternoon, carrying a five-gallon can of coffee, a mountain of sandwiches, and a large box of doughnuts to keep up the crew's energy until the next full meal.

Harvest was a period of anticipation, but also one of tension. The abiding dread, not unfounded, was that rain or snow would force the suspension of operations, and no one could know when or if dry conditions would return and permit the harvest to be completed. There was a pervasive sense of pressure to complete harvest operations as rapidly as possible

"Barefoot prairie boy"—Arthur Kroeger feeding the chickens, c.1941.

because until the grain was in the bins a whole season's effort and income were at risk.

An issue that sometimes gave rise to disputes during harvest was whether threshing operations should continue on Sunday. For Heinrich and Helena Kroeger, keeping the Sabbath was an important element of their religious observances; on Saturdays, floors in the house would be scrubbed and advance preparations made for Sunday dinner. However, the Kroegers did not press their beliefs to the point of insisting on a halt to harvest operations on Sundays.

Others were more severe in their approach. In some cases, it would be the operator of the threshing machine who would refuse on religious grounds to permit his crew to work on Sundays; in other cases, it would be the farmer whose crop was being threshed. Even when both parties were in agreement about keeping threshing operations going on the Sabbath, a piece of legislation known as *The Lord's Day Act* was a complicating factor. On September 14th, 1933, the RCMP constable based in Coronation issued a warning that the law gave no latitude, and that anyone found threshing on a Sunday would be charged. While the very thin presence of the RCMP in rural areas reduced the risk that such operations would be detected, there were cases in which farmers of a strongly religious disposition would file complaints with the police when they saw their neighbours engaged in Sunday threshing.

After the purchase of a cream separator in August 1937, the weekly "cream cheque" from the creamery in Coronation became an important part of the family's income. We had a herd of ten cows, and one of my duties at the age of ten was to milk five of them every morning and night; my sister Helen milked the other five. A pungent smell of fresh manure would greet us when we opened the barn door on winter mornings. One of my diversions when milking was to direct a stream of milk from the cow's udder to our barnyard cats, which would sit up on their hind legs as I raised the stream and gulp the milk that was squirted into their mouths. Then, when I resumed directing the milk into my pail, they would lick themselves clean.

The milk from the cows was run through a separator and the cream was collected in a five-gallon can. In summer, the full can would be attached to a rope and lowered down the well to keep it cool. Each week, our cans would be picked up and hauled to the creamery in Coronation, which would then mail a cheque to us. The skim milk left after the cream had been separated was consumed by the family. To this day, I have an aversion to skim milk.

For reasons that I never understood, my older brothers disliked horses, and would walk long distances rather than ride horseback. Only after they had grown up and left home was I free to start riding a horse to school. During the day, the horse would be tethered in the school barn and would feed on hay that I had brought in a sack. Whether going to school or rounding up our cows for milking, I always rode without a saddle or bridle, simply using a halter with a short length of rope to guide the horse. In lieu of boots and spurs, I would apply my heels—in summers, my bare feet—to the horse's ribs when I wanted it to trot.

One winter day as I was tying up my horse in the barn, I heard a rustling sound. In the corner of the barn was a muskrat. How it came to be there was a mystery, since there was no body of water within half a mile, and in any case the sloughs were all frozen over. My first thought was that I should kill it, since the pelt would fetch a good price, but I had no stomach for doing so. I turned away and went into the school. I never told anyone, for fear of being laughed at for my weakness.

On cold, clear winter nights the snow would sparkle and reflect the light of the moon, making it possible for us to see straw stacks in the fields half a mile away. On nights of threatening weather, or when a member of the family had taken a sleigh to Consort and was returning after dark, we would put a lamp in the upstairs window.

The prairies were overrun with rabbits during this period. In winter, their trails across our fields were clearly visible, which enabled Nick and Henry to set snares where the trails passed under the fences. In the spring the packed snow of the rabbit runs was the last to melt, and remained visible in the fields for a few days when all the rest had gone.

On the farm we had a rubber-tired wagon known as a Bennett buggy. During the 1930s, many farmers who could no longer afford to operate their cars removed the cabs and motors and converted the chassis into rubber-tired wagons that they named after the depression-era prime minister, R.B. Bennett. So far as I was concerned, however, the rubber-tired wagon we had inherited when we moved to the Day place was just a Bennett buggy. I was in my early twenties before I realized that the term had any political significance.

Life on the farm was isolated. Personal contacts were limited to a few neighbours and the other children at school. There was little personal stimulus, and I was often bored. The towns nearest to our farm were Monitor, twelve miles to the northeast, and Consort, twelve miles to the northwest. With a population of 300, Consort was the more important centre; Monitor was about half its size.

My parents or other members of the family went into town every week to purchase groceries and collect mail, but I seldom accompanied them. The trip could take two hours by sleigh in winter, and there was little if any spending money to purchase a chocolate bar at one of the stores. In addition, while I found the towns intriguing, they were also rather intimidating. People in town were sophisticated and worldly. The students at Consort High School wore black sweaters with a large orange C on the chest. It was said that some boys my age smoked. We were farm people, and Mennonites at that. How did one conduct oneself in a town?

We acquired an old pedal organ from somewhere, and Nick taught himself how to play it. On some evenings the family would sing hymns together, with Nick providing the accompaniment. In 1939, my father bought a battery radio for $30. It was a large expenditure for the time, but the new acquisition added considerably to our lives. My parents used it to listen to religious broadcasts, including the weekly broadcasts made at the time by Premier Aberhart from his Prophetic Bible Institute in Calgary. For the rest of us there were newscasts, radio plays, and, for me, after-school programs such as "The Lone Ranger," "Superman," and "The Shadow."

My sisters and brothers and I became regular listeners to Foster Hewitt's Saturday night hockey broadcasts from Maple Leaf Gardens in Toronto, and were ardent fans of Syl Apps, Turk Broda, and the Maple Leafs. I had never actually seen a hockey game of any kind, and the pictures in my mind as I followed the broadcasts proved not to be entirely accurate. When I was about twelve, I was somewhat surprised to learn that the net stood *on* the ice, and was not, as I had always visualized it, sunk into the ice like a cup in a golf green.

When large-scale settlement began in Alberta at the beginning of the twentieth century, one of the first tasks for the settlers who flooded in was to provide schools for their children. By 1938, over 3,000 one-room schools dotted the Alberta landscape.[2] I started school in the fall of 1938 and attended one-room rural schools for the next eight years. The nearest school to the Day place was Berryfield, which was a mile and three-quarters south of our house.

"The little white schoolhouse" of the prairies was typically a one-room wooden frame building, supplemented by an outdoor toilet for the boys and another one for the girls, and a barn to shelter the horses that some children rode to school. Inside the entrance were the girls' cloakroom on one side, and the boys' on the other, each with a row of hooks for coats. On the floor below the coats were boots and the Rogers Golden Syrup tins that served everyone as lunch pails. The smell of linseed oil, which was applied to the floors periodically to preserve the wood and perhaps to repel the snow tracked in by the students, was ever-present. A local resident, sometimes one of the older students, would be engaged to sweep and clean the schoolroom every day.

Sometimes a small additional structure would be provided to house the teacher, but more commonly teachers boarded with one of the local farm families, who were thereby able to claim credits against their school taxes. At the opening of the school year in September, a dance would sometimes be held in the local school house to raise money for the purchase of supplies. The schools doubled as community centres; they were variously used for box socials, church services, dances, weddings, funerals, polling stations, and meetings of the local branch of the United Farmers of Alberta or, in later years, the Social Credit League.

In later life when I encountered some of my former teachers I asked them the question I had often wondered about: "How on earth did you do it?" They had to provide instruction to a dozen or so students, sometimes many more, spanning eight grades. To cover the various subjects in the curriculum, they had to prepare and give about thirty lessons each day, rationing their time as best they could; the normal length of a period was twelve minutes. In addition, they might have to supervise one or two older students who were doing grade nine or ten by correspondence.

For new teachers recruited in Edmonton or Calgary, or in some cases Ontario, arriving in rural Alberta and beginning to teach in a one-room school could be a something of a shock. My teacher in grade four was an attractive young woman, Stella Kozicki, whose grandfather had immigrated to Canada from the Ukraine in 1891. She had lived all her life in

Berryfield School, 1941.

Stella Kozicki and her class at the Berryfield School in 1942. Arthur Kroeger is at the right end of the front row.

Calgary and had attended Normal School there, but a shortage of openings in Calgary had forced her to apply for a country school. Her fiancé was overseas with the armed forces.

Berryfield, which met most definitions of "rural and remote," was her first assignment. She was nineteen, homesick, lonely, and "cried a river," as she later put it. She lived in a room on the upper floor of my brother Nick's and his wife's farmhouse. On cold winter mornings, the water in her pitcher would be frozen.

For all the privations Stella experienced, she was a very effective teacher. She accurately described herself in retrospect as a disciplinarian, and she got the best out of her students. In later life she became president of the Alberta Catholic Women's League and played a prominent part in the national organization. When I asked Stella how she remembered me, she replied, "a serious little fellow who read a lot." I had never thought of myself as having been a particularly serious student in those years, but I took her at her word.

My teacher when I was in grades six and seven was a young woman named Eileen Bailey. Bright, articulate, and energetic, she had been raised on a farm near the Saskatchewan border and was herself a product of rural one-room schools. She had gone to Olds for grades eleven and twelve, and had then obtained an initial qualifying certificate by taking a three-month course at Normal School in Edmonton. Berryfield was her first school. She was nineteen, and recalls being "scared but happy."

Eileen described the daily routine at school as beginning with roll call, followed by scripture reading and the Lord's prayer. Instruction would begin with mathematics for the higher grades, which were then left to work on their own while she turned to the younger students. A good deal of cross-fertilization took place through the students in the lower grades listening to the instruction of those who were more advanced. In some schools, a sort of family atmosphere developed over time, with some of the older students becoming rather protective of the younger ones and helping them with their lessons. The last period on Fridays was reserved for spelling bees and geography quizzes.

The library in a one-room school normally consisted of a modest book-case on one wall. Eileen recalled that I used to read as extensively as Berryfield's limited stock of books allowed. She produced from the collection she had salvaged when the school closed a book entitled *Character* that I had apparently read when I was twelve, although I have no recollection of its contents. It was by one Samuel Smiles, a Victorian author whose works of an improving nature were distributed to schools throughout the British Empire. His other titles included *Thrift, Duty,* and *Self-Help.* None of these was among our school's holdings, but if they had been I might have read them as well, for want of alternatives.

There were sanctions for unsatisfactory conduct, including repeated failures to complete assignments. The mildest was detention at recess or after school. Significantly up the scale was "the strap"— a heavy strip of leather that was kept in every teacher's desk and applied to the palm of the children's hands when the situation warranted. Strappings were a normal instrument of discipline in the schools, and were usually admin-istered in front of the class. I have a personal recollection of another sanction, when two of my friends and I had our mouths washed out with soap for having said things that I can no longer recall.

One-room schools were not unique to the prairies; they were a stan-dard part of rural life across Canada. As educational institutions, they met only the most basic requirements. A report sent to the Department of Education in Edmonton in 1935 concerning rural schools in the part of the province where the Kroegers lived, stated: "The teacher has nothing to work with except a scarred and cracked blackboard, some chalk, and what material her ingenuity can devise."[3] Recreational equipment nor-mally was limited to a bat and a softball that had to be re-stitched from time to time, with the rudiments of a ball diamond being laid out in an adjacent pasture. Sometimes a school would also have a swing and a teeter-totter.

As the depression of the 1930s began to abate, the Alberta govern-ment initiated a program of immunization. Doctors with needles and vaccines made the rounds of all the rural schools. We were also supplied with "vitamin pills," apparently filled with cod liver oil, that we took without much enjoyment.

School attendance had to compete with other exigencies. I have already mentioned that at harvest time the girls stayed home from school to help their mothers with food preparation. My older brothers, in common with boys in most schools, would also be absent for weeks, sometimes for several months, during harvest season and again in the spring when the fields had to be seeded and cultivated.

It was rare for students, and particularly boys, to continue their schooling beyond the legal school-leaving age of fourteen. There was always work to be done on the farm, and going on to high school involved moving to town and finding a family to board with, as there were no dormitories before the late 1940s. Some girls found ways of going to high school and then went on to take teacher training at Normal School in Edmonton or Calgary, while for boys further education usually took the form of training to be a mechanic or a welder at one of the city's technical institutes. In reviewing 24 years of files of the *Consort Enterprise* ending in 1946, I found scarcely a single report of a local student going on to university.

Despite its limitations, the little white schoolhouse had important achievements to its credit. The Census of Alberta recorded that, during a five-year period in the 1920s, illiteracy among the "foreign born" population in rural areas fell from over 5,000 to 3,000. The one-room schools contributed to this increase in literacy by educating students of varying ages, particularly from the Slavic countries, who arrived in Canada with no previous schooling at all.

The prairies have a well-earned reputation for harsh winters. Temperatures of minus 25 to 30 degrees Celsius were a regular occurrence every winter and could persist for weeks at a time. Frozen fingers, toes, and faces were common, as students and teachers walked or rode horses for several miles through the snow. In each school, a designated student or sometimes the teacher had the task of getting to the school ahead of the rest and lighting the fire in the heater. When we arrived, the ink in our inkwells was usually frozen, and when necessary we would keep our coats and mittens on until the room had warmed up. Sometimes our lunches would also freeze on the way to school, in which case we would hold our sandwiches against the heater to thaw them at lunchtime. On one occasion, a large number of red-hot coals fell out of the heater and burned a large hole in the floor before it could be extinguished with snow.

I have a particularly clear recollection of setting out for school with my brother Peter one day when I was perhaps eight years old. It was a clear, brilliant morning. The air was still, and the snow sparkled in the winter sun. The temperature was minus 45 degrees Celsius. We walked a quarter of a mile and then, as we crested a small hill, we encountered an icy breeze. After a few minutes, we turned back and were soon safely at home. In retrospect, it seems foolhardy that we even set out on such a day, but at the time it seemed less remarkable.

Another day several years later, the temperature was minus 30 degrees, sharpened by a northwest wind that had developed during the afternoon. I had to face the wind when riding home on my horse. I was unable to fasten the ear flaps on my winter helmet because the strap was broken, and by the time I arrived home both ears were frozen solid. When they thawed they swelled to double their normal thickness, and the skin peeled off. My mother would not allow me to go to school for three days after that.

With the coming of spring, the boys at school always looked forward to shedding two items of apparel. One was the heavy winter underwear that we had donned in response to October's frosts. The other was our shoes. For the first few days, walking barefoot was a rather prickly business, but then we developed the necessary calluses and were carefree for the rest of the summer.

There were hazards. Sometimes the teacher would be told, for example, that "Herman can't come to school today. He stepped on a rusty nail." Tetanus shots were unknown to us; fortunately, no one ever came down with tetanus in our school.

A major event of the school year was the annual school picnic, which was held in late spring, or sometimes to mark the end of the school year. It was a community event, and participants included not only the school children but also parents and other adults from farms in the area. The site was often a slough (which on the prairies is pronounced, "slew," and refers to a body of water of modest size in a low-lying area) where trees and green grass grew in contrast to the brown pastures. Large quantities of home-made ice cream were one feature of the occasion, footraces and games another.

In the fall of 1942, our teacher at Berryfield was pregnant, so Peter and I had to attend another school, known as Willowbrook, until Christmas. It was a five-mile walk from our farm, unlike Berryfield which was less than two miles away. Far from regarding the change as a hardship, we treated it as an adventure. Peter set traps for weasels in the rock piles along the way. Our route had the novelty of taking us through a coulee (a deep valley cut into the surface of the prairie by a creek). On stormy days we were able to walk in the shelter of one of tributary valleys for the last mile to the school. Rabbits rustled in the willows along the creek, and one day as we were walking home we saw several coyotes in the winter twilight.

Another benefit of our time at Willowbrook was that the school had a different set of books than Berryfield. It was there that I first came upon Kipling's *Jungle Book*, with its stories of Mowgli, the boy raised by wolves, and his adventures in the animal kingdom. It was by far the most gripping piece of reading I had encountered up to that time, and I can still remember a good deal of the contents.

In the one-room schools, the annual Christmas concert was a highlight of the year. Preparations would begin weeks in advance of the appointed date. Desks were pushed together to create space at one end of the schoolroom, and men from local farms would come by to set up a stage of rough planks mounted on logs. Every student was given one or more parts: recitations, songs, pantomimes. Some events, such as singing Christmas carols, involved the entire school. Rehearsals were a happy alternative to schoolwork.

One normal feature of a Christmas concert was for the students to perform quadrille-type marches on the stage. At Willowbrook our teacher, Annie Tym, got her husband Sam to provide the accompanying music for the last few rehearsals. His favourite tune was "Marching through Georgia." At the time, it never occurred to me that there was anything incongruous about schoolchildren of Mennonite, Scandinavian, and other ethnic origins marching and counter-marching on a school stage in Alberta to a U.S. Civil War march played by a Ukrainian farmer on his violin.

Although most of the Mennonites the Kroegers knew were in the Naco/Sedalia area, there was one family, the Klassens, who lived half a mile from the Kroegers' new home. Mrs. Klassen was a relative of Heinrich's—a niece or a cousin (accounts differ). Heinrich's notebook recorded periodic visits to the Klassens during the Naco years, and the two families became near neighbours when the Kroegers moved north to the Day place.

Johann Klassen had grown up in Nieder (Lower) Chortiza, in the colony of the same name. During World War I, he had worked as a medical orderly in the Red Cross hospital in Dniepropetrovsk, where Heinrich Kroeger and other Mennonite young men had taken their basic training in the fall of 1914. During the civil war, Johann was at one point taken prisoner, but escaped his captors by jumping off a bridge and swimming to safety. During the same period, his wife saw her uncle bayoneted.

The Klassens were in the first group of Russlaender who had arrived in Rosthern in July 1923. He was 26, she 22. Like the Kroegers, they were to spend several years looking for a place to settle before acquiring their farm adjacent to the Day place. The family eventually grew to ten children.

While his wife was a quiet, gentle person, Johann was in some respects larger than life. He was broadchested, physically strong, and very hard-working. He was also a powerful personality. Sounds carried a long way on the prairie air, and we could sometimes hear him shouting orders to his children, and particularly the three eldest sons who helped him work the fields. He took great pride in his farm. In addition to the normal crops, he grew melons, strawberries, raspberries, and cucumbers. He also kept bees. By dint of his skill and energy, he managed to pay off the family's *Reiseschuldt*—a few years after arriving in Canada.

Relations between the two families were cordial during the ten years that we lived next to each other. Linked as we were by history, language, and our common Mennonite background, we tended to think of each other as members of the same extended family, and there was much visiting back and forth by the children as well as the parents. While my pals at Berryfield were two Polish boys, Joe and Ronald Ference, I also liked Herman, the Klassen boy nearest my age, and regarded him as something of an older brother. We would sometimes go to the coulee on their property to pick berries, or go shooting gophers together.

On one occasion, a student at Berryfield came into the school holding in her hand two dragonflies that were joined together at their ends. The students and the teacher gathered around and speculated as to the explanation. Herman took one look and went back to his desk at the other end of the room. Later he told me the explanation was simple: the two flies were mating. What then ensued was my introduction to the facts of life, as Herman explained animal and human reproduction to me. I was also friends with Herman's sister Mary, who was the closest to me in age; she recalls that when we were both about ten she was required to stay after school for some misdeed or other, and I waited for her so we could walk home together.

When the batteries on his radio went dead, Johann Klassen used to come to our house to listen to the news, particularly during the war when Hitler's armies occupied the region where the Mennonite colonies were located. Like many who had suffered through the post-revolutionary years in the USSR, he detested the Bolsheviks. On one visit to our house he held forth about how the Mennonites were culturally German and should therefore support Germany in the war against Stalin's Soviet Union. The colour rose in my sister Anne's face, and she finally slapped the table and exclaimed, "No! I'm a Canadian!" Her mother sharply rebuked her for failing to show respect, but on reflection later told her that she had been right.

Recollections of Johann Klassen differ. Some of his surviving children remember him as a disciplinarian with a violent temper; others remember him as a firm but loving father who brought them candy or other small presents when he returned from town. He was certainly capable of generosity: at one point during the depression he took a large wagonload of potatoes and melons to Consort for distribution to needy families.

In 1940, Mrs. Klassen gave birth to an eleventh child who was to have been named Elizabeth. Sadly, the child was stillborn. As was not uncommon at the time, Johann obtained permission to take the body home, and Heinrich Kroeger made a tiny coffin. The Klassen family gathered at the Kroegers. Mary remembers that Helena had placed pink geraniums in the coffin, one in the child's hand. Johann buried the baby on a knoll in his pasture and outlined the grave with small stones.

Johann was prone to intense headaches—a symptom of the high blood pressure that would eventually take his life. To obtain relief from the pain he would drink a dozen or more cups of strong black coffee. He was hospitalized in Calgary for several days after a mild stroke in 1940. A second stroke the following year was much more severe. His wife sat up nursing him through the nights, spelled off from time to time by Helena Kroeger. Johann was bedridden for several months and suffered hallucinations. During this time, the children were required to be very quiet when in the house.

He was a religious man who read the Bible regularly. When his children were approaching maturity, he sent them to the Bible college in Didsbury. Frieda, the eldest child, was the first to attend, followed by John, the eldest son. After John returned from the college in 1941, it was the turn of the second son, Rudolph. However, Rudolph became homesick, stole a bicycle, and rode it back to the family's farm.

The RCMP were notified by the owner of the bicycle, and a constable visited the Klassen farm. Like many Mennonites with experience of the Soviet Union, Johann Klassen and his wife were instinctively apprehensive about anyone in uniform. Their tension increased when they learned of the bicycle theft.

During the meeting, Johann's face twisted, and Mrs. Klassen saw that her husband was seriously ill. She persuaded the Constable to take him to the hospital in Consort, but a mile down the road the car became stuck in a mudhole, and the Constable had to walk back to the Klassen's farm to get horses to pull him out. By the time they arrived at the hospital, Johann's condition had seriously deteriorated, and he died shortly afterward. It was March 12th, 1942. He was forty-five.

Johann Klassen's funeral, with the coffin made by Heinrich Kroeger.

Heinrich Kroeger was called upon once more to make a coffin. I vividly recall him cutting and planing pieces of heavy new lumber that had been brought home from Consort. Helena lined the coffin with pink satin, and stuffed the lining with the shavings generated by Heinrich's plane. When the coffin was finished, it was painted with black enamel and left on two easels in the living room.

The living room was also where I slept during this period, my cot being located near a heater in the corner. I was nine years old at the time. That night, with the empty coffin nearby, was the most terrifying of my life. I slept only fitfully, and during my waking periods imagined that I heard a rapid ticking sound that I attributed to a "death watch beetle." To this day, I have no idea how this term came into my head.

The next day, while I was at school, Henry—who by this time owned a used car—drove into Consort to collect the body, which was placed in the coffin. To accommodate the coffin in the trunk, Henry had to take a hacksaw and cut a steel brace that ran across the back of the car. When

Henry returned to the farm, Nick shaved Johann's face in preparation for the funeral, at which the coffin would sit open. That night I again occupied my cot in the living room with the closed coffin nearby on its easels, but, exhausted from having been awake most of the previous night, I slept soundly.

The funeral was held in a small country church. Our teacher, Stella Kozicki, cut evergreen fronds, which were laid on the coffin. The Klassen family's grief was evident; Johann's eldest daughter sobbed loudly. A large number of farmers from the surrounding area attended. Burial was in the adjacent churchyard.

In 1947, one of the sons, Arthur Klassen, was stricken with a sudden illness and died abruptly after three days in hospital. The immediate assumption was that he had died of poliomyelitis. It was summer, and in the years before Salk vaccine summer was the polio season. The dreaded disease left some of its victims crippled and could be fatal. Public gatherings were often cancelled when a case of polio was reported because of a fear of contagion. In some cases, the opening of schools would be delayed until the colder weather of fall had dissipated the risk.

Fears of this kind dictated that Arthur's burial take place quickly and privately. At the request of the undertaker, my brother Peter borrowed a light pickup truck from Nick's and Henry's garage. He and the undertaker took the coffin with the body in it to the same small country church where Johann Klassen had been buried. Only the family were present. The funeral was held at night, and the coffin lid was kept closed. The minister conducted the brief service with a flashlight, which he then used to light the way to the hastily dug grave. The family was quarantined for three weeks.

Arthur's death marked the beginning of the end of the Klassens' time on their farm. The older sons began to look at other ways to make a living, such as trucking. The farm was sold, and family members left for other parts of Western Canada.

In the 1960s and 1970s, as improved roads gave local people access to churches in the towns, the little country church fell into disuse. Eventually a local farmer purchased and dismantled the building for the lumber.

Today, the churchyard is still fenced and mowed, but the wooden grave markers are gone and only a few stone monuments still stand. Johann Klassen and his son, like most others in the cemetery, lie in unmarked graves under a carpet of prairie sod.

FOURTEEN *Finding our Feet, 1936–1946*

Thus far has the Lord helped us.
—*I SAMUEL 7:12*

IN 1937, one of Heinrich and Helena's friends, Peter Kroker (no relation), presented them with a framed memento of their twenty-fifth anniversary. Using coloured foil from packages of cigarettes and candies, he cut out beautifully traced letters and then arrayed them on a black background to spell out their names and a biblical verse: "*Bis hieher hat uns der Herr Geholfen*" (Thus far has the Lord helped us). It was the same verse that the Mennonites had engraved on a monument they erected in Chortiza in 1889 to mark the hundredth anniversary of the colony's founding.

With its move to the Day place in November of 1936, the Kroeger family assumed significant financial obligations. The rent was to be $200 per year. Seeding the land would require money, as would the harvesting of a crop—should one be successful.

Nick was twenty-one at the time of the family's move. Having left school in 1929, he already had seven years of trying to make a living by one means or another. When he was sixteen, he had a full-time job milking twelve to fifteen cows for a farmer south of Monitor. He also helped to look after twenty hives of bees. His pay was $10 per month. Several years later, pelts from a large number of rabbits that he shot netted him over

The framed 25th wedding anniversary gift to Heinrich and Helena Kroeger made by a Mennonite friend from foil in tobacco packages.

$100; combined with his earnings on a threshing crew, this $100 enabled him not only to help support the family but also to purchase a used Model T Ford for $60. In December 1935, Heinrich recorded that Nick brought his car home on a sleigh because of the snow-choked roads.

In 1936, Nick traded his Model T car for a Model A Ford with a truck box, which enabled him to obtain work picking up cans of cream from farms in an area extending nearly to the Saskatchewan border. He delivered the cream to the central collection point in Monitor and was paid 25 cents per can. However, he was able to earn money this way only in the summer months, because in the winters the roads were choked with snow and farmers had to take their cream to Monitor by sleigh. Nick also tried to earn a living for a time as a travelling salesman for a company that produced the ointments and patent medicines then commonly used on prairie farms. His meagre earnings did not encourage him to continue.

In 1937, at the height of the drought, the principal crop in much of Alberta was Russian thistle. It grew to a height of two feet in our cultivated fields.

A rancher from near Monitor with 3,000 sheep cut and stacked our this-tles and engaged Nick to haul them to his holdings during the winter months. Each afternoon, Nick would load a large rack with thistles and place poles under the runners of the sleigh to keep them from freezing to the ground overnight. Early the next morning, he would hitch four horses to this heavy load and proceed with it to a rendezvous point some eight miles to the east, where he would be met by the farmer with an empty rack and fresh horses. They would exchange racks, and Nick would return to the farm, where he would load the empty rack with thistles for the next morning. He was paid $1 per load, an improvement on the $10 per month he had earned a few years before.

After the crop failure of 1937, Nick worked for a farmer, Fred Bleisner, for whom he milked twenty cows per day. During this period the govern-ment paid $5 per month to farmers who hired unemployed men.[4] What Nick got from this arrangement was his room and board. Even if paid employment had been available elsewhere, he might not have taken it at this stage, because he had developed an interest in the farmer's daughter, Lucille. A bright and vivacious young woman, she worked for the hotel in Monitor. Nick for his part was dark and good-looking. The two were married in the spring of 1939 and settled in a set of buildings on the Day place a quarter of a mile south of where the rest of the family was living.

For the next five years, Nick worked the fields on the Day place with Henry, and he also began raising a large number of pigs on his own, which he hauled to market in his Model A truck. Good crops in the early 1940s contributed to his earnings, although farming was still far from being lucrative. In 1944, Nick left the farm and joined Henry in purchasing, largely on credit, a vacant building in Consort, which they turned into a machine shop. This was the first step in a business partnership that was to last for the next twenty-four years.

Neither Nick nor Henry was called up for military service during the war. They benefited from a widespread exemption for young men engaged in farming; another factor was that they were both married with fami-lies. Had they been called up, the family would have been in a difficult situation. Heinrich's ill health would not have permitted him to manage the farm, and the next eldest son, George, was only fourteen when war broke out.

Born in 1917, Henry was lean of build and would remain so all his life, perhaps a consequence of the pace at which he always functioned. He could play a banjo, play chords on a piano and, like the rest of the family, had a good singing voice.

Of all the members of the family, Henry had the strongest drive. He was determined to escape the adverse circumstances in which he had grown up. He was restless in his quest for opportunity, and prided himself on always saving money, even when he was earning only a few dollars per month. In later life, he would often express regret at having had to leave school, saying he wished he had been able to go on and study law.

Henry always disliked the memory of our early years in Canada. He felt humiliated by what he regarded as the patronizing manner in which our family had been treated by other Mennonite families in the Naco/Sedalia area because of our father's ill health and his difficulties in coping with his new environment. This was not a sentiment that the rest of us shared when we looked back on that period, but Henry felt it intensely. In the early 1980s, when he was part of an Alberta government delegation visiting Moscow, he showed no interest in the fact that he was in the city where he had been born. Our origins in Europe belonged to the past. From an early age in Canada he was insistent that his brothers and sisters should speak English at home, notwithstanding his parents' desire to preserve the family's use of Low German.

In 1934, Henry began working for a farmer, Paul Peterson, who lived south of Consort and some miles west of the Day place. On his first day, he carried out a task Peterson had given him, and then went into the house and sat down. When Peterson came into the house shortly afterward and saw Henry sitting there, he said, "Well, if you can't find anything else to do, I guess I don't need you any more." His statement had a sobering effect, and Henry did not need to hear it twice. From then on, there were always fences that needed fixing, feed to be hauled, and machinery to be repaired. In later life, when he and Nick were operating their own business, Henry would sometimes recount this anecdote for the benefit of their employees.

In 1936, at the age of nineteen, Henry identified the vacant Day place as an opportunity and proceeded to arrange a lease. The next step was to find a means of farming it. He had managed to save $105 out of his meagre earnings in previous years, and he used this capital stake to acquire a used disk, a single-bottom plough, and harness for horses.

An employer had previously given two him horses in lieu of wages, and he had managed to purchase a third. However, he needed a fourth before he could begin operations. A horse was running loose in a nearby pasture, and when Henry's inquiries to the neighbours failed to identify its owner, he caught it and added it to his three. He also took possession of a small seed drill that had been left behind on a neighbouring farm when the owner abandoned the property and moved away. By the spring of 1937, he was ready to begin seeding.

In addition to fields on the Day place, Henry was interested in an adjoining quarter section, but was unable to find out who owned it. Neighbours told him he might as well seed it if he wanted to, since no one else was using it. Henry acted on this advice.

His improvisations that spring illustrate the social disintegration spreading across the prairies in the 1930s, as the drought and depression took their toll. Land that had been taken over by governments for unpaid taxes effectively belonged to no one and lay neglected. Over time it became covered with weeds, grass, and a tough low shrub known as buckbrush.

Henry's efforts to begin farming that spring ultimately came to naught because of a pervasive crop failure that year. The land he had seeded yielded only a scattering of blighted shoots, and the cattle were eventually turned out on the fields to eat what they could find. Towards the end of the summer, the owner of Henry's fourth horse turned up and reclaimed the animal. He was relieved that Henry had taken it in, as sixteen of his other horses had died that summer as a result of eating poisoned grain spread by farmers to kill grasshoppers.

After the failure of his first efforts to farm the Day place, Henry determined to search for opportunities elsewhere. On July 12th, after the cattle had been turned out to graze on what stunted crops existed, his father recorded, "Henry went to look for a farm and returned July 16th." Then, on August 3rd: "Henry went by bicycle to Rosemary." This was a reference to a trip that Henry and a friend made to explore prospects in southern Alberta.

They covered some 50 miles per day, and on the third day arrived in the region of the province where dams and irrigation systems had been built in the first part of the century. Their eyes widened at what they saw. After having pedalled past endless parched fields, drifted topsoil, emaciated livestock, and burned pastures, they now saw before them vistas of green: fields of grain, corn, melons, sugar beets, and other crops.

This experience made a lifelong impression on Henry. Over forty years later, when he was minister of transportation in the Lougheed government of 1979 to 1982, he developed a reputation as an advocate of diverting rivers in Northern Alberta to increase irrigation in the dry areas in the south and east of the province. His views met with a mixed reception. River diversion projects had been a staple of discussion on the prairies for much of the twentieth century, and in some quarters they still are.

However, the economic returns have seldom been found to warrant the costs involved; environmental considerations have also emerged as a major obstacle. Henry's advocacy of river diversion in the early 1980s must have seemed rather quixotic to many Alberta residents. However, those with personal memories of the searing drought of the 1930s and the psychological impact it had on individuals would at least have known, as the phrase has it, "where he was coming from."

In 1938, Henry benefited from a good harvest. He used the returns to purchase an old steel-wheeled tractor and to lease more land. In May 1940, his father recorded, "Henry came over with all the machinery for seeding." We no longer had to rely upon horses.

In 1939, Henry married Cleona Kelts, the daughter of a farmer who lived near Paul Peterson's place. For the first year, they lived in two rooms in the family house on the Day place, but then were able to move to a farm of their own.

In 1941, Henry's fortunes improved sharply as a result of events on the other side of the Atlantic. Whereas between 1914 and 1918 the disruptions of World War I in Europe had increased the market for Canadian wheat,

George Kroeger on Henry's tractor.

in 1940 the opposite happened. Hitler's armies swept through Western Europe and seized control of the continent from Norway to the Spanish border, with the result that Canadian grain exports to the region came to an abrupt end. Good crops from 1938 to 1940 had brought Canadian stocks of wheat and other grains to very high levels, far beyond what could be sold to Britain and the other remaining markets.

To head off a further increase in stocks, Mackenzie King's government in early 1941 used the *War Measures Act* to impose quotas for wheat deliveries. Under the Dominion Wheat Acreage Reduction Plan, farmers received cash payments for taking land out of production. Acreage sown to wheat that year fell to two-thirds of the 1940 level. The acreage payments were continued in succeeding years.[5]

This program resulted in Henry receiving a payment of $1,100 in the spring of 1941—a very large sum at the time. Using this money, and trading in various pieces of used equipment that he had assembled in previous years, he purchased a new Case tractor and a large disc-seeder. Thus equipped, he began to till and seed local farmers' fields on a commercial basis. Because of improved yields and prices in the post-drought period, a number of farmers were better off and could afford Henry's services. Wheat prices, which had stood at 61 cents in 1939, reached $1.23 in 1943.

Henry also used his new equipment to farm the Day place and the property where he and Cleona were now living. An unforgettable experience for me came at the age of eleven, when Henry allowed me to drive his tractor when he was working our fields. Until then, I had worked only with horses, and this was my first experience with farm machinery. On one occasion, just as I was heading out the door to join Henry as his tractor and disc approached the corner of the field nearest the house, my mother spoke to me about attending to some chores. "But Mom," I protested, with more than a little hyperbole, "Henry *needs* me." She relented and let me go.

Henry's years of farming and doing custom work for others came to an end in the summer of 1944, when he sold his machinery and went into partnership with Nick. Over the next two years, they acquired dealerships for Massey-Harris farm machinery (the company that would later become Massey-Ferguson), Dodge cars, and British-American Oil. In 1946, they added trucking services. Also in 1946, they purchased a sizable building on the corner of Consort's main street and moved their expanded business into it. During the winter months when activity was at a low level, Nick would go to the technical college in Calgary for courses in welding and mechanics. Henry for his part concentrated on sales and customer relations.

Thus the business was launched. It never made them wealthy, and at times their financial situation was precarious. Nevertheless, for many years the business was the principal source of financial support for our parents and the rest of the family. In particular, it provided the means for some of the younger members of the family, myself included, to pursue opportunities that would otherwise not have been open to us.

Among the documents that I found in my father's wooden box was an "Alberta Citizens Registration Covenant." Premier Aberhart's Social Credit government, which had taken office in 1935, issued what amounted to its own currency in the following year. The bills were described as Prosperity Certificates, and were referred to in the Covenant as "Alberta Credit." Under the Covenant, Albertans committed themselves to accept the certificates as remuneration, to use them in transactions, and to exchange

Heinrich Kroeger and his sons in front of Nick and Henry's business, Consort, 1950. Left to right: Nick, Henry, Heinrich, George, Peter, Arthur.

income received in Canadian currency for the certificates. The Covenant also stipulated, however, that the certificates could not be used for any kind of payment to the Alberta government, including taxes and fees.

The Social Credit government was committed to paying monthly dividends to Albertans "when circumstances permitted," and for this purpose recipients of the Covenant were required to complete forms providing detailed information about their personal income, debt, occupation, and—interestingly enough—ethnic origin.

The entire scheme came to naught within a year because of resistance on the part of the public and the business community. Heinrich Kroeger, however, duly submitted the information required, together with a signed and witnessed copy of the Covenant, retaining a copy for himself. It was an era when most immigrants did not choose to argue with governments.

Better times led to a modest improvement in the circumstances of the rest of the Kroeger family too. Although the two eldest sons were in charge of managing the farm, Heinrich played as active a part as his health permitted. Helena found her life growing easier as one offspring after another grew up and left home. She and Heinrich took the local train to visit Heinrich's uncle in Saskatchewan, and in 1940 Helena travelled to British Columbia to spend a month with her brother George Rempel and her sister Tina.

Prosperity was still some distance off, however. In 1939 and 1940, Heinrich recorded that he and Nick had done roadwork to meet their tax obligations without spending scarce cash. Helena for her part earned money in 1940 by working for ten days cleaning the school in Consort.

By the early 1940s, Helen and I were the only two members of the family still living at home full-time. Helen, who was then in her twenties, did a good deal of the outside work on the farm as well as helping mother in the house. She continued to live and work at home until mid-life; in 1967, she married Claude Thornton, the son of a family in the Sedalia area whose farm had been near the Kroegers' during the early 1930s. After their marriage, she and Claude lived in our family's house and cared for our father, who by then was a widower.

Born in 1923, Anne was the first member of the family to complete high school. In part, she was a beneficiary of the times: as a girl in the 1930s, she had less opportunity than her brothers to earn money to support the family, and so had the option of staying in school if she could find the means to do so. More important was her determination to pursue her education, and the tenacity she displayed in difficult circumstances.

At many rural schools, instruction extended only to grade eight, at the end of which students were required to pass province-wide examinations if they wished to go on to higher grades. Anne successfully did her examinations at Berryfield and then had to transfer to Willowbrook for grade nine. Willowbrook was five miles from our farm, and mother arranged for her to board at a farm closer to the school.

After completing grade nine, Anne was stymied. The nearest high school was in Consort, twelve miles away. For her to attend school there would

cost the family money, and she would have to find a place to board. She
spent a restless year at home, helping her mother and her sister Helen,
and also, as she put it, "continually pestering" her parents to let her go to
high school.

Eventually she got her wish. Her mother arranged for her to do house-
work for a Russian family who lived near Consort, in return for room
and board. The following year, Anne worked for a family in the town.
Sometimes she would get up at 4:00 AM to do laundry and ironing for her
employer before going to school. In her final year, after Nick and Henry
had opened their business, a set of rooms in their machine shop provided
a basic apartment for Anne, her brother Peter who was by that time also

attending Consort High School, and a Mennonite student whose parents were friends of the Kroegers.

Having successfully completed grade twelve, Anne then faced the problem of how to go on to Normal School in Calgary for training to become a teacher. Once again, help came from Nick and Henry. A good crop in the fall of 1944 enabled them to give her $120 for her tuition. She managed to find work in Calgary that enabled her to cover her accommodation costs of $30 per month plus $5 per month for streetcar fare.

In the spring of 1945, Anne returned from Calgary and took a two-month teaching assignment at a school north of Consort. The following September, she obtained a permanent position at a school near Hemaruka. There she met a local farmer's son who had just returned from wartime service in the Navy. She and Fred Dafoe were married in the spring of 1946.

The land in the Hemaruka area was no more than marginal, and making a living from farming was difficult. Anne taught for sixteen years, first at the two-room school in Hemaruka and after it closed in the school in the adjacent village of Youngstown. She was still raising her family when she began teaching, and she continued teaching after her children grew up, In summers, she would return to Normal School to take additional courses to improve her qualifications.

George was less than a year old when the family arrived in Canada. Like the rest of the family, he attended one-room schools. He started school in 1931. Heinrich's first note about George going to work for a neighbouring farmer was entered in 1937, when George was eleven. In 1940, George reached the legal school-leaving age and went to work for Henry.

The work was strenuous. Among his tasks in the first year was driving an eight-horse team, pulling a cultivator or in some cases a plough. Later he operated the tractor and equipment that Henry had purchased. During the summer of 1941, he and one of the older Klassen boys whom Henry had also hired worked around the clock, alternating twelve-hour shifts while Henry canvassed the surrounding area for new work.

When he was eighteen, George applied to join the RCMP. For unknown reasons, his acceptance did not come through for some two years. By that time, Nick and Henry had purchased a truck for their business and turned it over to George to operate, so he chose to remain with the business.

Two years later, George got married and moved to the Okanagan Valley in British Columbia, where he sold the truck and took work in the local sawmills. He later returned and worked for Henry and Nick's business. In 1954, George and his family returned to British Columbia, where he became maintenance supervisor for a large construction company.

Peter completed his high school and in July 1946 and at the age of eighteen began as a trainee with the local branch of the Royal Bank of Canada. His starting salary was $600 per year—$250 less than his sister earned in her first year as a teacher. In 1949, he was transferred to a branch of the Royal Bank in Edmonton, at a salary of $1,300.

Peter and Anne were the first members of the family to obtain "white collar" jobs.

The *Reiseschuldt*, the debt we owed to the Canadian Mennonite Board of Colonization for our passage to Canada, hung over our family continuously. During the early years in Canada, Heinrich's correspondence with the Board about his need to obtain a farm included references to the debt and his worry that it was growing because of interest costs. His hopes of obtaining a farm were disappointed, and as the acute poverty of the family continued there ceased to be any possibility of his making payments. All of us remember him and our mother often talking in worried tones about the *Reiseschuldt*.

From time to time he would receive reproachful letters from the Board, which was making strenuous efforts to continue reducing its debt to the CPR despite the adversities of the depression. These letters were among his papers at the end of his life. Particularly wounding was a reproach thrown at him in Low German by a fellow Mennonite who was angry about some passing matter or another: *"Du hast noch nicht diene Reisechuldt betohit."* (You still haven't paid your travel debt.)

As Nick's and Henry's financial situation began to improve in the late 1930s, they might have been able to begin making payments against the debt, but their focus was on getting themselves established. Both were newly married. When more money eventually came to hand, they used

Kroeger, Heinr. Heinr. S. 72.

1926.	Lf. Acc. # 32/3 - 1926 -Sept.20		Dr.	Cr.	Blnc
Dec. 31.	Transportation - Sept. 20	4864	675.25		
-.- "	Special levy -.- "	4865	6.00		
-.- .	Special expenses -.- "	4866	82.80	Dr.	764.05
1927 Dec. 31.	Interest due Dec. 31st, 1926	4602	13.37	Dr.	777.4
-.- .	Interest due	4602	46.65	Dr.	824.0
1928 Dec. 31.	Interest due	4185	49.45	Dr.	873.5
1929 Dec. 31.	Interest due	4816	52.41	Dr.	925.9
1930 Dec. 31.	Interest due		55.52	Dr.	981.4
1931 Dec. 31.	Interest due	7631	58.89	Dr.	1,040.3
1932 Dec. 31.	Interest due	7024	62.43	Dr.	1102.8
1933 Dec. 30	Interest due	9869	66.17	Dr.	1.168.9
1934 Dec. 31	Interest due	116.41	70.14	Dr.	1.239.1
1935 Dec. 31	Interest due	12.28	74.35	Dr.	1.313.4
1936 Dec. 31.	Interest due		78.87	Dr.	1392.
1937 Dec. 31.	Interest due		83.54	Dr.	1475.
1938 Dec. 31.	Interest due		88.55	Dr.	1,564.3
1939 Dec. 30	Interest due		93.86	Dr.	1,658.
1940 Dec. 31.	Interest due		99.49	Dr.	1757.
1941 Dec. 31.	Interest due		105.46	Dr.	1863
1942 July 11	Paym. $5.00 Pr. $2.10	30:11		7.10	1.856
Dec. 31	Interest due		111.89	Dr.	1.967.
1943 Mar. 3.	Paym. $26.40 Pr. $8.98 Gak.	10:23		35.38 Dr.	1.932.
1944 Feb. 25	-- $100.00 " $46.00 Dr.	9:39		146.00 Dr.	1786.
Dec. 31.	-.- $794.53 Pr. $1.108.05	45:2		1.902.58 Cr.	116.
1945 Jan. 30	Interest due		116.29		
	Total		2091.06	2091.06 --	-- --

Heinrich Kroeger's Reiseschuldt page in the account book. (Mennonite Heritage Centre, Winnipeg)

it to meet household needs, rent land, buy machinery, and repair dilapi-
dated buildings.

In time, however, they did turn their attention to the debt. They made
a first payment of $7.10 on July 11th, 1942, a second of $35.38 on March
3rd, 1943, and a third of $146.00 on February 25th, 1944. On the strength
of the good crop in the fall of that year, they paid off the final balance on
December 31st.

The debt, which had stood at $675.25 in September 1926 by 1944 had
reached $2,091.06. Its liquidation was one of many that helped the Board
clear its final obligations to the CPR in November 1946. The end of their
Reiseschuldt brought a palpable sense of relief to Heinrich and Helena.

FIFTEEN *Exile and Dispersal*

We bring our years to an end, as it were a tale that is told.
—*PSALM 90:9*

THE 1940S SAW THE END of the Mennonite colonies in the USSR and the dispersal of their populations.

During the 1930s, the pressures on the colonies had continued to increase as the First Five-Year Plan was implemented. The famine that Stalin deliberately inflicted on the Ukraine in 1931 and 1932 killed some five million people. It apparently had a less severe impact on the Mennonite communities than upon some others, perhaps because of the assistance the Mennonites gave each other. Several of my distant cousins, who were boys in Rosental during this period, recount that when they walked to school, sometimes they would see bodies of people who had died of starvation lying at the side of the street.

This was a period when the mere possession of a letter from abroad could elicit a sentence of four years' hard labour. Knocks on the door in the middle of the night and the arrests of heads of households became common occurrences. Some Mennonite fathers adopted the practice of keeping a packed bag by the door in anticipation of their turn. When it did come, many did not get much of an opportunity to use the contents of those bags, since arrest was often followed shortly afterward by execution.

In the first months of 1933, the Mennonite Colonization Board in Rosthern received some seven thousand letters from Mennonites in the USSR, pleading for help. No help could be provided. Appeals to the premiers and the federal government were unavailing, and the Canadian door remained firmly closed.[1]

In February 1936, Heinrich Kroeger received a letter from his younger brother Abram, who had stayed in the USSR. Abram recounted the difficulties they had experienced, and said that after many moves they were now living in a remote area on the edge of a forest northeast of Moscow. His son was in school, where he was doing well. Abram's wife was the manager of the local hospital, while he was working as a mechanic at the power station. He was losing his ability to speak German. They were in poor health and continued to feel the pain of their daughter's death in 1930.

It was the last time Heinrich heard from his brother. Nothing is known of the family's fate, but it is not difficult to imagine the possibilities. Stalin's purges reached full force in 1937, and ordinary farmers and workers, especially those of foreign descent, were caught up in them. In 1937, 351 residents of Chortiza were sent into exile, mostly to Siberia; in 1938, another 465 were sent.[2] Few of those exiled were ever heard of again. By the 1940s, Mennonites were a minority in Chortiza.

According to Heinrich, his sister Maria was also sent to Siberia during World War II and she died there in 1943. Heinrich said that one of Maria's sons was living in the Mennonite colony in Paraguay, and at one point he had me make inquiries about bringing the young man to Canada. However, second-degree relatives—nephews and cousins—were not eligible for sponsored immigration.

In June 1941, Hitler launched his armies across the borders of the USSR on a broad front. As the armies advanced, one of the Soviet regime's responses was to round up as many German-origin residents as possible and ship them to the east. Much of the population of the south Molochna was caught up in this sweep and exiled to Siberia, where they would spend the next fifteen years. In Chortiza and north Molochna, however, the advance of the Wehrmacht was so rapid that the deportations were just getting under way when the Germans swept in.[3]

After the brutalities of Stalin's regime over the years, the German invaders were in many quarters regarded as liberators. In the Ukraine, a military unit known as the Halychyna Division was formed and joined in operations against the Red Army. In the Baltic states, a Latvian Legion was formed and fought on the side of the Wehrmacht. A number of Cossack units also rallied to the German side.[4]

For the Mennonites, the German occupation brought a return to something resembling the life the colonists had once known. Independent farming resumed, employment in the factories increased, and the churches reopened.

Just two years later, this respite came to an end. After the defeat of the German army at Stalingrad, the Red Army began its inexorable advance. The Wehrmacht was ordered to retreat, and was authorized to evacuate with it some 350,000 German-origin residents.[5] Among them were the remaining residents of the Mennonite colonies, who no longer saw a future for themselves in the USSR. The evacuation of the Chortiza and Molochna colonies began in October 1943. With the evacuation of 1943, the Mennonite presence in the area effectively came to an end.

In all, some 35,000 colonists moved west with the retreating German army. The fortunate ones did so by train; others left in horse-drawn wagons that often had to travel by back roads because the main highways were used by the retreating army. Many of these wagons were driven by women, because years of deportations and executions of the men in the colonies had left half the Mennonite households without fathers.[6] As the Eastern European winter set in, the evacuees experienced continuous wet, cold, and hunger. Often the wagons had to struggle through deep mud. There were deaths from illness and from partisan attacks on the retreating German army.

By Christmas of 1943, the wagons had reached Poland, and some months later they crossed into Germany.

The Mennonites' refuge in Germany was to be of short duration. At the Yalta conference in 1945, Stalin secured an agreement from Roosevelt and Churchill stipulating that, after the end of hostilities, displaced nationals should be returned to their home countries. After the final defeat of Germany in May 1945, the Red Army set about rounding up former residents of the USSR.

Of the 35,000 Mennonites who had retreated with the German army, 12,000 managed to make their way into the Western zone and were thus beyond the reach of the Red dragnet. The remaining 23,000, together with other German-origin residents of the USSR, were loaded on trains and forcibly repatriated. In retribution for having left the USSR with the German occupiers, they were exiled to camps east of the Urals, primarily in Siberia. Conditions were those the gulags have become known for; the people were faced with malnutrition, wretched accommodations, bitterly cold winters, brutal treatment from guards, and a high death rate.

Ten years after the end of the war, as de-Stalinization got under way, the surviving Mennonite exiles in Siberia were among those released from the camps. There was however a restriction: they were not allowed to return to the areas where they once had lived. The result was a diaspora, and so the organized Mennonite presence in the country came to an end. What followed for many was intermarriage and assimilation.

The 12,000 Mennonites who managed to get to the Western zone of Germany and escape the Red Army lived through some difficult years, but their fate was incomparably better than that of their co-religionists who had been returned to the USSR. A number found temporary work of one kind or another in post-war Germany. During the next few years, approximately half made their way to Canada, while the other half settled in a Mennonite colony in Paraguay. As in the past, emigration to the United States was not an option because the Quota Act of the 1920s was still in force.

Remarkably, there are still identifiable groups of Mennonites in the former USSR. In 1965, the Canadian Embassy in Moscow sent an extensive report on a conversation one of its officers had with a Mennonite who stated that there were at the time about 45,000 practicing Mennonites in various parts of the country. In many cases, they were allied with other Protestant groups such as Baptists and Lutherans, and in some communities services were held in German. By the mid-1960s, the regime's hostility to religion had abated, with the result that the various Protestant groups were generally tolerated and were even given permission to hold conferences together from time to time.

In the last two decades of the twentieth century, liberalization and then the disintegration of the Soviet Union resulted in the emigration of large numbers of ethnic Germans to the West and particularly to Germany. Among them were up to 100,000 Mennonites and people of Mennonite descent. By the end of the 1990s, a few were beginning to make their way to Mennonite communities in southern Manitoba.

Today, only a few of the Ukrainian people living in the former Mennonite colonies have any knowledge of how the houses and villages they live in came into being. During the decades of Soviet rule, churches were turned into granaries and the houses of wealthy Mennonites became workers' clubs. The school for deaf mutes, established in Tiege before World War I, is now the headquarters of a collective farm, while the church at Ruckenau houses an oilseed press. Some of the mills built by Mennonite entrepreneurs before World War I are still in operation, as are a number of the schools and hospitals. The formerly Mennonite houses in places such as Chortiza and Rosental were stoutly constructed and many are still standing, although there are fewer with every passing decade. Visitors from Canada who are searching out their Mennonite roots are greeted with great hospitality and warmth, but few of the local residents have any sense of what the visits are really about.

SIXTEEN *Consort*

WITH THE ESTABLISHMENT of the garage in Consort and then its expansion to several dealerships and trucking services, Nick and Henry brought to an end their farming activities. There was no question of their father managing the farm on the Day place, so in 1946 they decided that the family should move into Consort. They purchased a lot, dug a basement, and poured a foundation.

The house in which the family was to live was a weathered building, about the size of a granary, which for some years had sat on an abandoned property adjacent to the Day place. Like many such buildings on the prairies in the 1930s, it effectively belonged to no one. Nick had moved it to his farmstead in 1943, and in 1946 he and Henry loaded it on a set of trailer wheels and moved it into Consort. They mounted it on the foundation they had prepared, and Heinrich helped with the construction of an additional two rooms at the back.

It became the home of our parents, together with Helen, and for a time, George, Peter, and me.

When we moved into Consort, I was fourteen. My days of milking cows were not yet over; we brought some elements of the farm with us. Partly to save the cost of buying milk, and partly to continue part of a familiar way of life, my parents kept two cows and quartered them in the town livery stable. They also brought the geese they had had on the farm.

These arrangements proved to be transitional, but while they lasted they caused me a good deal of discomfort. No one else in town milked cows. On one occasion, when I was with a group of boys my age, we heard the geese cackling in the distance. "Whose geese?" one of the boys wondered aloud. My face reddened, and I looked at the ground.

During those years, much of the financial support for our parents came from Nick's and Henry's garage. George and Peter also contributed as long as they lived at home, as did I from what I earned working at the garage after school and on Saturdays. Still, during the first years in Consort, money was in short supply.

In the summers of 1947 and 1948, oil companies sent seismic crews into the Consort area to test for oil-bearing formations. The crews were well paid by local standards and they spent freely. One of their needs was for someone to do their laundry, particularly because drilling operations regularly soaked their clothes with muddy water. My mother and Helen took the opportunity to supplement the family's income by taking in the crews' washing.

With the passage of a few years, my parents' lives became somewhat easier, particularly after they became eligible for the Old Age Pension, which was legislated in 1951. They settled into a modestly comfortable retirement.

Our father spent much of his time reading and corresponding with Mennonite friends and distant relatives in other parts of the country. Most days, he would walk downtown to see what was happening at his sons' garage, but he viewed events there in a detached way. The world around him was somewhat interesting, but it was not his world.

Quite often he would go to his wooden box and take out some papers, and at times he also took out the photograph album with the heavy, thick pages that had been a present from his maternal grandparents. He also liked to leaf through an illustrated history of the Mennonites in Russia, which included a photograph of the house in which he had once lived. The title of the book was *Alse Ihre Zeit Erfullt War*. The English translation of the book was entitled *In the Fullness of Time*.[1]

Our father was far from being the only one to remain focused on the past. Among the descendants of the Mennonites who came to Canada after the Russian revolution and civil war, a number recount that their fathers felt an irreparable sense of loss all their lives, and never managed to fully adjust to life in Canada. Interestingly, the anecdotal evidence suggests that the wives did better in making the transition.

Our mother continued to lead an active life in Consort, tending to her family, visiting friends, and engaging in church activities. There was no Mennonite church in the area, so she associated herself with the Full Gospel Church in Consort. She also liked to attend a week-long Full Gospel summer camp that was held every July on the grounds of a farm south of Veteran. The United Church was too bland for her and, at the other end of the spectrum, she was outspoken in her disapproval of the trappings such as icons, statues, and elaborate cassocks that characterized the Roman Catholic and Orthodox churches. Hers was the uncomplicated faith that is characteristic of many Mennonites.

As her children approached marriageable age, Helena would some-times express, as tactfully as she could, the hope that they would marry "one of our own kind." As things turned out, none did. This caused her some disappointment, and she occasionally allowed herself the observa-tion that, "English girls sure don't know much about cooking or sewing." Nevertheless, as new in-laws joined the family, she embraced them and made them welcome.

During my high school years, my married brothers and sister lived in the general area of Consort, so family reunions at Sunday dinners were a fairly regular occurrence. Mother continued to produce Mennonite food then and on other occasions, to my joy. I eventually lost my knowledge of Low German and my connection with the Mennonite Church, but dishes such as *varenyky* (small dough pockets filled with cottage cheese), *holubtsi* (cabbage rolls), *pannenkoeken* (large thin pancakes), and *perieschkje* (pastries filled with meat or fruit) remained lifelong favourites of mine, as did her homemade Mennonite sausage.

Despite our mother's sunny disposition, there was an undercurrent of fear in her life. Occasionally, her husband wrote letters about the fami-ly's activities for publication in a Mennonite weekly, *Der Bote*; when this happened, she expressed apprehension that the published letters could

Arthur Kroeger during his high school years in Consort.

enable the Soviet regime to find them, and she urged him to desist. The sight of a stranger on the street outside her home in Consort could cause her serious unease, and sometimes when there was an unexpected knock on the door she would take refuge in the basement.

Life in Consort proved to be less difficult than I had expected. I found that my schoolmates were congenial, and eventually I acquired a black high school sweater with a large orange "C" on the chest, thus becoming "like everyone else." I formed friendships that have continued to the present day, some sixty years later. I learned to skate, and eventually to play hockey—not particularly well, but well enough to qualify for a place on the Consort team. Our games were played on outdoor rinks, which made frozen noses and toes a normal part of the sport.

At school, I obtained marks that were respectable, particularly in view of the limited effort I put into my studies. As the youngest in the family, I had been spared the rigours and privations experienced by my older brothers and sisters. As a consequence, in Consort I drifted easily into behaving like other adolescents of the day. For much of the time—too much—I shot pool, played hockey, and hung around with my friends. If this proves that having things too easy is bad for you, so be it.

The high school in Consort had a complement of two teachers. When I began grade eleven, both were new arrivals. Mel Sillito and Fred Begoray had served in the armed forces during the war, and had then gone to the University of Alberta. When they came to Consort High School, they brought with them new ideas, including new approaches to vocational guidance, with tests of aptitude, personal preference, and IQ. They also talked about their experiences at university, which was a new concept for us.

In my own case, the tests yielded some indication of literary ability. My teachers suggested that I go on to university to develop this. By an accident of circumstance, there was evidence at hand in Consort that it was possible to make a living by writing. Ross Annett had come from Ontario to Consort in 1924 to be principal of the high school. He also wrote fiction as a sideline, with some success. His breakthrough came in 1937, when he sold a depression story entitled "It's got to rain sometime" to the *Saturday Evening Post* for the substantial sum of $500. Thus launched, he continued to write, and in the next two decades the *Post* carried over seventy of his stories. His son was one of my friends in high school, so I had first-hand knowledge of Ross Annett's success. I was intrigued by the thought that I too might be able to make a living this way.

But, if the idea of going to university aroused my interest, it had no comparable effect on my efforts at school. In 1950, when I was in grade twelve, lack of diligence led to my dropping two of the courses I needed for graduation. As a result, I spent the following year at Henry's and Nick's garage doing oil changes, assembling swathers, and driving a school bus. It was not work that I enjoyed or was much good at. The experience did however underline for me the desirability of getting away and going to university.

In July of 1951, I went to summer school in Red Deer to pick up my missing credits. Henry drove me to Red Deer, and during the three hours on the road he reviewed how he thought each member of our family was progressing. In each case, his assessment was positive, and he expressed optimism about our future. His message was no less clear for being left implicit: I had something to live up to.

During the next six weeks I applied myself to my studies, and when my marks came in at the end of the summer they provided a glimmer of evidence that my going to university might make some sense after all. I sent my application to Edmonton, and it was accepted.

And then the whole project was in jeopardy. On a morning in the first week of September, when I set off from town on my school bus run, heavy wet snow was falling. As I drove north, I could see the crops bending under the weight of the snow. The snow continued the next day, was followed by rain, then by a too-brief interval of sun, and then there was more snow. Before long, the crops lay flat in muddy fields. In late September, a frustrated farmer walked into a store in Consort and said in a loud voice to no one in particular, "My crop is down, and I'll pay $10,000 to anyone who can harvest it." There was no prospect that his offer would be taken up. It became clear that the crops would spend the winter in the fields, with what was left of them being harvested the following spring.

Nick and Henry faced a near-crisis situation. The prospect of excellent crops had enabled them to make very large sales of farm machinery. By early September, they had sold a record twenty-six combine harvesters, as well as tractors, swathers, and other equipment. Under prevailing arrangements, the farmers were able to take delivery of their machines over the summer and then pay for their purchases when they sold their grain in the fall. However, it became clear that there would be no grain sales in the fall of this year. Nevertheless, Henry and Nick still had to settle their account with Massey-Harris for the machinery they had received on consignment. The amount due was over $50,000. It was a very large sum at the time—the largest they had ever owed. The deadline for payment was October 1st.

In mid-September, Henry set out on a gruelling round of collections, stopping to see each customer to whom he had sold machinery. Because of the growth of the business since he and Nick had established it six years earlier, the territory he had to cover was very extensive, and at times he had someone drive him so he could sleep between calls.

During this period, farmers were unable to get bank loans for the purchase of farm equipment, so those whose crops were down had to obtain credit from commercial finance companies. Funds from these sources came at very high interest rates, but there was no alternative. Every morning in late September, when I came to work at the garage, there would be a new set of slips on the counter that Henry had left in the middle of the night, crediting the farmers he had called on with payment through a finance company contract. The amount from each contract went into the Kroeger brothers' account at the local bank, but when October 1st came there was still not enough money there to cover the post-dated cheque that had been sent to Massey-Harris several weeks earlier. Henry persuaded the bank manager to hold the cheque for another 48 hours. On October 3rd, the cheque was covered and successfully processed.

Registration week at the University of Alberta had come and gone, and it was still uncertain whether I would be able to attend. Nick and Henry had managed to avoid defaulting on their obligations, but money was in very short supply and, because of the failed harvest, business prospects were not good for the coming months. I went to see the local bank manager, but he was unable to help. Government loan programs for students still lay far in the future.

Another week went by.

The established practice in small Alberta towns at the time was for businesses to remain open on Saturday nights. On the Saturday night of Thanksgiving weekend, we turned out the lights at the garage and locked the front door at 10:30 PM. Nick and Henry repaired to the small office in the garage while I sat in the darkness by the counter. After about fifteen minutes Henry emerged and said, "Okay, it looks as though we can afford to send you."

The next day I packed and said goodbye to my parents. By this time, they had seen one after another of their children reach maturity and set out on their own. Still, there was some sadness, particularly on my mother's part, at the last son leaving home. They knew in a general way that I was taking an important step, but they couldn't comprehend exactly what I would be doing. Neither in Russia nor in Canada had they experienced anyone they knew going away to university.

Henry and Cleona drove me to a town near Edmonton, where Henry had business that afternoon. I took the bus the rest of the way, and it was night-time when I arrived at the campus. The darkened buildings looked very large and forbidding.

Finally, two weeks late, I could begin attending university.

SEVENTEEN *A Nightmare from the Past*

AFTER I GRADUATED from the University of Alberta, I spent two years in England at Oxford University. In February 1958, during my second year at Oxford, I received a telegram informing me that my mother was seriously ill. The trans-Atlantic telephone was rarely used in the 1950s, but in this case I called home and was connected with Nick.

He told me that she had died earlier that day. The cause of her death was a stroke, brought on by anxiety over a fatal shooting near Sedalia several days earlier. When word of the shooting reached our family, she reacted with intense fear, then fell unconscious and was taken to hospital. She seemed to be in a coma, although when Heinrich put his hand in hers, she responded by squeezing it. She died three days later.

Helena Kroeger had suffered from hypertension for many years. She was prone to severe headaches, which she treated by soaking cloths in vinegar and binding them around her forehead. She probably had also had several mini-strokes; at one time, she had experienced numbness in her arm, and on other occasions had had difficulty moving her fingers.

There was no question of my returning to Canada for the funeral. Transatlantic air travel was still fairly rare. The propeller-driven planes that existed were slow and flights were very expensive. However, I later obtained an account of the funeral from the family. The February day had been bitterly cold, with a strong wind and blowing snow. At the cemetery, a member of the family had tried to give my father the large fur hat that he always wore in winter. He abruptly pushed it away and remained bare-headed as his wife's coffin was lowered into the grave. She was buried wearing a simple gold ring that Heinrich had had made to replace the one taken from her by bandits during the Russian civil war.

After the funeral, the family in Canada made a tape-recording that they mailed to me. On it they had recorded messages, one of which was from my father. For the first time in many years, he reverted to speaking to me in Low German: "*Daut es seea schwa fe mie.*" (It is a very heavy burden for me.)

I shared his sense of loss. Mother had been a warm and loving person and a major présence in all our lives. She would be greatly missed. Upon learning of her death, I called an Australian couple who had become close friends and went to stay with them for several days at their house in an Oxford suburb.

When I returned to Canada the following summer, members of the family gave me a fuller account of the events that had led to Mother's stroke. This gave me a better picture of the circumstances, but I continued to find it puzzling that a shooting at a farm some twenty miles away, horrifying though it was, should have caused her to be so afraid. It was only when I acquired my father's papers in 1971 and began to get a picture of what he and my mother had gone through in Russia that I came to understand her reaction.

The farmer who had perpetrated the shooting, John Krukowski, had come to Canada from Poland in 1913, at the age of nineteen. He had had no schooling, and obtained little if any after his arrival. He was known in the area as a hard-working farmer who spoke English with a heavy accent, did not drink, read the Bible regularly, and had no significant brushes with the law.

He was proud of the success that hard work had brought him, and of the fact that it enabled him to be a major source of support for his children. He paid for his daughters' studies in Calgary and, when they married, gave each of them a gift of $7,000. However, his son Stanley had a special importance for him, as the person to whom he would one day turn over the substantial farm that he had built up. It was from this expectation that difficulties arose.

Stanley lived on the farm and operated it with his father, but as he progressed through his twenties and into his thirties he became increasingly independent-minded. Relations between the two became strained, and there were periodic quarrels. Things took a turn for the worse when, at the age of thirty-three, Stanley married the daughter of a farmer near Sedalia. The following spring the couple moved to their own farm, twelve miles west of the Krukowski family's property and near the farm that her parents owned. Krukowski felt that his son was being taken away from him.

Relations between father and son deteriorated further, and on January 31st, 1958, there was a quarrel between them over the removal of grain from a bin. It culminated in John trying to run over Stanley with his truck. John then drove the twelve miles to Stanley's farm, carrying a .38-calibre pistol. He entered the house and shot his daughter-in-law eight times. She fell down the basement steps with her four-month-old baby in her arms. The child's skull was crushed, and it later died.

When the shooting was discovered and the RCMP called, all that was known of Krukowski's whereabouts was that he had returned to his farm with the truck and had then set off on his tractor, taking a rifle as well as his pistol. As word spread, fears of his possible intentions swept through the surrounding area. People locked their doors and kept watch at their windows.

When later that evening Krukowski was located by the RCMP and arrested, he offered no resistance and talked freely about what he had done. When he left the farm that evening he had gone to look for his wife, whom he thought was visiting neighbours. He wanted to give her the combination to his safe. He then intended to use the rifle to take his own life, which he regarded as no longer worth living because, in the words of the judge who later presided at his trial, he "felt that all his aspirations had been shattered."[1]

When word reached Helena of shootings, killings, and a man on the loose with a gun, it brought back the years of anarchic violence that she and Heinrich had lived through in Russia after 1917. Those experiences had left psychic scars, which only occasionally manifested themselves but were nevertheless always there. For Helena, news of the violence on the Krukowski farm was a nightmare from the past, and that trauma took her life.

John Krukowski remained in custody until mid-June, when he was taken to the town of Hanna for his trial. The facts of the case were never in dispute. The only question was the state of Krukowski's mind. A psychiatrist testified that he found him emotionally disturbed, lacking in balance, and suffering from paranoia. A twenty-first-century jury might have been receptive to the defence's claim of insanity, but in 1958 the jury was not. After an hour's deliberation, it found John guilty of murder. He was sentenced to hang three months later, on September 15th, 1958.

On September 8th the federal government commuted his sentence to life imprisonment. John Krukowski served his life sentence in the Prince Albert penitentiary. In the early 1970s, he was released on what at the time was called compassionate parole because of his poor health. He entered a nursing home, and died there a few months later.

Heinrich Kroeger never forgave Prime Minister Diefenbaker's government for commuting Krukowski's sentence. Heinrich was a product of a time when capital punishment was an accepted component of the criminal justice system, and he strongly felt that it should have been applied in this case. He held John Krukowski directly responsible for his wife's death, and therefore deserving of the ultimate penalty. It was a view he continued to express to the end of his life.

EPILOGUE

NICK'S AND HENRY'S LAUNCH of their business in 1944 proved successful. By the mid-1950s, their growing sales had put them in the ranks of the major farm equipment dealers in the province. In 1960, they diversified by purchasing a farm south of Consort, not far from the area in which the family had lived during the early 1930s. In 1961, they bought a second farm and installed Nick's eldest son to operate it. In 1968, as their respective families came to maturity, they made the decision to split the partnership, with Nick and his sons taking the farms, and Henry and his sons taking the business in Consort.

January 14th, 2005, marked ninety years since Helena Kroeger had sent a telegram to her husband, then serving as a medical orderly in the czar's army, announcing Nick's birth. Nick spent his birthday with Lucille and his family in Consort, still in good health. Many friends braved a bitterly cold prairie day to attend a community reception to celebrate the occasion.

Henry had always had an interest in politics, and as early as 1957 had tried unsuccessfully to win a nomination for a federal riding. In 1974, he returned to politics and became the Progressive Conservative candidate in the provincial constituency where our family lived. He won his seat, and was re-elected in 1979. Premier Lougheed then appointed him Minister of Transportation.

Left to right: Federal Deputy Minister of Transport Arthur Kroeger in March 1980, his minister, Jean Luc Pepin, and his brother, Henry Kroeger, Alberta minister of transportation.

A few months later, I was appointed deputy minister in the federal Department of Transport. As a result, for the next few years Henry and I worked in related fields.

In the spring of 1980, Jean-Luc Pepin, my minister, and I travelled to Edmonton for a meeting with the Alberta government. Henry arranged for us to sit in the gallery of the Legislature and introduced us to his colleagues on the floor. In introducing me, he began by saying, "I started him out as a floor sweeper in our business back in 1950." He then added with a wry smile, "By the way, he didn't do that very well." His comment was quite accurate, and probably reflected an inner thought that the rather dubious investment he and Nick had made in sending me to university nearly thirty years earlier had turned out satisfactorily.

Henry thoroughly enjoyed being in government, and he gained the respect of his colleagues on both sides of the Legislature. Then, in the early 1980s, he developed cancer of the lymph system. He managed to continue with his ministerial duties while undergoing chemotherapy. The treatment was apparently successful, but after the 1982 election Premier Lougheed appointed him to the less demanding position of Chairman of the Water Resources Commission.

Several years later, the cancer returned. In August 1987, when I returned for Consort's 75th-anniversary homecoming, Henry and I had dinner together by ourselves. He reminisced at some length about his life in the 1920s and 1930s, and particularly his first attempts at farming in 1937 and 1938. A few weeks later, his resistance weakened by the cancer treatment, he fell seriously ill. I flew to Edmonton, but arrived just after he had died. He was seventy.

Anne and her husband eventually turned their farm over to one of their sons and retired to the town of Hanna.

George spent thirty years as supervisor of maintenance with Inland Construction in the Okanagan Valley of British Columbia.

Peter left the Royal Bank in 1950 to join Imperial Oil in Edmonton. He subsequently worked for several other companies before retiring in 1987 as an executive with Texaco Canada in Calgary.

Helen and her husband, Claude, lived at home in Consort, caring for our widowed father and later moving into the senior citizens' lodge. In 1997, Helen, who had never enjoyed robust health, died of heart failure at seventy-eight.

In the 1960s, the family's Kroeger clock ceased to function and for years it was stored away in a box. Eventually, the family came to realize the clock's significance as an heirloom. It was repaired, wound up, and put back into operation. Nick, as the eldest son, was entitled to take possession of it when our father died, and he subsequently passed it on to his eldest son. In 2005, the clock was 136 years old.

Peter and I for our part have succeeded in locating and purchasing Kroeger clocks for ourselves. His dates from 1904, mine from 1900. Both were made at the Kroeger clock works in Rosental.

Davey Jones left his farm in the late 1940s and moved into a small house in Consort. A few years later, he retired to a senior citizens' lodge in Youngstown, where he lived to an advanced age. Friends who visited him there, including Helen and Anne Kroeger, found him in good spirits, and reported that the grimy overalls that had been his trademark in his Naco days had given way to a suit.

When Jim Doolan retired in 1946, he reviewed the unpaid accounts that had accumulated in his store during the depression. Among them was one for some $60 in grocery purchases by the Kroeger family, which he took to Nick and Henry. They had been unaware that the family had left behind an unpaid bill in Naco when we moved to the Day place. The bill was promptly paid.

For my part, in 1957 at Oxford, I met a vivacious young Canadian student from Toronto named Gay Sellers. In 1958, we both returned to Canada to become Foreign Service Officers. Two years later, each of us was posted, she to the United Nations in New York and I to Geneva and then to India. We returned within a year of each other and were married in 1966.

During my years in the Foreign Service, I kept in touch with friends and family in Consort, and visited home regularly, particularly while my father was alive. In the summer of 1970, I left my wife and our two small daughters with her mother in Toronto and flew to Alberta. During my visit, I spent several days doing summer fallow on Nick's farm with a tractor and a large disc. When I shut down the tractor in the evening twilight and walked across the freshly turned soil to get in my pickup truck and drive back to Consort, it seemed as if I had never been gone.

Ours was a good marriage, but on Easter Sunday morning in 1972 Gay had an epileptic-type seizure. It was the first symptom of the brain tumour that would later take her life, in 1979. When Gay died, our two daughters were nine and eleven.

In the later years of his life, our father's health stabilized and actually improved, with only the attrition of sight and hearing that are normal with advancing age. As long as his wife was alive, she had looked after him and kept a close eye on his needs.

His mindset continued to be with the past. After his wife died in February 1958, he spent six weeks with cousins and Mennonite friends in Saskatchewan, reconnecting with the life he had known as a young man in Chortiza/Rosental.

During the years after he lost his wife he became markedly more self-reliant, and travelled a good deal to see his sons and daughters and their families. He had always been fond of small children, and one of the pleasures of his late years was the succession of grandchildren produced by his daughters and sons.

Usually our father's travels were in Alberta and British Columbia, where members of our family lived, but in 1966, shortly before I got married, he took a long-distance trip to visit me in Ottawa. I decided to drive him to Quebec City to see the place where he had landed in Canada. The visit failed to register with him. The traumas of his last years in Russia, the wrench of leaving, and the difficulties the family had experienced after arriving in Canada, had served to blank out any recollection of his arrival.

On one occasion during his last years, I sat down with him and had him take me through the photographs in the thick-paged album he had been given as a young man by his maternal grandparents. I made extensive notes as he spoke about each photo, and as he went on to reminisce about that period in his life. In subsequent years, I would often wish that I had done this with him more often.

In the fall of 1970, his health began to fail, and in December I flew home from Washington for his eighty-seventh birthday. A little over three months later, he died from the effects of a fall that had fractured his hip. It was at this point that I inherited the wooden box containing his papers.

When I had the papers translated and distributed copies to my brothers and sisters, it stimulated some interest in our family's history.

In 1995, with Anne, George and his wife Irene, and Peter and his daughter Diane, I joined a "Mennonite Heritage Cruise," which began in Kiev and sailed down the Dnieper River to south Ukraine, where the principal Mennonite colonies had been. As the ship came through the locks on the river at Zaporozhe and I was able to look across to the opposite

A former Mennonite church in the Molochna colony, built in 1892 near Petershagen, that was converted into a grain storage facility during the Communist years.

bank where my parents' village had been, I had strong, mixed feelings, including anticipation and curiosity, as I attempted to match what I was seeing with what I remembered from family photographs.

Our visit coincided with the seventy-fifth anniversary of the first meeting of the Mennonite Central Committee, and a special service of commemoration was held in the community centre, which had replaced the Chortiza Mennonite church during the Bolshevik years.

Alexandrovsk, which in our father's time had had a population of 50,000, had become Zaporozhe, an industrial city of over a million. It straddled both sides of the Dnieper, and Chortiza/Rosental had been absorbed into it. Nevertheless, the visit lent a reality to what the documents had told us.

We walked the streets of what had been our parents' village, using a 1915 map and my father's diaries to identify various buildings. All the buildings on the east side of the main street where our parents' house had stood were gone, presumably destroyed in World War II. However, a number of other buildings that figured in the diaries were still there. There were the schools, the village office from which the community's affairs had been managed, the building that had housed the credit union where Heinrich had obtained loans for his purchases of farm machinery, and the building that had once housed the Kroeger clock works.

Other parts of the village had changed greatly. The *Koloniesgarten*, where Heinrich had often spent Sunday evenings with his friends, was now an overgrown tangle of vegetation. On the site of the Chortiza Mennonite church stood a community centre. Some of the buildings that had housed the Mennonite farm machinery factories were still standing but much run down, and generally looked less impressive than the photos from the past. The gravestones from the cemeteries were gone, having been used for construction projects during the Soviet years.

It is now three generations since the Russlaender's exodus of the 1920s. This group, and those who had previously emigrated in the nineteenth and early twentieth centuries, have given Canada a Mennonite presence that is larger than is often recognized. For example, about 8 per cent of Manitoba's population today is Mennonite or of Mennonite descent. In other provinces, there are substantial Mennonite communities in places such as Coaldale, Rosthern, Leamington, and Abbotsford. Most residents of such communities have preserved their Low German language and religion. However, in urban centres assimilation has been fairly extensive among the large number of present-day Mennonites, and the Mennonite origins of many are invisible to the rest of the population.

For all Mennonites, the influences of the larger Canadian society have made themselves felt. One consequence is that pacifism is no longer a universal tenet. During World War II, while some 7,500 Mennonites declared themselves to be conscientious objectors, another 4,500 enlisted voluntarily in the armed forces.[1]

Alberta has changed greatly since the Kroeger family's early years in the Palliser Triangle. As families moved away over the years, the farms were consolidated into larger and larger units. Unused houses and barns

The site where Naco once stood. The surviving building was Jim Norton's garage.

were taken apart for their lumber or moved away as units. Along country roads in Alberta, some of the sites of former one-room schools have been commemorated by wrought iron arches bearing the names of the schools.

A census report in 1932 recorded a peak population of 85 in Naco. There followed a long period of decline as the depression took its toll. The train service was cut to three time a week in 1929, and then to once a week in 1931 as drought devastated crops. Thereafter, Friday was the day that farmers from the surrounding area came into own to pick up mail and supplies that the train had brought. Local merchants felt the decline in farmers' incomes. One business after another closed, and eventually one grain elevator was taken down.

With the passage of time, improved roads made access to larger towns easier. Train service came to an end in the 1950s, the remaining elevator was removed, and the track was pulled up. The last business closed in 1954, and the last resident moved away in 1963. A similar fate overtook Little Gem and Hemaruka to the west, and New Brigden to the east.

Consort has grown because of oil and gas discoveries in the area. It has become a regional centre, while most of the other communities in the area have lost population and businesses. South of Consort, the former Roland School has been preserved as a museum, complete with the desks, blackboard, strap, and Union Jack, all of which were standard school items in past years.

From a high hill on the road running south from Consort to Naco, it was for many years possible to see the wooden grain elevators of seven towns, four to the south on the Canadian National railway line, and three to the northeast on the Canadian Pacific line. Today all of those elevators are gone, the railway tracks have been taken up, and only vestiges of the towns remain.

In Monitor, where our family disembarked in September 1926, only the post office and a handful of residents remain. Sedalia's single remaining business is a general store; in this building, our parents bought groceries when we were living on the Monsees place from 1935 to 1936.

Berryfield school closed in 1945, and in 1949 was moved away to become a woodworking shop. Willowbrook is now the Full Gospel Church in Consort. The Klassen's house was purchased and moved into Consort, while their other farm buildings were dismantled. Only the hedges that surrounded their farmstead are still there, now heavily overgrown.

A memorial cairn stands on the site of Naco, attesting to the history of the community. A single building remains: Jim Norton's former garage, weathered and without windows or doors. Also discernible are the raised sites on which the grain elevators once stood. Running east-west past them is the right-of-way of the former railway, now covered with grass.

The house on the Day place, where we lived until 1946, is gone, as are the barn and all the other buildings. All that remains is a partially filled-in basement and a few discarded household artefacts in what was once our yard. When I visited the site with my brother George in the mid-1990s, he kicked at a piece of rusted metal protruding from the sod near where the house had stood. It proved to be a hub from the old wooden buggy that our parents left standing in the yard in 1946 when they moved into Consort. I took the hub back to Ottawa with me, and had it sand-blasted, lacquered, and mounted on a solid plastic base. It occupies a corner of my desk and holds my pens and pencils.

In 1998, I had Nick take me to the site of Davey Jones' farm. The only remaining evidence of habitation was a rusting bedspring in the prairie sod where Davey's house had once stood.

Notes

ONE *Before the Flood*

1. James Urry, *None But Saints: The Transformation of Mennonite Life in Russia, 1789–1889* (Winnipeg: Hyperion Press, 1989), 47.

2. Urry, *Saints*, 70, 129, 133, and Appendix 1, 282–88.

3. *Journal of Mennonite Studies*, Vol. 1, 1983, J.W. Friesen: "Studies in Mennonite Education," 133–38; J. Friesen, ed., *Mennonites in Russia, 1788–1988: Essays in Honour of Gerhard Lohrenz* (Winnipeg, CMBC Publications, 1989), 75–94.

4. Urry, *Saints*,71.

5. Frank Epp, *Mennonite Exodus* (Altona, Manitoba: D.W. Friesen and Sons for the Canadian Mennonite Relief and Immigration Council, 1962), 21.

6. H. Smith, *The Story of the Mennonites*, 4th ed. (Newton, Kansas: Mennonite Publications Office, 1957), 462–64.

7. N. Kroeker, *First Mennonite Villages in Russia* (Cloverdale, B.C: printed by D.W. Friesen and Sons, 1981), 142–44.

8. Kroeker, *Villages*, 63; David G. Rempel, *A Mennonite Family in Tsarist Russia and the Soviet Union* (Toronto: University of Toronto Press, 2002), 91.

9. James Urry, "Through the Eye of a Needle: Wealth and the Mennonite Experience in Imperial Russia," *Journal of Mennonite Studies* 3 (1985), 7–35; J. Friesen, *Essays*, 147–48; D. Rempel, *Tsarist*, 118.

10. Urrey, *Saints*, p. 27.

11. F. Epp, *Exodus*, 3.

TWO *War, 1914–1918*

1. J. Friesen, *Essays*, 120.

2. A. Reimer in *Journal of Mennonite Studies*, vol. 11, 1993 .

3. J. Urry, *Saints*, 268.

4. John B. Toews, *Czars, Soviets, and Mennonites* (Newton, Kansas: Faith and Life Press, 1982), 63–64.

5. A. Reimer, in *Journal of Mennonite Studies* 2 (1993); Orlando Figes, *A People's Tragedy* (London: Random House, 1996), 271.

6. L. Klippenstein, *Mennonite Alternative Service in Russia* (Kitchener, Ontario: Pandora Press, 2002), 27–30.

7. A. Reimer in *Journal of Mennonite Studies* 2 (1993); Smith, *Story*, 479.

8. R. Massie, *Nicholas and Alexandra* (New York: Dell, 1969), 309.

9. Figes, *Tragedy*, 263.

10. Quoted in Toews, *Czars*, 70 (parantheses are in Toews).

11. I. Deutscher, *The Prophet Armed—Trotsky, 1879–1921* (London: Oxford University Press, 1954), 330.

THREE *Civil War, 1918–1920*

1. E. Mawdsley, *The Russian Civil War*, 2nd ed. (Edinburgh: Birlinn, 2000), 4; Massie, *Nicholas*, 322.

2. J. Toews, *Lost Fatherland* (Scottdale, Pennsylvania: Herald Press, 1967), 26.

3. D. Neufeld, *A Russian Dance of Death*, trans. Al Reimer (Winnipeg: Hyperion Press, 1980), 9.

4. O. Subtelny, *Ukraine: A History*, 2nd ed. (Toronto: University of Toronto Press, 1994), 360; M. Palij, *The Anarchism of Nestor Makhno* (Seattle: University of Washington Press, 1976), 110–12.

5. Figes, *Tragedy*, 662.

6. Peters, *Nestor Makhno* (Winnipeg: Echo Books, 1970), 68–70.

7. Neufeld, *Dance*, 14, 17.

8. D. Rempel, *Tsarist Russia*, 221.

9. *Preservings* 21 (Dec. 2002), Winnipeg: Mennonite Heritage Centre.

10. Ibid.

11. G. Schroeder, *Miracles of Grace and Judgment* (Tennessee: Kingsport Press, 1974), 50–51, 84, 118, 178.

12. D. Rempel, *Tsarist Russia*, 227; Schroeder, *Miracles*, 114–16; *Preservings* 21 (Dec. 2002).

13. G. Lohrenz, *Zagradovka*, trans. V. Doerksen, Echo Historical Series (Winnipeg: CMBC Publications, 1980), 93–100.

14. Toews, *Fatherland*, 36; Toews, *Czars*, 91.

15. Palij, *Anarchism*, 210; Peters, *Makhno*, 67; Schroeder, *Miracles*, 138.

16. F. Epp, *Exodus*, 37.

17. Toews, *Czars*, 112–13.

18. *Preservings* 21 (Dec. 2002).

19. Palij, *Anarchism*, 244; *Journal of Mennonite Studies* 6 (1988), 216; Sputnik Library http://www.spunk.org/library/writers/makhno/sp001781.

20. H. Bruce Lincoln, *Red Victory* (New York: Simon and Schuster, 1989), 305; Figes, *Tragedy*, 677–79.

21. I. Deutscher, *The Prophet Unarmed—Trotsky, 1921–1929* (London: Oxford University Press, 1959), 4.

FOUR *Hay for Butter, 1920–1924*

1. Deutscher, *Prophet Armed*, 399.
2. Figes, *Tragedy*, 753, 776–77.
3. Toews, *Czars*, 112–14.
4. Schroeder, *Miracles*, 206.
5. Figes, *Tragedy*, 779.
6. F. Epp, *Exodus*, 42.
7. Toews, *Czars*, 113.
8. I. Deutscher, *Stalin: A Political Biography*, 2nd ed. (London, Oxford University Press, 1967), 209.
9. Schroeder, *Miracles*, 206, 231–32.
10. D. Rempel, *Tsarist Russia*, 114.
11. Toews, *Fatherland*, 86–87.

FIVE *Opening the Way*

1. J. Toews, *Fatherland*, 163.
2. J. Toews, *With Courage to Spare: The Life of B.B. Janz* (Winnipeg: Christian Press, 1978), 41.
3. F. Epp, *Exodus*, 95–99.
4. National Archives of Canada (NAC), Microfilm C.7330, correspondence with Secretary, Department of Colonization and Immigration, January 1921.
5. Janet Dench, "A hundred years of immigration to Canada, 1900–1999," Canadian Council for Refugees. http://www.web.net/~ccr/history.html.
6. National Archives of Canada, Microfilm C.4715, memo of July 25, 1923.
7. H. Harder, *David Toews Was Here* (Winnipeg: CMBC Publications, 2003), 111.
8. NAC, MG26J1, Volume 82, microfilm reel 2250, p. 69574. Mennonite Heritage Centre (MHC), Volume 1269, file 602.
9. MHC Archives, Vol. 1269, file 600.
10. *Canadian Pacific Staff Bulletin*, January, 1939, obituary of Col. Dennis.
11. F. Epp, *Exodus*, 107.
12. Canadian Pacific Railway (CPR) Archives, Annual Report to Shareholders, May 2, 1923.

13. *Manitoba Historical Society News and Reports* 6 (Fall 1983).

14. MHC Archives, Vol. 1394, file 1555, speech by David Toews, 1938.

15. Ibid.

16. H. Harder, *Toews*, 120.

SIX *Even the Strong Wept*

1. F. Epp, *Exodus*, 142.

2. Kroeker, *Villages*, 227.

3. F. Epp, *Mennonites in Canada, 1920–1940* (Toronto: Macmillan, 2003), 170.

4. Newspaper *Kurzemes vards*, Liepaja, No. 148, July 8, 1923, 3.

5. NAC, Microfilm C-7350, report of July 6th, 1923 from the Immigration Office in Riga.

6. NAC, Microfilm C-7350, letter from the Immigration Office, Antwerp, July 11, 1923.

7. MHC Archives, Vol. 1271, File 608.

8. CPR Archives, Info file C-150.

9. F. Epp, *Exodus*, 185.

10. *Canadian Pacific Staff Bulletin*, October 1, 1937.

11. Toews, *Fatherland*, 164.

12. Toews, *With Courage*, 56.

13. MHC Archives, Volume 1271, file 609, memorandum from Dr. Drury, June 22, 1926.

14. J.A. Harder, *From Kleefeld with Love*, Kitchener, Ontario, Pandora Press, 2003, 33. This account captures the spirit of many such crossings under the Red Gate.

15. Privately printed.

16. CPR Archives, Bulletins 1923–25, HE 1001 C23, Bulletin 186, 11.

17. O. Figes, *Natasha's Dance* (London: Penguin Books, 2003), 528–29; R. Johnson, *New Mecca, New Babylon* (Kingston and Montreal, McGill-Queen's University Press, 1988); National Archives of Canada, microfilm reel 4715, memos of August 31 and September 7, 1923.

SEVEN *The Great Lone Land*

1. *Census of Agriculture*, 1925, Vol. 5, 82.

2. Ted Byfield, ed. *Alberta in the 20th Century, Volume Five: Brownlee and the Triumph of Populism, 1920–1930* (Edmonton: United Western Communications, 1996), map on inside cover and p. 308.

3. *Consort Enterprise*, June 14, 1931.

4. R. Bryce, *Maturing in Hard Times*, Institute of Public Administration of Canada, (Kingston and Montreal, McGill-Queen's University Press, 1986), 23.

5. H. Palmer, *Alberta, A New History* (Edmonton: Hurtig, 1990), 247.

EIGHT *To Be at Home Somewhere, 1926–1930*

1. MHC Archives, Vol. 1286.
2. David C. Jones, ed., *We'll All be Buried Down Here,* (Calgary: Historical Society of Alberta, 1986), xxxvi.
3. Palmer, *Alberta,* 210.
4. *Alberta in the 20th Century,* 4; D. Jones, *Buried,* 155, 170; D. Jones, *Empire of Dust* (Calgary: University of Calgary Press, 2002), 210–13.
5. Glenbow Archives, file 1175, letter of May 23, 1927.
6. Heinrich Kroeger's correspondence may be found in the MHC Archives, Boxes 1053, 1175, 1244, 1250.
7. MHC Archives, Volume 1244, Envelope 449.
8. Ibid.; see also Vol. 1389, File 1533.

NINE *Boiled Apple Peels, 1930–1934*

1. J. Gorman, *A Land Reclaimed* (Hanna, AB: Gorman and Gorman, 1988), 57–61.
2. The accounts of events in Naco are drawn largely from the files of the *Consort Enterprise* for the 1920s and 1930s.

TEN *Russian Thistle and Relief, 1934–1939*

1. T.C. Douglas in R.D. Francis and H. Ganzevoort, eds., *The Dirty Thirties in Prairie Canada* (Vancouver: Tantalus Research, 1980), 166.
2. Provinicial Archives of Alberta (PAA), Acc. 78.133, Box 71, circular dated April 8, 1935, and Acc. 73.07, Box 28, file 347, circular of October 16, 1935.
3. G. Britnell & V. Fowke, *Canadian Agriculture in War and Peace, 1935–50* (Stanford University Press, 1962), 65–72; B. Neatby, *The Politics of Chaos* (Toronto: MacMillan, 1972), 28; Byfield, ed., *Alberta in the 20th Century, Volume Five,* 9.
4. G. Friesen, *The Canadian Prairies* (Toronto: University of Toronto Press, 1987), 318.
5. *Consort Enterprise,* March 6, 1924.
6. Quoted in D. Guest, *The Emergence of Social Security in Canada,* 3rd ed. (Vancouver: University of British Columbia Press, 1999), 39.
7. Bryce, *Maturing,* 174.
8. Ibid., 26.
9. PAA, Acc. 78.133, Box 71, File 554C, memo of April 8, 1935.
10. Ibid.
11. PAA, Acc. 73.07, Box 28, files 342, 345, 346, 347.
12. PAA, Acc. 73.07, Box 71, File 554C, memo of June 1, 1931.
13. Neatby, *Politics,* 33–34.

14. Janet Dench, Canadian Council for Refugees; L. Glassford, *Reaction and Reform* (Toronto: University of Toronto Press, 1992), 122.

15. *Consort Enterprise*, August 12, 1937.

16. Material in this section is drawn from the Annual Reports of the Alberta Division of the Red Cross, supplied by National Headquarters of the Canadian Red Cross, Ottawa.

17. Bryce, *Maturing*, 56; G. Friesen, *Prairies*, 388.

18. PAA, Acc. 78.133, Box 71, letter of June 13, 1934, and Box 161, File 1167c, letter of December 19, 1938; Acc. 79.334, Box 47, letter of August 29, 1932; *Consort Enterprise*, November 5, 1931.

19. *Consort Enterprise*, November 5, 1931; see also T.C. Douglas in Francis and Ganzevoort, eds., *The Dirty Thirties in Prairie Canada*, 166.

20. B. Little, "Social Spending now following a new pattern," *Toronto Globe and Mail*, November 18, 2002; Guest, *Social Security*, 101.

21. Bryce, *Maturing*, 174–76; Ernest Watkins, *R.B. Bennet* (London: Secker and Warburg, 1963),185; Britnell & Fowke, *Agriculture*, 73.

22. J. Struthers, *No Fault of their Own* (Toronto: University of Toronto Press, 1983), 168.

ELEVEN *The Door Closes*

1. F. Epp, *Exodus*, 242.

2. *Consort Enterprise*, February 13, 1930.

3. Subtelny, *Ukraine*, 410.

4. F. Epp, *Exodus*, 225.

5. Ibid., 231–36.

6. F. Epp, *Mennonites*, 307.

7. F. Epp, *Exodus*, 150.

8. H. Harder, *Toews*, 182, 250, 255–56.

9. Ibid., 163.

10. Byfield, *Alberta in the 20th century, Volume Six*, 24.

11. Esther Epp-Tiessen, *A Leader for his Time* (Winnipeg: CMBC Publications, 2001), 172.

12. H. Harder, *Toews*, 291.

13. Ibid., 117–18.

TWELVE *British Subjects and Aliens*

1. J. Gray, *Boomtime: Peopling the Canadian Prairies* (Saskatoon: Western Producer Prairie Books, 1979), 33–34.

2. J. Thompson, *Forging the Prairie West* (Toronto: Oxford University Press), 77.

3. G. Friesen, *Prairies*, 405, and Glenbow Archives, Box 112, File 1041, Article, June 2, 1928.

4. *Consort Enterprise*, February 22, 1915.

5. CPR Archives, Bulletin 189, October 1, 1924, 8.

6. R. Bothwell, *Canada 1900–1945* (Toronto: University of Toronto Press, 1987), 58.

7. *Hill Times*, Ottawa, March 10, 2003, 15.

8. PAA, Acc. 78.133, Box 71, File 554B, Memo of June 1, 1931.

9. *Consort Enterprise*, March 3, 1927; Glenbow Archives, File 615.

10. R.D. Francis and H. Palmer, eds. *The Prairie West*, 2nd ed. (Edmonton: University of Alberta Press), 1992, 325.

11. The records of Heinrich Kroeger's naturalization are in the citizenship archives of the department of Secretary of State, File 7444.

12. *Consort Enterprise*, May 24, 1939.

13. G. Friesen, *Prairies*, 272–73; Palmer, *Alberta*, 312–13.

14. Centre for Mennonite Brethren Studies, C.F. Klassen photo collection NPS 52-01.

15. CPR Archives, Staff Bulletin, October 1, 1937.

16. All references to the IODE are drawn from Provinicial Archives of Alberta Acc. 77, 248.2–248.3.

THIRTEEN *Farms, Schools, and Neighbours*

1. *Consort Enterprise*, October 9, 1941.

2. J. Charyk, *Pulse of the Community* (Saskatoon: Prairie Books, The Western Producer, 1970), 315.

3. J. Burnet, *Next Year Country* (Toronto, University of Toronto Press, 1951), 135.

FOURTEEN *Finding our Feet, 1936–1946*

1. D. Jones, *Empire* 124–25.

2. Alberta Archives 78.133, Box 104, Files 804b and 807a and b; see also federal Order-in-Council P.C. 2456 of April 8th, 1941.

FIFTEEN *Exile and Dispersal*

1. Harder, *Toews*, 208.

2. F. Epp, *Exodus*, 268.

3. Toews, *Czars*, 171.

4. Subtelny, *Ukraine*, 461; John Ure, *The Cossacks* (London: Constable, 1999), 26, 222–23; F. Stambrook, ed. *A Sharing of Diversities*, Canadian Plains Research Centre (Regina: University of Regina, 1999), xiv.

5. Smith, 520.

6. M. Epp, "Moving Forward, Looking Backward," *Journal of Mennonites Studies* 16 (1998).

SIXTEEN *Consort*

1. Quiring, Walter. *In the Fullness of Time: 150 Years of Mennonite Sojourn in Russia.*
    (Kitchener, ON: A. Klassen), 1974.

SEVENTEEN *A Nightmare from the Past*

1. All material in this section is drawn from police reports and court records in the
    National Archives of Canada, RG 13, Vol. 1769, File VL2PT2, including Order-in-
    Council P.C. 1958–1248.

EPILOGUE

1. T.D. Regehr, "Lost Sons" in *Mennonite Quarterly Review* (October 1992), 465.

Bibliography

Birdsell, Sandra. *The Russländer*. Toronto: Emblem Editions, McClelland and Stewart, 2001.

Black, Larry. *The Peasant Kingdom*. Penumbra Press, 2001.

Bothwell, Robert, I. Drummond, & J. English. *Canada 1900–1945*. Toronto: University of Toronto Press, 1987.

Britnell, G. & V. Fowke: *Canadian Agriculture in War and Peace, 1935–50*. Stanford: Stanford University Press, 1962.

Bryce, Robert. *Maturing in Hard Times*. Institute of Public Administration of Canada. Kingston and Montreal: McGill-Queen's University Press, 1986.

Burnet, Jean. *Next Year Country*. Toronto, University of Toronto Press, 1951.

Byfield, Ted, ed. *Alberta in the 20th Century, A Journalistic History of the Province in 13 Volumes, Volume Five: Brownlee and the Triumph of Populism: 1920–1930*. Edmonton: United Western Communications, 1996.

———. *Alberta in the 20th Century, A Journalistic History of the Province in 13 Volumes, Volume Six: 1930–1935*. Edmonton: United Western Communications, 1998.

Consort Enterprise. Files 1922–46. National Library and Archives, Canada.

Carr, Donald. "Dry and Dusty." Bruce Peel Special Collections Library, University of Alberta.

Charyk, John C. *Pulse of the Community*. Saskatoon: Prairie Books, Western Producer, 1970.

———. *Those Bittersweet School Days*. Saskatoon: Western Producer Prairie Books, 1977.

Dench, Janet. *A Hundred Years of Immigration to Canada 1900–1999*. Canadian Council for Refugees. http://www.web.net/~ccr/history.html.

Deutscher, Isaac. *Stalin: A Political Biography*. 2nd ed., London: Oxford University Press, 1967.

———. *The Prophet Armed—Trotsky, 1879–1921*. London: Oxford University Press, 1954.

———. *The Prophet Unarmed—Trotsky, 1921–1929*. London: Oxford University Press, 1959.

Dyck, J.J. *Add One Cossack and Stir*. Toronto: Britannia Printers, 1972.

Epp, Frank H. *Mennonites in Canada, 1920–1940*. Toronto: Macmillan, 1982.

———. *Mennonite Exodus: The Rescue and Resettlement of the Russian Mennonites since the Communist Revolution*. Altona, MB: Canadian Mennonite Relief and Immigration Council, 1962.

Epp, M. "Moving Forward, Looking Backward." *Journal of Mennonite Studies* 16 (1998).

Epp, Reuben. *The Story of Low German and Plautdietsch: Tracing a Language across the Globe*. Hillsboro, KS: Reader's Press, 1993.

Epp-Tiessen, Esther. *A Leader for his Time*. Winnipeg: CMBC Publications, 2001.

Figes, Orlando. *A People's Tragedy*. London: Random House, 1996.

———. *Natasha's Dance*. London: Penguin Books, 2003.

Francis, R.D. & H. Ganzevoort, eds. *The Dirty Thirties in Prairie Canada*. Vancouver: Tantalus Research, 1980.

Francis, R.D. & H. Palmer, eds. *The Prairie West*. 2nd ed. Edmonton: University of Alberta Press, 1992.

Friesen, Gerald. *The Canadian Prairies*. Toronto: University of Toronto Press, 1987.

Friesen, John, ed. *Mennonites in Russia, 1788–1988: Essays in Honour of Gerhard Lohrenz*. Winnipeg: CMBC Publications, 1989.

Friesen, J.W. "Studies in Mennonite Education." *Journal of Mennonite Studies* 1, 1983, pp. 133–38.

Glassford, L.A. *Reaction and Reform*. Toronto: University of Toronto Press, 1992.

Gorman, Jack. *A Land Reclaimed*. Hanna, AB: Gorman and Gorman, 1988.

Gray, James H. *Boomtime: Peopling the Canadian Prairies*. Saskatoon: Western Producer Prairie Books, 1979.

———. *The Roar of the Twenties*. Toronto: MacMillan, 1975.

———. *Men Against the Desert*. Saskatoon: Western Producer Prairie Books, 1967.

Guest, Dennis. *The Emergence of Social Security in Canada*. 3rd ed. Vancouver: University of British Columbia Press, 1999.

Harder, Helmut. *David Toews Was Here*. Winnipeg: CMBC Publications, 2002.

Harder, J.A. *From Kleefeld with Love*. Kitchener, Ontario: Pandora Press, 2003.

Horsch, J. *Mennonites in Europe*. Vol. 1, 2nd ed., Scottdale, Pennsylvania: Mennonite Publishing House, 1950.

Johnson, R. *New Mecca, New Babylon*. Kingston and Montreal: McGill-Queen's University Press, 1988.

Jones, David C. *Empire of Dust*. University of Calgary Press, 2002.

Jones, David C., ed. *We'll All be Buried Down Here*. Calgary: Historical Society of Alberta, 1986.

Klippenstein, Lawrence. *Mennonite Alternative Service in Russia*. Kitchener, Ontario: Pandora Press, 2002.

Kroeker, N.J. *First Mennonite Villages in Russia*. Cloverdale, BC: printed by D.W. Friesen and Sons, 1981.

Kropinske, Earl & Ella Kropinske, *Schools of the Neutrals*. Monitor, AB: Privately printed, 1995.

Lincoln, H. Bruce. *Red Victory*. New York: Simon and Schuster, 1989.

Lohrenz, Gerhard. *Zagradovka*. trans. V. Doerksen. Echo Historical Series. Winnipeg: CMBC Publications, 1980.

MacEwan, Grant. *Between the Red and the Rockies*. Saskatoon: Western Producer Prairie Books, 1979.

MacGregor, James. *A History of Alberta*. rev. ed. Edmonton: Hurtig, 1981.

Massie, Robert. *Nicholas and Alexandra*. New York: Dell, 1969.

Mawdsley, Evan. *The Russian Civil War*. 2nd ed. Edinburgh: Birlinn, 2000.

Mennonite Historical Atlas. 2nd ed. Winnipeg: Springfield, 1996.

Neatby, H. Blair. *The Politics of Chaos*. Toronto: MacMillan, 1972.

Neufeld, Dietrich. *A Russian Dance of Death*. trans. Al Reimer. Winnipeg: Hyperion Press, 1980.

Palij, Michael. *The Anarchism of Nestor Makhno*. Seattle: University of Washington Press, 1976.

Palmer, Howard. *Alberta, A New History*. Edmonton: Hurtig, 1990.

Peters, Victor. *Nestor Makhno*. Winnipeg: Echo Books, 1970.

Preservings (historical journal). Winnipeg: Mennonite Heritage Centre.

Radzinski, E. *Stalin*. trans. H.T. Willetts. New York: Doubleday, 1996.

Regehr, T.D. "Lost Sons." *Mennonite Quarterly Review* (October 1992).

Regehr, T.D. *Mennonites in Canada, 1939–1970*. Toronto: University of Toronto Press, 1996.

———. *Peace, Order, and Good Government*. Winnipeg: CMBC Publications, 2000.

Reimer, A. "Sanitatsdienst and Selbstschutz." *Journal of Mennonite Studies* 2 (1993).

Reimer, Al. *My Harp is Turned to Mourning*. Winnipeg: Windflower Communications, 1990.

Rempel, David G. *A Mennonite Family in Tsarist Russia and the Soviet Union*. Toronto: University of Toronto Press, 2002.

Rempel, Peter Gerhard. *Forever Summer, Forever Sunday: Peter Gerhard Rempel's Photographs of Mennonites in Russia, 1890–1917*. St. Jacobs, ON: Sand Hill Books, 1981.

Schapansky, H. *The Old Colony (Chortiza) of Russia*. Rosenort, Manitoba: Printed by Country Graphics and Printing, 2001.

Schroeder, Gerhard. *Miracles of Grace and Judgment*. Tennessee: Kingsport Press, 1974.

Smith, H. *The Story of the Mennonites*, 4th ed. Newton, KS: Mennonite Publications Office, 1957.

Sputnik Library, http://www.spunk.org/library/writers/makhno/sp001781.

Stambrook, F., ed. *A Sharing of Diversities*. Canadian Plains Research Centre, University of Regina, 1999.

Struthers, James. *No Fault of their Own.* Toronto: University of Toronto Press, 1983.

Subtelny, Orest. *Ukraine. A History.* 2nd ed. Toronto: University of Toronto Press, 1994.

Taubman, W. *Kruschev.* New York: Norton, 2003.

Thompson, J.H. *Forging the Prairie West.* Toronto: Oxford University Press, 1998.

Toews, John B. *Czars, Soviets, and Mennonites.* Newton, Kansas: Faith and Life Press, 1982.

———. *Lost Fatherland.* Scottdale, PA: Herald Press, 1967.

———. *With Courage to Spare: The Life of B.B. Janz.* Winnipeg: Christian Press, 1978.

Trotsky, Leon. *The History of the Russian Revolution.* trans. Max Eastman. Toronto: Pathfinder, 1980.

———. *Ma vie.* trans. Maurice Parijanine. Paris: Editions Gallimard, 1953.

Tuchman, Barbara. *The Guns of August.* New York: Dell, 1962.

Ure, John. *The Cossacks.* London: Constable, 1999.

Urry, James. *None But Saints: The Transformation of Mennonite Life in Russia, 1789–1889.* Winnipeg: Hyperion Press, 1989.

Urry, James. "Through the eye of a needle: wealth and the Mennonite experience in Imperial Russia." *Journal of Mennonite Studies* 3 (1985), 7–35.

Wardhaugh, R.A. *Mackenzie King and the Prairie West.* Toronto: University of Toronto Press, 2000.

Watkins, Ernest. *R.B. Bennet.* London: Secker and Warburg, 1963.

Archival Sources

Canadian Pacific Railway (CPR) Archives, Montreal.

Centre for Mennonite Brethern Studies.

Glenbow Archives, Calgary.

Mennonite Heritage Centre (MHC) Archives, Winnipeg.

National Archives of Canada (NAC), Ottawa.

Provincial Archives of Alberta (PAA), Edmonton.

Index   *Photos are indicated in italics.*